LINKED LIVES

LINKED LIVES

Adult Daughters and Their Mothers

LUCY ROSE FISCHER, Ph.D.

HARPER & ROW, PUBLISHERS New York
Cambridge, Philadelphia, San Francisco, London,
Mexico City, São Paulo, Singapore, Sydney

1817

To the memories of

Jerry A. Rose, *my brother*   Helen Rose, *my mother*

Henry Rose, *my father*

FIRST EDITION

Designed by Ruth Bornschlegel

Library of Congress Cataloging-in-Publication Data

Fischer, Lucy Rose.
    Linked lives.

    Bibliography: p.
    Includes index.
    1. Adult children—United States.   2. Mothers and
daughters—United States.   I. Title.
HQ799.97.U5F57   1986   306.8′743   85-45634
ISBN 0-06-015571-X

86 87 88 89 90 HC 10 9 8 7 6 5 4 3 2 1

Contents

PREFACE *xi*

ACKNOWLEDGMENTS *xv*

1 MOTHERS' LIVES/DAUGHTERS' LIVES *1*

DAUGHTERS AS MOTHERS *2*

A SPECIAL CLOSENESS *5*

"ADULT CHILDREN" AND "POST-PARENTS" *8*

FAMILY TIES OVER TIME *11*

2 THE ADOLESCENT YEARS *14*

HOLDING ON AND LETTING GO *15*

    Attachment in the Mother-Daughter Bond 20
    Adolescent Daughters Detaching from Their Mothers 22
    Intimacy plus Separation 24
    From the Viewpoint of the Mothers 25

ATYPICAL MOTHERS AND DAUGHTERS *26*

    A Remote Mother 27
    A Highly Involved Mother and Daughter 27
    "Invested" Mother-Daughter Pairs 29

DAUGHTERS PROTECTING MOTHERS *32*

    Teenage Daughters as Confidantes 32
    Problems with Parents 35

THE "METAMORPHOSIS" OF DAUGHTERS *39*

    The Reproductive Bond 39
    Fathers as "Sexual Guardians" 41
    Keeping the Mother in the Dark 43

THE YEARS BETWEEN *44*

3 MATURATION, MARRIAGE, AND MOTHERHOOD 46

A TYPOLOGY OF SYMMETRY AND ASYMMETRY 47

Responsible Mothers/Dependent Daughters 49
Responsible Daughters/Dependent Mothers 53
Mothers and Daughters with Peerlike Friendships 55
Mutual Mothering 58
Beyond the Typology 60
Type X—"Uninvolved" Daughters 63

MARRIED DAUGHTERS VERSUS SINGLE DAUGHTERS 64

DAUGHTERS WITH CHILDREN 73

PEERSHIP AND PARENTING 79

4 GENDER AND GENERATION 81

MOTHERS AS ROLE MODELS 83

Role Models in Adolescence 83
Young Adult Daughters Identifying with Their Mothers 85
Her Mother, Herself 87
Daughters Wanting to Be Different 89

THE IMPORTANCE OF HUSBANDS 91

Women's Work 92
Power and Priority 96
Husbands and Mothers as Confidants 97
The Confidentiality of Husbands 101

BETWEEN GENERATIONS 104

Cohort and Generation 105
The Meaning of Motherhood 110

HOW MUCH HAS CHANGED? 115

5 HER MOTHER VERSUS HIS 117

"WHY MOTHERS-IN-LAW ARE WONDERFUL PEOPLE" 118

INTERACTIONS WITH MOTHERS-IN-LAW 120

In-law Friendships 120

Minimally Involved In-law Relationships 122
Substitute Mothers 123

NOT QUITE DAUGHTERS 125
Conflict about Children 126
Alice: The Unhappy Daughter-in-law 130
The Caution of In-laws 131
Linda: The "Good" Daughter-in-law 132
Mothers versus Mothers-in-law 135

WHAT CAN GRANDMOTHERS DO? 140
How Grandmothers Help 141
Grandmothers as Experts 146

MARRIED DAUGHTERS AS MEDIATORS 150

THE OTHER MOTHER 154

6 WHEN MOTHERS BECOME FRAIL 156

BECOMING FRAIL 157

REVERSING ROLES 161

DAUGHTERS IN THE MIDDLE 167

WHO'S IN CHARGE? 173
An Independent Woman 174
Power and Reciprocity 177

FAMILIES AND HOSPITALS 185
An Angry Family 188
The Caregiving Alliance 191

THE FINAL STAGE 194

7 MOTHERS AND DAUGHTERS AS WOMEN 196

APPENDIX A: **Research on Mothers and Daughters** 202
A Study of Young Adult Daughters and Their Mothers 202
A Study of Parent Caregiving and Posthospital Care 204

APPENDIX B: A Note About Qualitative Research and
Life-History Data *205*

NOTES *208*

REFERENCES *221*

INDEX *227*

Tables

1. Indicators of Involvement between Adolescent Daughters and Their Mothers versus Their Fathers   17

2. "Attachment" and "Separation" between Adolescent Daughters and Their Mothers   21

3. Characteristics of Four Types of Adult-Daughter/Mother Relationships   48

4. Cross-tabulation of Mother-Daughter Relationships by Level of Reciprocity in Giving and Receiving   50

5. Cross-tabulation of Mother-Daughter Relationships by Daughter's Marital/Parental Status   64

6. Cross-tabulation of Mother-Daughter Relationships by Daughter's Age   65

7. Daughters' Rating of Themselves as Being Very Similar to or Very Different from Their Mothers   86

8. Awareness of Daughter's "Saying or Doing Something that Seems Just Like" Her Mother—from the Perspectives of the Daughter and Her Husband   87

9. Participation of Daughter's Husband in "Female" Household Chores by Parental and Work Status   93

10. Husband's Participation in Child Care, by Wife's Work Status   94

11. Confidants for Daughter's Husband by Parental Status   98

12. Confidants for Married Daughter by Parental Status   99

13. Types of Careers for Mothers and Daughters   108

14. Amount of Help Exchanged between Mothers and Daughters and between Mothers-in-law and Daughters-in-law   145

15. Comparison of Advice Asking and Advice Offering, by the Paired Perspectives of Daughters and Mothers and Daughters-in-law and Mothers-in-law   149

Figures

1. Conflict with Mothers and Mothers-in-law, by Daughters' Parenthood Status   128

2. Amount of Conflict from Perspectives of Daughters, Mothers, Daughters-in-law and Mothers-in-law   129

Preface

The research for this book began about ten years ago. I was interested in the sociology of aging; and I wanted to find out how people change and develop over the course of their adult years. I stumbled onto the topic of mothers and daughters almost by accident. It seemed to me that the best way for a sociologist to study adult development would be to look at how relationships change in adulthood. I chose to study mothers and daughters because this relationship is both long enduring and emotionally close. This was the central idea behind my study of their "linked lives"—that mothers and daughters are important in each other's lives and that their relationships are subject to change as they both grow older.

My first pilot study on the mother-daughter relationship ended with a sad irony. In the summer of 1976, I was finishing a paper on mothers and daughters based on eleven interviews. I was pulling the last page from my typewriter when the telephone rang. I heard my sister in New York telling me: "Mother is dead." It did not seem possible. She was just in her mid-sixties and we always had thought of her as very young. My mind went from that telephone call to my typewriter—where I just had been thinking about my mother, wanting to tell her what I had learned about mothers and daughters.

Nearly two years later—in 1978—I began a larger and more elaborate research project on the mother-daughter relationship. For that project, I did extensive interviews with about forty young adult daughters and most of their mothers. My main question concerned the impact of the daughter's motherhood: What happens to the mother-daughter relationship when the daughter becomes a mother herself?

Because my own mother had died so recently, I was worried about doing those interviews. Would I start crying, inappropriately and unprofessionally, in the middle of an interview? That never happened. Often a mother or daughter would talk about painful experiences and I would listen in sympathy. But their experiences were different from my own; and my grief about my mother was a separate matter. But I did learn a great deal about myself and my own family from doing this research—especially as I began to analyze the interviews. I learned how my family experiences were echoed in other families. Even more important, I began to have a sense about variability across families and why relationships differ.

I was a graduate student at the University of Massachusetts, in Amherst, when I did my study on young adult daughters and their mothers. I spent about eight months doing over eighty interviews—which meant driving all around small towns in western Massachusetts. Each interview took between two and four hours. Some of my interviews were done under "battle conditions." Interviewing daughters who had toddlers meant that there were frequent interruptions as their children needed their attention. In a few cases, the children spent their time banging on my tape recorder.

I wrote up this research as my doctoral dissertation and later I published articles on my findings in professional journals. In the meantime, I had started teaching in the Sociology Department at the University of Minnesota, Minneapolis, where I continued to do research on relationships between adult children and their parents. In 1982, I did another study on mothers and daughters, which I have used for the last part of this book. In that research I examined a later-life transition in the mother-daughter relationship: How does their relationship change when the mother becomes frail and the daughter becomes a caregiver to her parent?

When I began my research on mothers and daughters, I chose the topic mostly because I thought it was interesting theoretically— as a way of understanding adult development. When I presented my initial findings to other sociologists, I expected to engage in theoretical discussions about aging, development, and family structure. But I often found that my colleagues wanted to talk both about sociology and about their personal experiences with their own mothers or daughters. Women, in particular, seem to be intrigued by this topic. After I had published articles in professional journals, I began to receive invitations to appear on television and radio talk shows, and I was interviewed many times by journalists from newspapers and magazines. All of this interest convinced me that I ought to put together a book on my mother-daughter research.

I have written this book both for sociologists and for other people who have a personal or professional interest in the topic of mothers and daughters. Addressing a mixed audience has been a challenge—and sometimes a problem. At times I have felt frustrated when a theoretical idea or technical aspect of my research design seemed too complex to describe in simple terms. But there also has been an important advantage to writing a book in plain English. The technical language that we use as professionals can be useful but it also can be a crutch. When I have to translate my writing into plain talk, I often am able to see which ideas are really clear and what concepts just sounded good because they were dressed up in fancy terms.

I have described both of my research projects in Appendix A. I also have added "A Note about Qualitative Research and Life-History Data," which is in Appendix B.

Acknowledgments

I have had help with this book from many sources. I want to give my first thanks to the people I cannot name—the people who spent many hours sharing their experiences and their insights on family relationships. Sometimes I have given them names in the text; these are all made up. Occasionally, I have disguised a few details in their statements (such as the names of places). But for the most part, I have quoted their own words and my understanding of mothers and daughters has come from interpreting what they told me about their relationships.

I also am grateful to many of my colleagues and students, who have helped at various stages in doing this book. Two people, in particular, have been instrumental in helping me with this project: Alice Rossi and Reuben Hill. Alice Rossi supervised my doctoral dissertation at the University of Massachusetts. One of the leading feminist sociologists in this country, Rossi was an invaluable mentor. As I worked on the design and analysis of my dissertation, she critiqued my written materials with incredible speed, subjected my work to serious criticism, and also generously shared her insights. When I came to the University of Minnesota, Reuben Hill became in some ways another mentor, as well as a colleague. Hill, one of the founders of family sociology, was a kind of walking encyclopedia in this field. He died shortly after I completed the final manuscript of *Linked Lives*. He contributed to this book not only by reading and critiquing many of the chapters but also by sharing his knowledge and ideas with me over the years.

Other colleagues who have talked over specific ideas about this work and have helped in other ways with the book include Albert Chevan, Cynthia Deitsch, Mary Ford, Naomi Gerstel, Jan Greenberg, Anthony Harris, Carol Hoffman, Margaret Huyck, Robert Kennedy, Michael Lewis, Jane London, Helen Mederer, Paul Rosenblatt, Beth Schneider, Leah Shamgar-Handelman, Jane Silverman, Richard Tessler, and Carol Woehrer. I also have received much useful feedback on my research when I presented papers at professional meetings. I am particularly grateful to my colleagues in the Midwest Council for Social Research on Aging—an organization that has facilitated my professional development. I assigned portions of the manuscript for *Linked Lives* in a sociology course called "Aging and Intergenerational Dynamics," and my students suggested a number of useful revisions. I have worked with two editors: Sallie Coolidge, at Harper & Row, and Mark S. Fischer, my husband. Each of them contributed a fresh and critical eye to the writing of this book.

I have had a number of grants to support my research on mothers and daughters: a dissertation grant from the University of Massachusetts (1978), three small grants from the Graduate School of the University of Minnesota (1979–82), a postdoctoral fellowship from the National Institute on Aging in coordination with the Midwest Council for Social Research on Aging (1980–81), a grant from the All-University Council on Aging/CURA at the University of Minnesota (1982), and a Faculty Summer Research Fellowship from the University of Minnesota (1984).

In writing this book, I have been supported and encouraged by my husband, Mark; our son, Jeremy; other members of our extended family; and also many friends. I have described mothers and daughters as having "linked lives." But our lives are also linked with others—with all those who love us and whom we love.

*Hold your parents tenderly, for the world will seem
a strange and lonely place when they're gone.*

Belle of Amherst: A Play Based on the Life
of Emily Dickinson, BY WILLIAM LUCE

Although *Linked Lives* is factually accurate, all names, locations, and other identifying characteristics of the interview subjects mentioned in *Linked Lives* have been changed.

1

MOTHERS' LIVES/ DAUGHTERS' LIVES

Recently, I led a workshop for a small group of women on the topic "Mothers and Daughters." We were discussing evidence that mothers and adult daughters tend to become closer and have less conflict after the daughter becomes a mother herself. But one of the women in the workshop said that her experience with her mother had been very different. She described her mother as "cold and distant." All her life, she found herself searching for something that was not there—a quality of love and caring that her mother would or could not give her. "When I became a mother," she said, "I realized how *easy* it was to love that child in my arms. It took no effort or will. It was then that I realized how strange my relationship with my mother really was . . . It was one of the most striking things in my life. . . . Most of the changes we go through are gradual. This was one of the few things that came crashing down on me. Nothing had prepared me for how I felt about this kid. And the contrast was immediately apparent . . . Why was it so *difficult* for her to love me?"

Another woman, in the same workshop, also said that her experiences with her mother were unusual. She had been an adolescent during World War II and had spent those years with her mother in concentration camps in Poland. Although they both survived the concentration camps, her mother died shortly after the war. She said: "What I felt was this sense of utter injustice. I was just devastated by the fact that she lived through so much and then didn't get to enjoy anything." Several years later, after she had a daughter of her own, she too saw her mother in a new way: "I realized what a terrible thing it must have been for my mother to see me suffer—you understand, it's the selflessness of motherhood. It was different for me—I had only myself to worry about. . . . Sometimes I felt angry at my mother; if she hadn't given me life I wouldn't be in this fix. But I realize, when you're a mother, that your own life isn't that important."

The stories told by the women in that workshop were *all* different—reflecting their unique experiences and the personal idiosyncrasies of people in different families. Nonetheless, there seemed to be some common threads among these different mother-daughter relationships. This book discusses how family structure and gender roles shape the relationships between adult daughters and their mothers and how variability in family structure also accounts for the diversity among their experiences.

DAUGHTERS AS MOTHERS

Some of the most interesting work on mothers and daughters was done over two decades ago by British sociologists and anthropologists[1] who were studying family relationships in working-class communities. They reported that when daughters become mothers they experience a renewed closeness to their own mothers. For example, in a book by Peter Willmott and Michael Young, *Family and Class in a London Society,* which was published in 1960, an elderly mother in London reflected:

> A daughter alters when she gets married and has children of her own. She seems to feel closer to her mother than before. They seem to understand each other more.

A comparable point was made in several classical works by psychologists. Freud,[2] in his explanations of the psychology of women, noted: "Under the influence of woman's becoming a mother herself, an identification with her own mother may be revived, against which she had striven up till the time of her marriage . . ." These classical studies and essays suggest that the daughter's motherhood provides a source of identification between mother and daughter.

However, in recent years, there have been major changes in

family structure and in the roles of men and women. Divorce rates have risen and there is increasing participation of women in the paid labor force. How can we assume that the roles of mothers and daughters are the same across generations? Much of the evidence for mother-daughter closeness comes from the studies done in the 1950s of British working-class communities.[3] There are a number of fundamental differences between British and American family systems—differences that are compounded when we take into account such factors as social class and the impact of social change. It is not clear how social class affects mother-daughter relationships. In working-class families, husbands and wives often do *not* have emotionally close relationships. In these families, then, mother-daughter intimacy seems to compensate women for the lack of emotional support from their husbands. But other research has shown that more educated families tend to have more egalitarian marital relationships. We might ask: Are mothers and daughters closely attached to one another *only* in certain communities—in stable, close-knit working-class families?

Nonetheless, although such factors as social class and social change clearly affect family relationships, current research shows that gender continues to be a central factor in family life. One aspect of family roles that does not seem to vary greatly or to have changed much is the fact that mothers and women take prime responsibility for caring for small children. A recent study of relationships between mothers and young children highlights the *absence* of differences among social classes: ". . . the obligations in the mother-role—exclusive responsibility for the children, responsibility for them all the time—largely override class differences . . ."[4] Other research also has indicated that even in modern marriages, with "dual career" couples, mothers continue to have prime responsibility for child care—especially with infants and very young children.[5] This mothering responsibility is an important factor in the continuing attachment between generations of mothers and daughters.

In *The Reproduction of Mothering,* Nancy Chodorow has combined a sociological perspective and psychoanalytic theory to explain why it is that women, and not men, are "primary caregivers." She suggests that there are fundamental differences in personality between women and men. According to Chodorow, men view themselves as separate and distinct from others; women define themselves through their relationships with others. She asserts that these personality differences are derived from an important feature of family structure: both daughters and sons are much more familiar with their mothers than their fathers. Therefore, daughters develop their identity as females by continuing their identification with their mothers. Conversely, sons establish their identity as males through a process of negation—by denying their similarity to their mothers. Chodorow argues that the structure of family relationships is a crucial factor in creating a psychological basis for mothering:

> Women's capacities for mothering and abilities to get gratification from it are strongly internalized and psychologically enforced, and are built developmentally into feminine psychic structure. Women are prepared psychologically for mothering through the developmental situation in which they grow up, and in which women have mothered them.[6]

There are other theories—biological and sociological—to explain why it is that women mother. It is not my purpose here to argue about which theory is correct. Like Chodorow, however, I am interested in the implications of family structure. A central fact about family structure is that women mother; and this fact provides a framework for the continuity of a special closeness between mothers and adult daughters.

In my workshop, the daughter who described her mother as "cold and distant" and the woman who had been in a concentration camp with her mother both conveyed an intuitive understanding of how their relationships with their mothers had changed when they became mothers themselves. The pull of mother-daughter identity is illustrated, paradoxically, by the daughter who said that her mother was "cold" and that she did *not* feel closer with her mother after the birth of her child. Although she saw herself as very different as a mother, their roles had become parallel. Becoming a mother created a dramatic shift in this daughter's perspective—despite her unresolved feelings about her mother. Similarly, the woman who had been in a concentration camp with her mother also found that she identified with her mother in a new way—from the perspective of motherhood.

These two stories illustrate the dualistic nature of mother-daughter identity. They are both about motherhood, experienced from the dual perspectives of "object" and "subject." When daughters become mothers, they shift from being the loved object to becoming *also* the subject—the one who loves as a mother. The word "also" is crucial here. The daughter-to-mother transition is sequential and additive. The daughter remains her mother's child—in memory and/or in an ongoing relationship with her mother—at the same time that she establishes a mothering relationship with her own child.

Myra Leifer,[7] in *The Psychological Effects of Motherhood,* reported that new mothers seem to have a need to be "mothered" by their own mothers. One of the young mothers in her sample commented about her mother's visit: "She mothered me more than the baby, and that was very luxurious." The implication is that mothers help prepare their daughters emotionally for motherhood. By reinforcing their daughters' position as objects of love, mothers may help establish their daughters in their subject roles—as givers of "mother love" to their own children.

In one sense, when daughters become mothers, they become "colleagues" with their mothers: both of them are adults and have ostensibly the same role. As mothers themselves, the daughters are the "selfless" supporters and nurturers of their own children. But in another sense, the daughters can never "catch up." When they become mothers, their mothers remain their mothers and also become grandmothers: Their family roles are mutually contingent and, in their generational positions, they are always a phase apart.

A SPECIAL CLOSENESS

How special or unique is the mother-daughter relationship? A number of recent theorists[8] have suggested that mothers and daughters tend to be too close and that "healthy" development requires loosening their emotional hold on each other. Other researchers have described the mother-daughter bond more positively—as the closest and most important relationship in interactions with kin. For example, Willmott and Young,[9] from their observations on family life in London in the late 1950s, commented on the "striking" interdependence of mothers and daughters. They noted that if the mother is sick, it is the daughter who comes to help. They also said that daughters see their mothers more often than sons do, and maternal grandparents see their grandchildren more than paternal grandparents do. Similarly, Peter Townsend, another anthropologist who was studying British family life around the same time, described family relationships as dominated by women—with the mother-daughter bond as the linchpin of family interactions. He wrote:

> Men, young as well as old, rarely occupied a vital role in family care. The system was chiefly organized around female relations. At its focal point stood the old woman . . . she usually retained important functions as housewife, mother and grandmother (even after her husband had retired from his central role). In her social and occupational life she had experienced much less change than had the man.[10]

About ten years later the sociologist Bert Adams found a similar pattern in the United States. In his book *Kinship in an Urban Setting,* which was based on research in a southern city, he said that females maintain ties among kin, and mothers and daughters tend to have especially close relationships. He also pointed out that close mother-daughter attachments persist across social class and generational differences. Adult children in white-collar families are more likely to live at a distance from their parents than the sons and daughters of blue-collar families. But daughters appear to be "kin-keepers" (that is, maintain contact) more than sons with both geographically near and distant relatives.[11]

There are other, more recent, studies from social gerontologists that provide further evidence for a special closeness between adult daughters and their mothers. Virtually all current studies of elderly parents have shown that daughters are much more likely than sons to be caregivers for their elderly parents—especially for their mothers.[12]

However, there are several reasons to raise questions about

just how close adult daughters and their mothers really are. First of all, at least one study has challenged the notion that kinship interactions are centered around women. Rosenberg and Anspach,[13] in their book *Working Class Kinship,* which is based on a large random survey, reported that husbands and wives usually see their relatives together and make joint decisions about whom to visit. (Nonetheless, they did find that married couples visit with wives' kin more than husbands' kin.) Second, even those who describe the mother-daughter bond as central in kinship also note that, in general, there are strong ties between adult children (daughters *and* sons) and their parents (mothers *and* fathers). For both daughters and sons, their attachment to their parents is unlikely to disappear just because the "children" are grown and have left their parents' home.[14] Finally, a number of studies have hinted that there are boundaries or limitations around mother-daughter intimacy. For example, the British anthropologist Raymond Firth and his co-researchers commented:

> . . . what is particularly significant in the social relations of married children is the way in which superficial harmony covers a range of disparate attitudes. Common in our material was the expression on the part of married son or daughter that relations with a parent were friendly but superficial; that he or she liked the parent but did not feel they could discuss intimate matters with him or her . . . Many of our informants expressed this feeling of duty to parents . . .[15]

In the United States, most older parents say that the type of relationship they want with their children is "intimacy at a distance"—that is, they want to live near but not with their children.[16] The wording of this phrase suggests a reconciliation of opposing themes in relationships between adult children and their parents. It seems that both generations try to maintain their attachments with one another and, at the same time, they recognize the boundaries that separate them.

If mothers and daughters tend to have special bonds—which are closer than other ties between kin—this has to be because of their shared roles as women in the family—especially their roles as mothers. As mothers, they occupy a similar position in family structure; they engage in comparable tasks and responsibilities; and they share the emotional experience of mother love. This means that there is a "reproductive bond" that links mothers and daughters across generations in the family.

But there are barriers between mothers and daughters—and these limitations to mother-daughter intimacy also come from their family roles. Their reproductive bond competes with the heterosexual bond between husband and wife. For a daughter, her new motherhood may intensify her attachment to her own mother. But at the same time, and even more significantly, the birth of her child reinforces her marital commitment and increases her dependence on her husband.[17]

One conclusion we might draw is that mothers and their adult daughters tend to have relationships that are *both* emotionally close and emotionally distant. In effect, the structure of family relationships simultaneously seems to sustain mother-daughter attachments and impose barriers between them. One purpose of this book is to understand the meaning of this apparent contradiction.

"ADULT CHILDREN" AND "POST-PARENTS"

This summer a woman I know was in a serious automobile accident. As she was lying on the ground, she said to her husband, who also had been injured: "I've broken my back. I'm going to die. Take care of the children." At the time of the accident, her "children" were thirty-eight and forty-one! It is possible, of course, that she was delirious and had projected herself back in time. Even so, it is striking that her first thoughts concerned her responsibility as a mother.*

The terms we use—"adult children" and "post-parents"— reveal the paradox. The mother-child (or parent-child) hierarchy is defined by the fact that the parent is responsible for the child. As children grow older, the nature of maternal or parental responsibility changes—until, at some point, parents launch their children and surrender day-to-day responsibility for their care. But the incident

---

* Both the husband and wife with the broken backs eventually did recover.

of the woman with the broken back illustrates the continuity of parental responsibility—at least in a symbolic and emotional sense.

In various ways, adult sons and daughters in our society appear to negate the parent-child hierarchy. Young adult children almost always establish independent residences when they marry, and often before. Moreover, married sons and daughters generally neither expect nor receive substantial economic support from their parents. In fact, as both the children and their parents grow older, it becomes increasingly likely that children give more help to their parents than vice versa.[18] A number of surveys have found that adult children generally express feelings of filial responsibility toward their parents. When elderly parents become frail, adult children, particularly daughters, often provide care to their parents, either having their parents in the same household or supervising care in the parents' home. Thus, in terms of the external components of their lives— where they live, economic support, and other kinds of help—the parent-child hierarchy seems to all but disappear.

However, in terms of their emotional relationships, it is not so clear that most grown children and their parents are able to have adult-to-adult peerlike relationships. There is at least implicit evidence, from various sources, that the parent-child asymmetry may be preserved well into the child's adulthood. For example, several sociologists have noted that adult children who provide care to their parents often seem to feel uncomfortable about their parents' dependence on them.[19] Also, reports from a number of clinical psychologists have indicated that adult children continue to seek their parents' approval. Several of these studies have implied that daughters, until at least age forty or so, often sustain some sense of child position in their relationships with their mothers. One clinical study found that relationships with mothers were better if the mothers demonstrated "approval of" and "interest in" their adult daughters—behaviors that might be interpreted as a continuity of mothering. Another study showed that adult children tend to judge their parents on the basis of the quality of parenting they received—also suggesting that they continue to view them more as parents than as peers.[20]

In some ways mothers may have less difficulty than fathers

in developing peerlike relationships with their children. Possibly, mothers' relationships with their growing children may be less hierarchical than fathers' relationships—specifically, in terms of power. Families differ in the amount of power that parents can exert over their children. In some but not all cultures, the father is clearly supposed to be the "boss." But, though the power structure varies, in virtually all societies mothers have more involvement with their children. This means that mothers—compared to fathers—can rely more on affection and less on the use of power in gaining compliance from their children.[21] Presumably, then, when the children are grown, the vertical nature of relationships with fathers needs to be radically restructured, while relationships with mothers are already more nearly horizontal.

But in another sense, motherhood entails a much more asymmetrical or imbalanced relationship than fatherhood. The psychologist Alice Balint[22] has noted that from the perspective of the infant, the "ideal mother has no interests of her own." This does not mean, of course, that women as mothers in actuality have no self-interests. But the nurturance associated with mothering is asymmetrical—with the infant/child entitled to absolute dependence and the mother ideally (from the child's point of view) all-giving. According to several theorists, adults as well as children continue to attribute "selflessness" to women as mothers. Dorothy Dinnerstein, in *The Mermaid and the Minotaur,* asserts that mothers are viewed as both necessary and intrusive—that is, they have "the dual role of indispensable quasi-human supporter and quasi-human enemy of the human self."[23]

Among the various intergenerational pairs (mother-daughter, father-daughter, father-son, and mother-son), mothers and daughters are likely to be the most involved in each other's lives. It is because of their involvement that both mothers and daughters are confronted with choices about treating each other as peers or not. Thus, if there is a tension or inconsistency between peership and parenting in relationships between adult children and their parents, this tension is likely to be more emotionally complex between mothers and daughters than in other relationships between generations.

FAMILY TIES OVER TIME

A central question in my research has been: How do mother-daughter relationships change? In addressing this question, I have found conflicting and confusing images—both when I review the research literature and when I talk to women about their personal experiences. There appear to be two sets of contradictory predictions about the life course of the mother-daughter relationship:

The first set of contradictions is about emotional closeness versus distance:

Mothers and daughters remain close to each other over the years. (OR) *Mothers and daughters grow apart over the years.*

The second set of contradictions concerns parenting versus peership:

Mothers and daughters continue to treat each other as parent and child. (OR) *Mothers and daughters become like peers when the daughters are adults.*[24]

Which statements are true? One type of answer is obvious: Mother-daughter relationships vary. Some mothers and daughters have close relationships; others feel distant from each other. In a similar way, in some families the young adult children are treated as equals; in others the daughters or sons are never seen as fully adult, no matter how old they are. Such factors as social class and ethnic background, along with differences in personality, are likely to account for variability across families. But the most obvious explanation—that families differ—does not really explain the contradictions. In my interviews with adult daughters and their mothers, I have been struck by the contradictions that appear within the same relationships. It seems that most mothers and daughters are both close and distant, and most are both peerlike and parental at the same time.

Throughout this book, I will argue that these contradictions are inherent in the mother-daughter relationship and that they emerge from underlying characteristics of family structure. The mother-daughter relationship is part of a larger family structure. When daughters marry and have children of their own, new members are added to their families—spouses, in-laws, and grandchildren. When mothers become frail, there are new roles and responsibilities for members of their families. Thus, as daughters mature and mothers age, the structure of their family relationships changes.

A "family structure" can be defined objectively—with such characteristics as the number of family members, their roles or positions (mother, father, daughter, etc.), and their relative ages. Over time, there are alterations in family structure. Some of the changes are gradual and subtle: A child becomes a little older and a bit more independent. A mother begins to feel the effects of age; perhaps she is not able to walk or to see or to hear quite as well as she used to. There is a continuous process of change in family life, which is almost impossible to measure or study. But some of the transformations are much more visible: When daughters marry and have children of their own, they establish new households and new family ties. This transposition of family structure creates new conditions for their relationships with their mothers. In a similar way, there are changes in family structure when mothers age and become frail. When elderly mothers are hospitalized and require care after they leave the hospital, there is a change in the objective conditions of their lives. And this change is likely to have an impact on their relationships with their daughters.

What I have just described are changes in the objective characteristics of family structure. But there is also a subjective dimension to family life. Each of us carries in our head a symbolic representation of our family. For most of us, our subjective interpretations are based largely on the objective characteristics of our own family. But our symbolic images incorporate not just what our family is like now, but also a sense of our family over time.[25] It is in this sense that we can understand the contradictory nature of the mother-daughter relationship. Mothers and daughters share a long and intimate past. The relationship between adult daughters and their mothers emerges from both the current structure of family life and the structure of their relationships in the past.

A friend of mine used to love to talk about her mother's blue couch. Although she was married and had been living in another state, she always knew that she could go "home"—to her mother and her mother's blue couch. Often, when she needed comforting, she would travel home and sit on that couch, talking with her mother—so that she became, at least for a while, the same child, the daughter who had a place to go "home" to.

For my friend, that blue couch symbolized her relationship with her mother when she was a child, and part of her remained in this earlier relationship. In her current life there were many experiences and feelings that she preferred to confide in friends and to keep secret from her mother. At least in part, she preserved her special intimacy with her mother by maintaining her distance— geographical and emotional. Moreover, despite her desire for the comfort represented by that couch, in most of her interactions with her mother she certainly would not want to be treated like a child. But in her relationship with her mother there was a merging of past and present. She was both a child and an adult.

In interviewing adult daughters and their mothers, I never came across another story about a blue couch. In fact, as I commented in the beginning of this chapter, there is a different set of experiences for every mother-daughter relationship. But there are common themes, which emerge from the underlying structure of family roles. The daughters and mothers in my study, by describing their individual experiences, revealed the structural contradictions in their relationships. The opposing themes and contradictory expectations that are found in relationships between adult daughters and their mothers begin to be expressed during the adolescent years.

2

THE ADOLESCENT YEARS

My interviews with young adult daughters and their mothers began with a number of questions about their relationships during the daughters' childhood and adolescence. Their experiences during the adolescent years provide a framework and background for understanding their adult relationships. In order to understand how relationships between adult daughters and their mothers have changed, we need to see what kinds of family experiences came before the daughter's adulthood. Moreover, families differ, and these differences set the stage for later transitions in mother-daughter relationships.

The information for this chapter is largely retrospective; and we have to be concerned both that people forget and that they remember selectively—recalling the past to fit the present. Nonetheless, the mothers and daughters did tend to refer to comparable events in their lives. In a number of cases, however, the same events were perceived or interpreted in different ways. In any case, I was not asking about a very distant past; for most of the daughters, adolescence was just a few years before.

In some ways, adolescence brings a kind of metamorphosis to family relationships, as daughters and mothers both view the development that has occurred already and envision the changes that are yet to come. For about a year or so in early adolescence, the physiological changes in a girl are startling—rapid growth, menarche, and the development of breasts, wider hips, and pubic hair. Menstrual cycles in early puberty tend to be irregular and may contribute to volatile moods in teenage daughters.[1]

The social transformation of adolescence takes much longer and is more ambiguous than the physiological development. The sociologist Ralph Turner, in *Family Interaction,*[2] has suggested that much of the difficulty in relationships between adolescents and their parents derives from opposing definitions of the adolescent's status as adult or child:

> The adolescent self-conception typically centers on future achievement, which is displaced in time into the present. The adolescent characteristically thinks of himself as already in large part what he is to become. He demands that others interact with him on the assumption that he has already achieved the wisdom, the responsibility, and the versatility that represent his personal goal . . . But unlike youth, parents do not merge the future into the present in their conception of the adolescent. The bias instead is in the opposite direction, the accumulated memory of past images dominating the parent's anticipations regarding behavior in the immediate present. As a consequence, the parent deals with the adolescent as he has been but not quite as he is now.

These comments apply to parents' relationships with both daughters and sons. In some ways, the issues that emerge in adolescence are similar for mothers and fathers and for daughters and sons. All of these parent-child relationships need to be renegotiated as the adolescent approaches adulthood. But gender is an important factor in family life. I did not interview sons about their adolescent relationships with their parents. However, in my interviews with the daughters, I asked almost as many questions about their fathers as about their mothers; and the comparison of mother-daughter and father-daughter relationships shows how gender structures family interactions.

HOLDING ON AND LETTING GO

Nancy Chodorow, in *The Reproduction of Mothering,* has argued that the issue of separation in adolescence tends to be more difficult for daughters than for sons. According to her psychoanalytic perspective, the process of establishing psychological distance occurs early in male development—during the resolution of the oedipal phase for preschool-age boys. Daughters, however, do not need to establish the same measure of psychological distinctness when they are small children; and, in fact, they never fully develop a separate sense of self. Chodorow characterizes mothers' attitudes toward their adolescent daughters as "ambivalent" in that "They desire both to keep daughters close and to push them into adulthood. This ambivalence in turn creates more anxiety in their daughters and provokes attempts by these daughters to break away."[3]

In depicting the adolescent years, most of the mothers and daughters in my study characterized their relationships in terms of both holding on and letting go—that is, endeavoring to maintain an ongoing attachment while, at the same time, also engaging in a process of separation. The dynamic quality of this process is evoked when we compare daughters' relationships with their mothers versus those with their fathers. Other studies have shown that both daughters and sons tend to feel closer to their mothers than their fathers.[4] My research indicated much more continuity in relationships with mothers than with fathers. In the mother-daughter bond, there tends to be an ongoing intimate attachment throughout the daughter's adolescence. But it is also true that daughters engage in a separation struggle much more with their mothers than with their fathers.

One indicator of mother-daughter closeness is daughters' tendency to "confide" in their mothers. Table 1a shows that the daughters, as teenagers, were far more likely to confide "a lot" in their mothers than in their fathers. Conversely, they were much more likely to say that they confided "not at all" in their fathers than in their mothers. Although most of the daughters stated that they confide in their mothers more "now" (as young adults), nonetheless, as teenagers, almost all of them confided considerably more in their mothers than in their fathers.

As the daughters discussed their childhood and teenage years, they portrayed a sharp division of roles within their families. Most of the daughters indicated that their fathers were considerably less involved in their upbringing than their mothers. A third of the daughters could not give any description of their fathers' method of disciplining, whereas all of them could describe how their mothers

Table 1. Indicators of Involvement between Adolescent
Daughters and Their Mothers versus Their Fathers

(A)	DAUGHTERS CONFIDED IN:	
	Mothers	*Fathers*
A lot	14	1
Some	26	17
Not at all	3	21
Total	43	39

(B)	DAUGHTERS ARGUED WITH:	
	Mothers	*Fathers*
Most of the time	14	1
Occasionally	24	7
Almost never	5	31
Total	43	39

(C)	PRAISE AND CRITICISM FROM:	
	Mothers	*Fathers*
Received praise	28 (43)	23 (39)
Received criticism	31 (43)	13 (39)

disciplined them. Often it seemed that the father was something of
an adjunct parent—with the mother in charge and setting the tone
for the way the children were to be reared. A number of daughters
made statements to the effect: "I think my father pretty much left
it up to my mother . . ." Even working mothers tended to have
prime responsibility for home and children.[5]

Many of the daughters who did describe their fathers' involvement in their upbringing also implied that the fathers' role was
secondary. For instance, one daughter, when asked, "Was your
father involved in things you did?" replied:

> Not to the extent my mother was. He's very quiet. He's into
> everything in town but as far as home things . . . it's kind of hard.
> I think he's awkward . . . as to saying things like "I love you"

     ... things like that. He was involved but kind of behind my mother.

There is, of course, a range of feelings toward fathers (and mothers). The daughter quoted above implies that there is an underlying sense of warmth in her relationship with her father, but he is not emotionally expressive—in contrast to her mother, who does express open affection. Some of the other daughters described their fathers in more hostile terms; for example, one daughter quipped: "He didn't care what other people did around him—as long as it didn't interfere with his time." But although there was a range of feelings for both parents, what is clear across virtually *all* of the families is that the daughters grew up with greater involvement, familiarity, and intimacy with their mothers than with their fathers.

    The fathers were not necessarily stricter than the mothers. But the fathers' "limits"—in terms of emotional responses—may have been less known. Several of the daughters stated that as children they thought of their fathers as strict and fearsome; it was only later that they "discovered" that there was nothing to be frightened of. The father's status as something of an outsider allows him to "come in" with authority.

    Nancy Friday,[6] in her popular book *My Mother, Myself,* suggested that fathers may be particularly valued because of their outsider status:

> Daddy is godlike, not just because he's distant and has this attractive sexual quality, but because like executives who let underlings deliver the bad news while they themselves announce promotions and raises, mother has had to do the day-to-day discipline, withholding allowances and pleasures when we are naughty, forcing us to eat and do things we don't like. When dad comes home from work, we may be at the end of our rope with mother. He enters with a clean slate.

A number of the daughters saw their fathers as often being tired and having other concerns. "He wanted to be easygoing and playful with us but he would get tied up with his own needs and . . . his way had to go." When the father's time in the family is brief, his time may be imbued with a sense of importance not given to the mother's time. In contrast, mothers tend to have "fire department duty"—that is, always being on call. The mother's time may be perceived as having no bounds and therefore little value.

In contrast to adolescent daughters' relationships with fathers, mothers and adolescent daughters appear to experience a continuity of strong attachment. But the daughter's greater intimacy with her mother also means that her struggle for detachment is played out much more with her mother than with her father. Both my respondents and other researchers[7] have portrayed adolescence as a time for breaking away from childhood attachments to parents. Not all daughters argue a great deal with their mothers. As Table 1b shows, about a third of the daughters reported arguing "most of the time" with their mothers. But this table also shows that the daughters were considerably more likely to argue with their mothers than with their fathers—undoubtedly because mothers were more available and were viewed as more approachable. Daughters also were more likely to refer to their teenage years as the "worst age" in relationships with their mothers than in relationships with their fathers.

In addition, mothers were viewed as more intrusive than fathers. Although the daughters reported similar amounts of praise from both parents, about twice as many indicated being criticized by mothers as by fathers. (See Table 1c.) The greater amount of criticism tends to center around one factor: messiness. Either the daughter's room was a mess or her hair or clothes were too sloppy. It seems to be rare for fathers to have commented on this—and when they did it was usually in support of the mothers. Criticism, particularly over this issue, may well be part of the mother's supervisory role—caring for home and children. Indeed, the mother's domestic role is the reason for her greater involvement with the children. The mother's criticisms seem to carry a dual and contradictory message: first, that the daughter ought to be more responsible and grown up (and thus be less "messy"), but, second, that the daughter is still a child and still in need of her mother's supervision.

The day-to-day involvement of mothers and daughters—from infancy through adolescence—creates a sense of mutual accessibility. Their familiarity with each other leaves the mother approachable for argument and the daughter accessible to criticism. It is through the intimacy of their involvement that mothers and daughters experience developmental struggles—particularly during the daughter's adolescence. Fathers and daughters tend to lack this intensity of involvement and, as a consequence, the father-daughter bond may be both less intimate and less difficult emotionally.

Attachment in the Mother-Daughter Bond So far I have talked about mother-daughter attachment by default—that is, daughters appear to be close to their mothers in contrast to fathers' lesser involvement in their lives. But how much "attachment" or "closeness" is there across mother-daughter relationships? Since emotions are difficult to measure, I have constructed two behavioral indicators of attachment from the interview data: (a) spending time alone with the mother and (b) receiving praise from the mother. When we spend time alone with someone, we can develop a unique set of shared meanings—experiences that we alone understand together.[8] Giving praise is a type of support and this kind of communication tends to lead to positive feelings.[9]

These behavioral indicators suggest that there is at least some form of attachment in most relationships between adolescent daughters and their mother. Table 2a shows that four-fifths of the daughters reported spending time alone with and/or receiving praise from their mothers. (This is the sum of the "highly involved" and the "somewhat involved" cases.) Mother-daughter closeness reflects the structure of gender roles in the family in two ways. First of all, time spent alone with and praise from mothers (for both daughters and sons) emerges from the obligations of the mother role—that is, the mother's accessibility and care. Second, the specific content of mother-daughter closeness, at least to some extent, often is associated with feminine activities (such as shopping) and the encouragement of femininity in the daughter. Most of the mothers and daughters spent time with each other in "typically" feminine activities—with shopping by far the most common activity, followed by baking, cooking, and sewing—in addition to just "sitting and talking." Praise from mothers centered on daughters' appearance and/or accomplishments (such as grades, sewing, etc.).

Table 2. "Attachment" and "Separation" between Adolescent Daughters and Their Mothers

(A) TYPES OF RELATIONSHIPS BETWEEN
ADOLESCENT DAUGHTERS AND THEIR MOTHERS—
IN TERMS OF PATTERNS OF "ATTACHMENT"

"Highly Involved" Relationships	
Daughters who spent time alone with *and*	
received praise from their mothers	22
"Somewhat Involved" Relationships	
Daughters who spent time alone with *or*	
received praise	13
"Remote" Relationships	
Daughters neither spending time alone	
with *nor* being praised	8
Total	43

(B) WAYS THAT ADOLESCENT DAUGHTERS ACHIEVE
EMOTIONAL SEPARATION FROM THEIR MOTHERS*

Implicit Way of Separating	
Censorship	39
Explicit Ways of Separating	
Conflict	15
Emotional withdrawal	15
Total	69

(C) TYPES OF MOTHER/ADOLESCENT-DAUGHTER
RELATIONSHIPS IN TERMS OF THEIR *COMBINATION*
OF "ATTACHMENT" AND "SEPARATION"

"The Most Common"	
Involvement plus censorship	29
"Invested"	
Involvement with no censorship	6
"Remote"	
Low involvement and censorship	8
Neither involvement nor censorship	0
Total	43

* Does not add up because more than one answer given by each respondent.

Adolescent Daughters Detaching from Their Mothers   If most mothers and daughters maintain a sense of closeness and attachment, there is another pattern that is equally prevalent—that is, for daughters to impose limits on their intimacy with their mothers. I noted above that almost all the daughters as teenagers confided at least somewhat in their mothers. But it is also true that almost all daughters engaged in some form of self-conscious censorship in terms of *what* they confided. For instance, one daughter noted: "There was nothing I couldn't tell her—a lot I just didn't tell her." Another said:

> It wasn't that I had secrets but I wasn't really at ease. I don't know why. If she asked a direct question I would probably tell her. But I wouldn't tell her secret thoughts.
> *What wouldn't you talk about?*
> Things I would wonder about—sex. I was never really comfortable talking with her [as a teenager] . . .

Only a few daughters said that they would and could tell their mothers anything. This overwhelming pattern of "censorship" constitutes an implicit way of achieving separation: The daughter quietly refuses to share certain of her feelings and experiences with her mother. The daughters who engaged in a form of censorship implied both that they could not expect their mothers to understand their feelings and also that their mothers probably wanted them to maintain some measure of privacy. Through their censorship, then, they did not explicitly reject their mothers' intimacy but rather they created a sense of separation implicitly, by placing boundaries around their intimate involvement. (See Table 2b.)

However, most of the daughters did not engage only in this implicit pattern of detachment. There is a stereotypical image of adolescence as a time of conflict and rebellion, characterized by the daughter's emotional volatility. About a third of the daughters described themselves as arguing with their mothers "almost all the time" during their adolescent years. For these daughters, the overt conflict constituted an explicit challenge to their mothers—in terms of both their intimate involvement and their authority relationship.

One daughter noted that as a teenager she seemed to be arguing with her mother "sixty percent of the time . . . it was very often about boyfriends . . . and what Mother expected of me, what her goals and aspirations were—when she'd want me to go bicycling through Europe and I'd want to stay home for the summer or whether it was an attitude about people in school or something like that . . ."

The arguments between mothers and adolescent daughters varied both in intensity and in specific topic (picking up rooms, boyfriends, daughters' plans for an evening, a summer, a lifetime). But the underlying issue was the mother's right to supervise and take part in her daughter's life. A high degree of conflict is likely to signify a daughter's "rebellion"—that is, her assertion of separation and independence from her mother.

There is, moreover, one other strategy of explicit separation, and that is for the daughter to withdraw emotionally from her mother. About a third of the daughters described themselves as emotionally withdrawing from their mothers—not just by mildly censoring what they said, but by overtly pushing their mothers away. The daughters who were emotionally withdrawn tried to build a defensive wall around themselves—presenting themselves to their mothers as shy, private, and stubborn. One daughter, when asked how much she confided in her mother, stated:

> Nothing unless she pulled it out of me. I didn't want to confide at all.
> *Would she try to pull it out?*
> Yes, sometimes. I do remember an incident coming home and being very upset about this boy who didn't have anything to do with me and I liked him and I had my door closed and she tried to come in and calm me down and just ask what was the matter and I felt at this time it was very private and I didn't want to tell her and eventually I did . . . But at that time I had my own private feelings and she wasn't aware of that.

The incident quoted above reflects the delicate balance between attachment and detachment. The mother, faced with a closed door, must choose between her concern for her daughter (reflecting her intimate attachment) and the symbolic boundary—the closed door.

In two-thirds of the cases the daughters' attempt at separation was explicit—entailing overt conflict and/or a process of emotional withdrawal. Thus, most of the daughters not only censored their confidences with their mothers, but also rejected their mothers more explicitly—either through conflict and/or by withdrawing emotionally.

Intimacy plus Separation   Overall, the most common pattern for adolescent daughters and their mothers is a juxtaposition of intimate involvement and separation. Table 2c shows that two-thirds of the cases fall into this pattern—that is, some form of involvement (time alone with and/or praise)—plus some strategy for detachment (with at least some censorship by the daughters).

Furthermore, in most of these families, there was not just quiet censorship, but either conflict or emotional withdrawal or both. For most of these families, relationships between mothers and adolescent daughters appeared to be characterized by both affection and some measure of interpersonal difficulty. For about a third of the families, the daughter's adolescence was experienced as a battlefield. An important point to make from these findings is that maintaining a balance between attachment and detachment may require a considerable amount of effort.

Most of the daughters had close friendships with their peers—girl friends, boyfriends, or both. They shared feelings and experiences with these friends that they kept secret from their mothers. But, despite their growth away from their families—through their attachment to peers—it is clear that most of the daughters made some "room" in their lives for their mothers (and vice versa). The daughter's process of separation takes place against a background of mother-daughter intimacy: Mothers (much more than fathers) are argued against, withdrawn from, and rebuffed—while at the same time daughters continue to rely on their mothers' nurturance. For most of the daughters, it is the stability of their mothers' attachment to them that allows them to go through the process of separation and develop a sense of independence.[10]

From the Viewpoint of the Mothers Adolescent daughters and their mothers confront a similar "developmental task"[11]—simultaneously "holding on" and "letting go." The mother's task is largely reflective and reactive. It is the daughters who are trying to separate by, in various ways, resisting their mothers' hold on them. An important issue to explore is how mothers respond and adjust to their daughters' attempts at breaking away.

There appear to be three types of responses from mothers: (1) normative explanations, (2) evidence of denial, and (3) feelings of rejection. The most commonly expressed reaction is normative—that is, stating that the daughter has a right to establish boundaries and that, culturally and developmentally, mothers ought to expect their daughters to go through some form of separation process. For instance, one mother of four daughters noted: "There's a lot of confiding from children when they're growing up, but in their teen years they share more with their friends or sisters than with their mothers." A number of the mothers indicated that they were not surprised by their daughters' striving for privacy. (This expectation of privacy was noted especially by mothers who tended themselves to be inexpressive and private with their feelings.)

Several mothers seemed to deny that their daughters were trying to set some distance between them. One example is the case of the daughter who said she confided "nothing" unless her mother "pulled it out of her." This mother and daughter presented very different pictures of their past and present relationship. The mother depicted their relationship as consistently very close, while the daughter described her relationship with her mother as cool—saying that she has always felt much closer to her father. Such inconsistencies were found for several mother-daughter pairs.[12]

About a quarter of the mothers (eleven out of the thirty-nine mothers interviewed) indicated that they felt a sense of rejection or helplessness as their daughters went through adolescence. In various ways, a number of these mothers expressed a feeling of being "left out." For example, one mother of six daughters noted that "There were a lot of conversations upstairs—above my head."

Another mother complained about her daughter's not being "the confiding type." This mother felt shut out by the shell of privacy that her daughter had erected around herself. She stated: "I thought I used to confide in her [the daughter] a lot. I tried to get very close to her because she was my whole life—but she wouldn't confide in me much." Such responses from mothers were found only in those cases where the daughter's separation process was explicit—with the daughter arguing a lot or building a tight shell of privacy around herself.

These three types of reactions are not necessarily mutually exclusive. That is, some of the mothers who talked about feelings of rejection softened these admissions with normative explanations. For instance, one mother said that "sometimes I felt left out" but added the qualification "but I expected that." Conversely, mothers who did not talk about feeling hurt were not necessarily free from pain. The expressions of rejection and helplessness were spontaneous responses—the mothers were not asked explicitly if they felt hurt by their daughters' actions during the adolescent years. It is possible that respondents might either repress such negative feelings from their memories or selectively represent themselves in a more positive, socially desirable way during the interview. Other research[13] suggests that mothers with teenagers in their homes experience anxiety and lowered self-esteem.

ATYPICAL MOTHERS AND DAUGHTERS

I have noted that "holding on and letting go" is the most common pattern in relationships between adolescent daughters and their mothers. But about a third of the mothers and daughters in my sample varied from this pattern. It is important to examine these atypical cases for two reasons: First of all, we need to emphasize the variability in mother-daughter relationships and not make the mistake of assuming that there are universal and invariant features of these relationships. Second, we need to examine under what circumstances mothers and daughters deviate from the most common patterns. These atypical or deviating families can help to illuminate the underlying processes in mother-daughter interactions.

About a fifth of the daughters said that as teenagers they spent virtually no time alone with their mothers and that their mothers did not give them any praise. In their descriptions of their teenage years these daughters tended to indicate both a minimal affective involvement with their mothers and a lack of self-esteem. In reviewing these families, I was struck by what was *not* there— that is, a sense of warmth and pleasure in these mother-daughter relationships. In order to give a sense of the qualitative differences between remote and involved mother-daughter pairs, I will compare two families, one remote and one highly involved—that is, where the daughter reports that she both spent time alone with and received praise from her mother.

A Remote Mother When Alice was a young girl, her mother was widowed and her mother's life seemed to center on a struggle for financial survival. She had little education and, over the years, worked at several low-skilled jobs. Alice depicted her mother as inexpressive, both physically—no hugging or kissing—and verbally. The mother consented to be interviewed reluctantly and gave curt answers to all the questions. She described her feelings about being a mother with the words: "I did what I had to do. That's the story of my life." Alice, when asked, "What did you enjoy doing with your mother as a teenager?" answered: "We didn't do anything together. She was always working or tired." When asked if her mother praised her, she said: "I don't think she praised me for anything. There wasn't anything to praise me for."

A Highly Involved Mother and Daughter Mrs. Kormer was married to a professional man and, despite some brief difficulties in his career, their family enjoyed financial security. Mrs. Kormer was college-educated and worked at least part-time most of her life. She described motherhood as "the most important part of my life— well, being a wife first, a mother second. It was never a conflict for me being a mother and being a professional. I didn't go back full-time until Judy [youngest daughter] was in college. For me it was very important being with the kids." Judy said that as a teenager she enjoyed shopping and baking with her mother; and when asked about praise, she replied: "She often said things about my being pretty and having a nice figure and general things about being bright or sharp."

These two young women, at the time of my interviews with them, were both soft-spoken and both appeared to be intelligent and moderately attractive. Thus, the differences in praise seem to reflect not their innate qualities but the nature of their mother-daughter attachments. What is evident in the involved mother-daughter pair and missing in the remote mother and daughter is a *sense of joy* in their relationship. We need to ask, why should this be so? Why do some mothers and daughters *not* have a strong sense of attachment and intimacy?

One important factor is personality. In some of the families the lack of emotional involvement seemed to be related to the mother's personality. The highly involved mothers were more likely to be rated by their daughters as expressive and openly affectionate, while the remote mothers tended to be described as private and inexpressive. The daughter's personality also affected the relationship. In two of the remote pairs, the remoteness appeared to be initiated by the daughters. In those pairs, the daughters, from an early age, appeared to reject emotional involvement with their mothers, so that the lack of time alone with the mother and the lack of support seem to reflect the daughter's personal characteristics.

Another variable is social class, a factor that differentiates the two pairs just discussed. The first mother's lack of resources—both financial and educational—clearly affected her relationship with her daughter. But social class is not necessarily a determining factor. Middle-class families include both remote and highly involved mothers and daughters, and the same is true for lower-class families.

There are also differences between the remote and highly involved mother-daughter pairs in terms of the structure of their family systems. In comparing the structures of these families, I noticed two striking differences: First of all, the remote families are somewhat larger—an average of four children, in contrast to an average of three children for the more involved mother-daughter pairs. And second, the remote mothers and daughters are much more likely to be in families that have experienced marital disruption.

Half of the remote mothers were widowed or divorced before the daughters' adolescent years. In contrast, *none* of the highly involved mothers was widowed or divorced during the daughter's childhood or adolescence. (There were two highly involved mothers who were divorced *after* the daughter had reached adolescence.)

My sample is small, so we have to be careful about drawing broad conclusions. Also, I think that problems in mother-daughter relationships are not caused directly by the mother's lack of a husband. But these findings suggest how the mother-daughter relationship is shaped by the larger family system of which it is a part. Half of these mothers were generational "isolates"—having no generational peer in their nuclear families. When a husband/father is lacking, there is no backup support for parental responsibilities. Also, with relatively large families, these mothers may have been worn down by competing demands on their time. Thus, the remote mothers were both overloaded and undersupported by their families.

"Invested" Mother-Daughter Pairs I noted above that most adolescent daughters use at least some measure of censorship in their confidences with their mothers. Six daughters said that they censored nothing. In all but one of these families, the daughters and mothers also reported that their confiding was mutual. For these relationships, this pattern of mutual confiding has persisted from the daughter's adolescence into young adulthood. Thus, these mothers and daughters have a long and continuous history of strong emotional investment in each other. I am calling these "invested" mother-daughter pairs—recognizing, however, that there is variability among these relationships. Other researchers have described a pattern of tight friendship between mothers and daughters in working-class families.[14] The invested mothers and daughters fit that image. In my study, however, these relationships are extreme in the extent to which there is such a high level of mutual investment. They are unusual even for working-class mothers and daughters in my study. In these families, the mothers were highly invested in their daughters—to the exclusion of other relationships. Moreover, most of these daughters as young adults have retained a symbiotic kind of relationship with their mothers.

The invested and the remote relationships seem to reflect very different kinds of family alliances. Specifically, these families differ markedly in terms of the position of the father. In the invested pairs, there tended to be a tight *mother-daughter alliance against the father*. In all of these families, the daughters, by the time they were adolescents, had taken on rather adultlike relationships with their mothers. In half of these invested relationships, the father was alcoholic or otherwise irrational. (In contrast, there were problem fathers in only two of the other thirty-seven families.) In the other families the father's role was very traditional—being a provider but having little emotional involvement with his daughter (or perhaps with his wife).

Because of their intense closeness, the daughters in invested relationships were probably often aware of their mothers' moods. In one family, for instance, with a very traditional father, the mother talked about needing someone to talk to when she was angry with the father:

> You know sometimes you have arguments with your husband and you have to talk to somebody. I would never run her father down or anything . . . He was involved in the Moose lodge and he got involved in different things and I would say I wish he could be home . . . She agreed with me—though she understood it as well as I did. She would say, Well, Dad felt good . . . and he can't always be with us. I think she was very understanding that way.

In this family, the alliance between mother and daughter supports the traditional father role: Together they justify the father's frequent absence from the home while at the same time providing emotional support for each other—diminishing, particularly for the mother, the need for the father to be around.

This kind of mother-daughter alliance is seen even more explicitly in families with problem fathers. These daughters tended to be given private, secret information about their fathers. For instance, one daughter told about learning that her father refused to have sex with her mother:

> My mother told me that he was masturbating upstairs and they hadn't had sex for a long time. That, of course, was none of my

business. But I mentioned to my father that I thought there were an awful lot of Kleenexes in the laundry lately . . . My mother was complaining that she had to do all the handkerchiefs . . . She washed them and she ironed them and my father was using them to masturbate upstairs and then he'd throw them under the bed and she'd have to clean them up. I didn't think that was her job. So when she told me I got angry with my father. I didn't confront him directly . . . but I let him know that I knew . . .

In this family there seems to be some confusion about the boundaries around the husband-wife dyad. The daughter indicates her awareness of these boundary problems; she admits that it was "none of my business" to know about her father's sexuality. The mother describes herself as highly invested in her children—with a marriage that was more empty than conflictful. Both the mother and daughter indicated that they had an unusually close relationship. But while the mother depicted her relationship with her daughter as "more like a girl friend; I felt the same age as my children," the daughter saw herself as her mother's protector. The daughter was furious with her father on her mother's behalf—thus forging an alliance against the father.

In contrast, in most of the remote families there seemed to be no mother-daughter alliance. In those families in which the remoteness appeared to be initiated by the daughters, the daughters' strongest family alliances were with their fathers. But in half of these families there was no father present. The lack of a father meant that there could be no father-mother alliance which would define the mother's generational position in relation to the children. At the same time, the lack of a father meant that there could be no mother-daughter alliance against a father.

In most mother-daughter relationships there is a delicate balance between attachment and separation. The father's position may be critical in helping to define this balance. First of all, the father's economic support for the family provides a context for the mother-child intimate involvement. Second, the presence of a father who is less intimately involved than the mother helps to define the mother-daughter relationship as special. Thus there is an implicit contrast so that the daughter (or son) learns about intimacy according to a sense of relativity—the mother, because of the nature of her role (and despite variability in personality) in most families is more involved with her children than is the father. Finally, the father's emotional relationship with the mother places boundaries around the mother's needs for emotional investment in her children and helps to create generational subsystems in the family. In most families, there are a number of possibilities for subsystems: husband-wife; mother-child; father-child; and child-child. In the atypical families (those with remote or invested mother-daughter relationships), the husband-wife relationship is either lacking or there is some problem in that relationship. Under these circumstances, there may be more pressure on the mother-daughter relationship—so that either the daughter's relationship with her mother is diminished or the mother comes to be overly invested in her relationship with her daughter. In either type of case, the difficulties in the mother-daughter relationship are related to the structure of family relationships and the fact that these families appear to lack clear generational boundaries.

DAUGHTERS PROTECTING MOTHERS

Adolescence entails problems of definition and timing: How and when does the daughter (or son) emerge from childhood into adulthood? There is no clear passage into adulthood in our society—despite some nominal rites of passage, such as confirmation or bar mitzvah or ages for driving, drinking, and voting. Most of the mothers and daughters indicated that their relationships were asymmetrical or hierarchical during the daughter's adolescence, with the daughter defined as a "child." But one consequence of the daughter's transition to sexual and social maturity is that, eventually, the daughter will need to be treated as an adult.

Teenage Daughters as Confidantes   One indicator of peer-like relationships between mothers and their maturing daughters is the extent to which mothers confide in their daughters. Most of the mothers in my study insisted that they did *not* confide in their adolescent daughters. The central factor was that they were not peers. One mother, asked about confiding in her daughter as a teenager, said: "Not about my problems. We would talk about *her* things." Many of the mothers made normative statements about the inappropriateness of confiding in "children":

> I never believed in it at that age—giving the child any trouble that I might have had. . . . Like if her father and I had an argument I didn't believe in imposing it on them [the children]. The arguments they heard—they heard openly, but other than that I would never tell them till they were older. Now I tell them—life isn't a bed of roses for anybody—the good with the bad. Then I didn't want to create a feeling against either one of us for something I might confide. What they didn't know wouldn't hurt them.

While this statement is full of clichés about life and may not reveal actual behavior, what is significant is the mother's attitude of *protectiveness*. This mother was attempting to shelter her daughter (and sons) from potentially disturbing information about the parents' marriage. At the same time, she was protecting her family as a unit by maintaining generational boundaries.

Only about a third of the mothers and fathers confided at all in their adolescent daughters. But there were some important differences. First of all, according to the accounts of the daughters, most of the mothers who confided in their daughters confided a *lot;* the fathers who confided in their daughters confided a *little*. Second, for many of the fathers who were said to have confided a "little," the context did not necessarily imply a strong and exclusive bond of intimacy between father and daughter: There was a tendency for fathers *not* to single out one daughter, and the content of what the father confided often focused on workday activities rather than feelings. Thus, for instance, a father might be said to "confide" in the whole family around the dinner table about his day at work. Conversely, mothers who treated their daughters as confidantes tended to share more personal experiences and feelings in one-to-one dialogues. Finally, the content of confiding between father and daughter was often intellectual rather than emotional. This is suggested by the fact that father's education[15] is an important factor in the amount of confiding between father and daughter. The daughters did more confiding in college-educated than in less-educated fathers. Conversely, education was not a factor in how much the daughters confided in their mothers. (If we argued that educated fathers were just more expressive, why would this not apply to mothers?) While a few of the daughters said that they shared emotional issues with their fathers, most—if they talked with their fathers—tended to focus on such issues as school achievements, politics, and current events.

The lack of intense mutual confiding between most fathers and daughters indicates not only less intimacy than between mothers and daughters but possibly also more of a hierarchical relationship. That mothers chose to confide a lot or not at all in their teenage daughters suggests that those mothers who did confide in their teenage daughters were interacting with their daughters more or less as peers.

In almost all cases of mothers' confiding in their teenage daughters, the daughter's relationship with the father was extreme—either very positive or very negative. There are two variables that are associated with the likelihood of mothers' confiding in teenage daughters: (1) having a problem husband/father and (2) daughter's birth order. Both of these relate to the structure of family relationships and the orientation of the father in the family.

The mothers confided in their adolescent daughters in virtually *all* of the families where there were ongoing and blatant problems with the fathers. Possibly these mothers lacked confidantes, in that their husbands may have been emotionally unavailable. But these mothers' reliance on their daughters does not seem to be explained simply by the lack of adult confidantes, because the mothers without husbands (through widowhood or divorce) did *not* confide in their daughters. Thus the daughters with problem fathers seemed to become confidantes not just to fill a vacuum—an empty place in a family system—but because these daughters had become involved in family alliances. The daughters with problem fathers were witnesses in their parents' marital difficulties and were drawn into an emotional alliance with their mothers.

The second variable, birth order, is also an important component of family structure. Mothers were considerably more likely to confide in oldest daughters as teenagers than middle or youngest daughters. Nearly three-quarters of the mothers confided in oldest and only daughters as adolescents; by comparison between one-quarter and one-third confided in middle and youngest daughters. About the same proportion of oldest and middle daughters confided in their mothers as teenagers—so that the confiding by mothers appears to be an indicator of peership, not just attachment.

Birth order affects the daughter's family position in that oldest daughters are more likely than middle daughters to have especially close relationships with their fathers. When there are no sons in the family, fathers often seem to treat their oldest and only daughters as "substitute sons" and give them attention and encouragement for their achievements. When a daughter has a distinct and close relationship with her father, mother-daughter confiding is counter-balanced by father-daughter closeness, creating a family triangle in which there are alliances—or close bonds—among all family members.

There may be another reason why mothers are more likely to confide in oldest daughters—the daughter's imputed maturity. Mothers who confided in their daughters almost always pointed to their "exceptional maturity." It is possible that mothers perceive oldest daughters as mature at a relatively early age. Oldest daughters often are expected to take on adultlike responsibilities, such as taking care of younger siblings. Moreover, parents of oldest and only daughters are likely to be inexperienced and naive in their expectations. Mothers of oldest daughters may compare them to their younger siblings and, within that comparison, think they are already grown up.

Problems with Parents The daughters were selected from a "normal"—that is, nonclinical—population. The majority portrayed their family lives as reasonably happy. There were a number of daughters, however, who described major problems with one of their parents. Six of the daughters described their mothers in generally negative terms; seven portrayed their fathers very negatively. (Each of these daughters spoke negatively about only one of her parents.) These daughters differed from the others in two ways: First, they made many more negative statements about either the mother or the father in discussing their childhood and adolescent years than the other daughters; and, second, in these daughter interviews, there was a continuing tone of hostility or resentment toward the one parent. In addition, the mothers who were described negatively were rated lower by their daughters on a "mothering ability" scale than were the other mothers.[16]

These negative perceptions came from the single perspective of the daughters. In one family, the mother and daughter were "estranged"—had had almost no contact with each other for several years; this mother declined to be interviewed. In the interviews with the other mothers who were portrayed negatively, there was little or no evidence that the mothers were aware of their daughters' negative feelings toward them.

The bases for the negative feelings were different for mothers versus fathers. The fathers were alcoholic, abusive and/or philandering—in all cases extremely uninvolved with their families. The negative characteristics of the mothers were less concrete and more subtle; they were portrayed, implicitly, as either hostile (too strict) or selfish (not sufficiently interested in the daughter).

What appears to be common to the experience of having a problem father or mother is that the daughter turns to and is closer with the other parent—especially during the adolescent years. The fact that this is true in all families with problem fathers is not too surprising, since most daughters are closer to their mothers anyway. With the problem mothers, in half of the families the father was not around—through either death or divorce. In all of the other families, the daughters reported having been much closer with their fathers than with their mothers.

However, faced with one problem parent, daughters "turn to" mothers and fathers in very different ways. When the mother was the problem, fathers were turned to for protection—that is, they relied on their fathers for emotional support and they used their fathers as allies in conflict with their mothers. When the father was the problem, daughters were protective of their mothers—that is, the daughters were leaned on emotionally; their alliance would give the mother some measure of power over the father; and sometimes they were asked to serve as intermediaries—presenting the mother's needs to the father.

The daughters who had problem mothers liked to spend time alone with their fathers but gave no hint that they were trying to "protect" their fathers. One daughter who became estranged from her mother said about her father:

> He kind of spoiled me, whereby I could go to him and say, look what she's doing to me. I felt that he was always put in the middle, having to decide between her and me . . . A couple of times she threw me out and he'd always call me up and say come home . . .

In this family, the daughter's tie with her father gave her leverage in her arguments: Her mother could not permanently "throw her out" when the father could invite her home again. In this family, the father was caught in the middle—playing an intermediary role. Several other daughters—including some who later reconciled with their mothers—also saw their fathers as potentially strong allies, especially in their adolescent battles against their mothers. We can infer from the descriptions of the teenage years that being caught in the middle was often uncomfortable for these fathers. But the father's ability to "step in" with authority could sometimes be used to the daughter's advantage—giving a favored daughter special privileges, such as use of the family car.

In contrast, daughters with problem fathers became confidantes and advice givers to their mothers. Four of the six daughters with problem fathers counseled their mothers to seek a divorce. In another family, a daughter was asked by her mother to "save" her parents' marriage by interceding with the father—a difficult role for an adolescent girl. The protectiveness of some of the daughters is illustrated by the following description by a mother who eventually divorced her alcoholic and abusive husband:

> When she was in college she tried to show me what was wrong. She brought me reading matter. She thought I should have a life of my own. When I finally put him out of the house she made a remark that I'll always remember. She said: "That's the first time anyone told him what to do." Because the judge made him leave. He always did the telling.
> *How did you feel when she said that?*
> It felt good.

There seemed to be a sense of helplessness on the part of this mother. The daughter's remark about "the first time anyone told him what to do" (and the mother's implicit agreement with this statement) shows that the mother exercised little control in her marriage. Indeed, her dependence on her husband for financial support meant that this mother had little power to change her situation. She divorced her alcoholic and abusive husband only *after* her eight children were grown. At the time of the interview, she indicated that her financial resources were poor; despite court orders her husband rarely sent her alimony and she had few skills with which to earn much money on her own.

Another mother, asked if she confided in her daughter, said:

> She saw almost everything. When she was in college I'd tell her everything—when I saw her on weekends. If we hadn't had each other I would have thrown in the towel long ago. If not for her—a mother has to stay if she has a little girl. Otherwise I might have left. But those people who tell you to keep a marriage together are wrong!

On the one hand, this mother is saying, what would I do without her—that is, the daughter is leaned on, like a friend (or, perhaps, like a parent figure). But in the next breath she is asserting that she remained in her marriage because of her responsibility to her daughter. She attributes her problems, at least in part, to her role as mother.

These families illustrate both the differential power in family relationships and the complexity of peership between mothers and daughters. It seems that fathers do not need protection, mothers do. Daughters (and also possibly sons) with problem fathers may be pulled into adultlike alliances in their families because of the mothers' helpless, powerless or martyrlike position.[17] In contrast, the daughter may lean on her father (if a father is available) and it is the father's *hierarchical* position that makes his support particularly valuable. The European-born psychoanalyst, Frieda Fromm-Reichmann[18] described American mothers as family "leaders" and fathers as the confidants of their children. But even if American fathers do not wield the authority of traditional European fathers, nonetheless their relationships with their children are likely to be more hierarchical than mother-child relationships—just because the father tends to be something of an "outsider" to inner family dynamics.

THE "METAMORPHOSIS" OF DAUGHTERS

The daughter's developing sexuality creates a problem in the mother-daughter relationship: How do mother and daughter maintain a sense of continuity and stability in their family life in the face of the daughter's physiological and social "metamorphosis"? The daughter's physical development has a dual and contradictory meaning for the mother-daughter relationship: It represents both their bond as females and the greatest barrier between them— their heterosexuality. Their identity as females potentially provides a "reproductive bond" which links generations of mothers and daughters. But the daughter's sexual maturation also means a development away from her childhood tie with her mother. For both mother and daughter, heterosexuality orients them toward an intimacy with male partners—an intimacy from which each excludes the other. Furthermore, the daughter's sexual development connotes another paradox: The daughter's process of maturation specifically evokes the mother's parental role—teaching the daughter about sexual reproduction and about the use of menstrual pads or tampons—while it marks the beginning of the end of the daughter's status as child.

The Reproductive Bond Most of the daughters—four-fifths—learned about menstruation from their mothers. Daughters are taught about their reproductive functions by their mothers in part because providing training in hygiene tends to be part of the mother's role and in part because menstruation is part of the "business" of females in the families.

Mothers are not the only source of information about female reproductive functions. Almost all of the daughters said that they had seen a film in school (an indication of our common cultural heritage). Some had learned from sisters, a few from friends; occasionally a mother would explain the "facts" to more than one daughter at a time. Many of the mothers gave their daughters booklets put out by manufacturers of sanitary napkins. But whatever the source of information, it was almost always female; even films in school tend to be shown in sex-segregated groups.

Although the mothers were usually involved in initiating their daughters into the menstrual process, they were more often ill at ease than open and comfortable in their explanations. The fact that mothers generally do give their daughters at least the rudiments of reproductive knowledge suggests that teaching a daughter about female self-care is specifically part of a mother's role. Two daughters reported reaching menarche before the process had been explained to them. The reaction of these daughters included anger at their mothers—from which we can infer an expectation of maternal involvement. A number of the daughters learned about menstrual cycles from their mothers "just before" starting their first period. One daughter remarked: "I think I was twelve. She told me one day before I started. I asked my mother how she knew. I imagine my mother checking my underwear since I [was] ten . . ." This quote illustrates the familiarity of mothers' involvement with their daughters—a familiarity facilitated both by the mother's domestic role in the family (handling the laundry) and by their shared identity as females. But the discomfort of mothers in providing explanations may indicate ambivalence both about sexuality in general and about the meaning of sexuality in the mother-daughter relationship.

Open mother-daughter discussions about the daughter's (or mother's) sexual activities are exceptions, representing either rare relationships (there were just a few cases of mothers who were very open about sexuality) or "accidents"—especially, a premarital pregnancy. One daughter described an unusual confession she made to her mother:

> When Jerry and I were going out together, I think we had some sort of sexual relations and after that I had some terrible pains in my stomach and I was so scared and so she called my brother to bring me to the hospital because she thought I had appendicitis. And then I thought: "Afterwards what happens if I go to the hospital and the doctor tells my mother that I've been fooling

around—she'd kill me because I didn't tell her first." So I told her and it was the hardest thing I ever did in my entire life—to tell her because I was so ashamed and I was crying and saying I'm sorry. She was so cool about the whole thing. She said, "You're a young girl and you think that you love him and maybe you do. That's a human emotion and you just have to learn how to deal with it. You shouldn't be ashamed of yourself."
Did she approve?
She wouldn't really say but I know that she doesn't really approve of that. She wouldn't say—go live with a guy. She doesn't approve of that, but she knows what's going on. I know she knows what went on with me and Jerry before we were married . . . That made me love her more—she didn't sit back and say you should never do that.

This incident probably is unusual both in the mother's tolerance and in the daughter's need to confess. (We might wonder: Were her stomachaches psychosomatic—representing her guilty secret?) Nonetheless, this situation illustrates a daughter's ambivalence and confusion about how to reconcile her sexuality with the intimacy in her relationship with her mother. Despite the intense intimacy of this particular mother-daughter relationship (this is one of the invested pairs), the daughter would not ordinarily tell her mother about "fooling around" with her boyfriend (showing that even invested daughters who say they confided everything to their mothers nonetheless did use some censorship). This daughter is caught in a triangle—between her attachments to her boyfriend and her mother. Her confession to her mother is a violation of her intimacy with her boyfriend "Jerry." But she is not comfortable keeping this secret—feeling that both her behavior and her silence violate her mother's expectations. At the same time, she is aware that her sexual behavior is acceptable within her own cohort; she acknowledges that even her mother "knows what's going on."

Fathers as "Sexual Guardians" For most daughters any aspect of sexuality seems to be an even more embarrassing topic with fathers than with mothers. A number of the daughters, for instance, mentioned that they were mortified to know that their fathers had learned of their menstruating. Almost all of the daughters said that they learned nothing about sexuality from their fathers. For fathers, having teenage daughters in the household may pose a problem—with intimacy constricted by the fear (or temptation) of violating incest norms.

Nonetheless, the position of fathers vis-à-vis their daughters' sexuality may be in one sense less complex: Fathers seem to recognize and define their daughter's heterosexuality more clearly than mothers. There are two indicators of fathers' greater acknowledgment of their daughters' sexuality. First, it tended to be fathers, rather than mothers, who forbade daughters wearing clothing that might be construed as sexually seductive, such as bikinis or too short miniskirts. Second, in at least several families the fathers appeared to serve as "sexual guardians" or "gatekeepers" in interactions with the daughters' potential boyfriends. One daughter recalled:

> My father was the one that would give them the rundown. He would say, "Hi, how are ya," and make conversation. Then when I got home from a date he would say, "I like this guy because . . ." "I don't like this guy because . . ."
> *How did that make you feel?*
> Very upset. I didn't like it at all.

Another daughter said:

> Boyfriends—he [father] would come over and he would not really talk to them. He would say, "Hello, how are you? I'm Mr. Johnson." Then he would sit down and he would sort of grunt when they would talk to him. Guys in high school are so nervous. They would have to sit there. I was never there when they were going through it. I would come down and they would be sitting with their hands in their laps. Any guy that would come over to take me out for a date. It wasn't that he didn't take an interest in who I was going out with. It's more that he's shy and he didn't know what to say to them. But they figured he didn't like them on sight.
> *Was he critical of guys you were going out with?*
> He was—very. If he didn't like someone he would tell me. And it would be up to me to tell them that I couldn't go out with them anymore. I think it would be better to have the father rant and rave and say, "You're not going out with my daughter." It's

worse to say to someone, "I can't go out with you. My father won't let me."

What was your mother like with your dates?

She's very outgoing and friendly. It was fortunate because she'd come into the room and start a conversation and they could ignore my father.

Mothers were much more likely than fathers to be portrayed as friendly toward their daughters' dates and as trying to create a good impression. In a number of families, both daughters and mothers noted that the mothers disapproved of their daughters' boyfriends but they voiced this disapproval only after the dating relationship had ended.

There are several reasons why at least some fathers might serve as gatekeepers. First, fathers, as well as mothers, may be concerned with evaluating the daughters' boyfriends as potential husbands. Second, in families with traditional gender roles, fathers may have more "power" and be viewed as having a right to demand compliance. Conversely, the mother's power, with both daughters and sons, is likely to be based on ties of affection—so that the mother who openly states her disapproval risks not only a loss of respect but a loss of intimacy. Finally there is the issue of fathers' recognition of the daughters' sexuality. Possibly, fathers project onto young male suitors their own inappropriate sexual desires. Fathers may want to modulate and moderate their daughters' sexuality for their own sake—to avoid accentuating their daughters' sexual presence.

Keeping the Mother in the Dark In discussing the mother's role in the daughter's sexual development, we have to differentiate between two related yet quite distinct issues: menstruation and sexual intercourse. Whereas four-fifths of the daughters learned something about menstruation from their mothers, almost half of the daughters learned nothing at all about sexuality from their mothers. Only a few learned about the pleasures of sexuality. For most mothers and daughters, silence about sexuality is maintained until the daughter's pregnancy—when the focus turns again to their "reproductive bond" as females in the family.

After early adolescence, sexuality tends to be a carefully skirted issue in the mother-daughter relationship. Much of the dynamic in their relationship entails *keeping the mother in the dark about the daughter's sexuality*. Most daughters do not tell their mothers about their sexual involvements; and mothers and daughters seem to have an implicit, mutual agreement not to discuss sexuality. Other studies have found that mothers know little about their daughters' sexuality and therefore they systematically underestimate their daughters' level of sexual activity.[19]

Adolescent daughters often talk with their mothers about dating, other experiences that involve boys or boyfriends, and the special clothes that are needed for proms, etc. But most daughters do not talk at all about their sexual experiences with their mothers, despite their intimacy on other issues. It is as if heterosexuality is not only not part of the mother-daughter bond but even constitutes a threat to their intimacy. Also, perhaps conversely, mother-daughter intimacy may be a threat to the daughter's potentiality for heterosexual development.[20] Not until the daughter experiences pregnancy and birth do mothers and daughters tend to openly share their experiences related to sexual reproduction.

Silence about sexuality can be understood as a strategy for maintaining continuity in the mother-daughter relationship. "Keeping the mother in the dark" about the daughter's sexuality serves as a holding pattern—a way of conserving their relationship and avoiding an important source of tension. By ignoring the sexual arrangements that pull the daughter away from her mother, mother and daughter can maintain their sense of closeness with each other. They also sustain their parent-child hierarchy by avoiding the clearest evidence of the daughter's adulthood—her sexuality. Thus, mother and daughter maintain a fiction of continuity in their family relationships, while minimizing the enormous changes that have occurred.[21]

THE YEARS BETWEEN

By the time daughters are ready to leave home, they already have begun to renegotiate their relationships with their mothers. The daughter's developing sexuality symbolizes the beginning of the end of being a child in her family home. The teenage years, the years between childhood and adulthood, are full of ambiguities—with mothers and daughters trying both to hold on to each other and to let go.

Most daughters feel close to their mothers, from childhood through adulthood—including adolescence. The popular imagery of the adolescent years as a time of overt conflict and rebellion seems to be something of an exaggeration. In my study about a third of the daughters said that as teenagers they argued with their mothers "almost all the time"; so the majority of these daughters as teenagers were not arguing constantly with their mothers. Even so, most of the daughters also said that the worst time in their relationships with their mothers was when they were teenagers. This means that as they matured and when they married and had children of their own, their relationships with their mothers got better!

3

MATURATION, MARRIAGE, AND MOTHERHOOD

In the years following adolescence, several changes seem to happen almost all at once in the daughters' lives. They leave home; they establish relationships with men; they marry; they have children. How does the mother-daughter relationship change as a result of these new developments? Several mothers and daughters referred to each other as "friends"—making statements like "We've become more friends than mother and daughter." The young adult daughters that I interviewed ranged in age between twenty-one and thirty-one. But, although they may have had the legal status of adult, it seemed to me that they did not necessarily interact with their parents as peers. Even for those who claimed that they were friends, their mother-daughter relationships appeared to be different from other forms of friendships.

Gunhilde Hagestad,[1] however, has suggested that as children mature and enter adulthood they become friends with their parents. She interviewed college students and their parents and found that daughters and sons often provide emotional support to both their mothers and their fathers. Hagestad remarked that, for many parents, the "emptying of the nest" means a gain of a friend more than the loss of a child.

Potentially, when daughters marry and have children of their own, they and their mothers become "role colleagues." They are both adults, they occupy similar positions in family relationships, and they share both the instrumental and emotional experiences of motherhood. Because of the similarity of their roles in adulthood, mothers and daughters may have more in common—and therefore more of a basis for friendship—than fathers and daughters, mothers and sons, or fathers and sons.

In our society, friends tend to be age peers.[2] Obviously, a daughter can never catch up to her mother's age. More important, a different type of reciprocity seems to be expected in interactions with friends than with relatives. If people exchange goods or services with friends, they usually expect an approximately equal return.[3] In interactions with relatives, the rules of reciprocity seem to be much more complicated, and the give and take among kin may be spread out across generations. The caregiving that each of us receives from our parents is never really "paid back" through filial responsibility. Instead, we pass on this debt by being parents ourselves and providing care for our own children.

This chapter examines both the frequency and conditions of mother-daughter "friendships." Do all—or any—mothers and young adult daughters develop peer friendships? To what extent do daughters establish collegial relationships with their mothers when they become mothers themselves? How do the daughters' age and maturation affect the parent-child nature of relationships with their mothers? What is the impact of such factors as social class and geographical distance on the possibility of mother-daughter "friendship"?

A TYPOLOGY OF SYMMETRY AND ASYMMETRY

My in-depth interviews with mothers and daughters gave me portraits of each case—both highlighting their individual features and also suggesting certain patterns in terms of the "quality" of these relationships. Most of the relationships seem to fit into four distinct patterns or types:

> Type I *Responsible Mothers/Dependent Daughters*
> Type II *Responsible Daughters/Dependent Mothers*
> Type III *Peerlike Friendships*
> Type IV *Mutual Mothering*

The underlying characteristic that differentiates these four types is a "hierarchy of responsibility"—that is, the extent to which one

Table 3. **Characteristics of Four Types of Adult-Daughter/Mother Relationships**

TYPES OF MOTHER-DAUGHTER RELATIONSHIPS	RECIPROCITY	CONTROL	FOCUS OF CONCERN	TOTAL
I. Responsible mothers/ dependent daughters	Mother gives	Mother supervises	Daughter-focused	11
II. Responsible daughters/ dependent mothers	Daughter gives	Daughter supervises	Mother-focused	5
III. Peerlike	Both give/ both receive	Neither supervises	Mutual concern	6
IV. Mutual mothering	Both give/ both receive	Both supervise	Mutual responsibility	15
Total				37

member of the pair is responsible for the other.

There is, in addition, a residual category—Type X—comprised of relatively "noninvolved" mothers and daughters. In these relationships the issue of peership or friendship was difficult to assess because these daughters and mothers see each other rarely and seem to have little emotional involvement in each other's lives.

I created this typology by analyzing the interview transcripts both qualitatively, in terms of descriptions of their experiences, and quantitatively, by examining the distribution of specific variables. Table 3 describes these mother-daughter relationships in terms of three variables: *reciprocity; control;* and *focus of concern.* By reciprocity, I mean the extent to which there is an equal or unequal give and take of goods and services. In relationship Types I and II there are unreciprocated exchanges, whereas in Types III and IV both mothers and daughters try to be givers and receivers. "Control" means the extent to which the mother and/or the daughter attempts to supervise or control the other's behavior.

"Focus of Concern" refers to their subjective perceptions of one another—that is, who is most talked about or thought about in their relationship.

Responsible Mothers/Dependent Daughters   Eleven of the forty-three relationships might be described as "pretransitional," in the sense that the mother continues to view herself as responsible for her daughter and the daughter, at least implicitly, acknowledges the relationship as asymmetrical. These eleven relationships represent a continuity from the daughters' adolescent relationships with their mothers. They are pretransitional in the sense that the daughter's status as child or adult is still being negotiated. It must be emphasized, however, that this categorization is relative—that is, the daughters are more dependent on their mothers than other daughters. However, at least in some measure, *all* of the daughters, including these, view themselves as adults.

These eleven relationships have the following characteristics: (a) they tend to be low on reciprocity; (b) the mother continues to supervise the daughter's behavior; and (c) in comparison to other daughters, these daughters tend to be more daughter-focused. The focus on the daughter means both that the mothers view themselves as responsible for meeting their daughters' needs and that daughters' perceptions of their mothers are distorted by their own needs.

Almost all of these daughters receive more types of help from their mothers than they give to their mothers—as is shown in Table 4. This table was constructed from a questionnaire item in which the daughters were asked to check off types of help that they received from their mothers and types that they gave to their mothers. These data provide a rough indicator of giving and receiving. (The respondents were not asked to indicate how much or how frequently they gave each type of help, but only whether or not each type was given and/or received.) The differences among the types that emerge from the questionnaire largely support the interpretations from the interview data.

From the interviews, it seemed that a number of the mothers in this group catered to their daughters' physical and emotional needs. The pattern of nonreciprocity was epitomized by one family

Table 4. Cross-tabulation of Mother-Daughter Relationships by Level of Reciprocity in Giving and Receiving

TYPES OF MOTHER-DAUGHTER RELATIONSHIPS	MOTHER GIVES MORE	EQUAL GIVING/ RECEIVING	DAUGHTER GIVES MORE	TOTAL
I. Responsible mothers/ dependent daughters	10	0	1	11
II. Responsible daughters/dependent mothers	0	1	4	5
III. Peerlike	1	1	4	6
IV. Mutual mothering	7	2	6	15

Note: Data are from daughter questionnaires.

with a daughter living in her mother's apartment. The daughter was a student at a local college; her mother was divorced and worked full-time. The household arrangement was clearly not a symmetrical roommate situation. The mother expressed a responsibility to take care of her daughter, commenting: "I feel that she's up to her neck with her studies. She used to do the dishes, but I feel that I should do all the work." Although this relationship represents something of an extreme in terms of the mother's orientation of self-sacrifice, in various ways the other relationships in this category also were characterized by a lack of reciprocity. The mothers appeared to view the daughters as needing to be cared for; the daughters also seemed to see themselves as recipients rather than givers of help. In contrast to other daughters, these daughters received more services from their mothers and provided fewer in return.

In some families, the mothers resisted daughters' attempts at reciprocity. For example, one recently married daughter related an incident involving herself, her mother, and her unmarried sister. One afternoon, while she (the married sister) was visiting (using the washing machine in her mother's home), her younger sister surprised their mother by shampooing the rug. The daughter telling the story expressed irritation at her mother's response when she came home: "Why did you do that? I'll do it when I'm ready to do it . . . I can do it myself." This mother, in her separate interview, described her help to her married daughter, noting: "I help her by doing her laundry, putting her things in the washer and dryer . . . I don't mind. But I'll be glad when she has her own washing machine. I don't mind though." This mother's orientation of self-sacrifice serves to maintain an unequal relationship with her daughters. Moreover, her ambivalence about her continuing mothering role creates a debt in her daughters that they are not allowed to repay.

Type I relationships tended to be hierarchical—with mothers supervising their daughters' behavior and giving a considerable amount of advice. Like most of the other daughters, these daughters both asked for and received advice from their mothers. One of these daughters quipped, when asked whether or not her mother gave her advice: "Oh yes—unasked for, asked for—mothers always give you advice whether you want it or not . . . she knows personal things about me . . . she just every so often would give me digs." For this daughter, one subject of maternal advice is the daughter's weight. Her mother said: "One thing bothers me—she's overweight. Maybe I hurt her when I say something. But she always had a beautiful figure. When she's eating, I say—Ellen, please. Maybe that bothers her." These daughters did not necessarily accept their mothers' advice easily or eagerly. But what is striking about these relationships is that they are mother-dominated—with the mothers assuming a largely one-sided right and responsibility to offer direction to their daughters' lives.

The mother's supervision or control over young adult daughters is illustrated by another case of mother and daughter in the same household. In this family, both mother and daughter work and the daughter also takes evening classes. The daughter noted conflicts over cleaning. The issue here is not the relative neatness of mother and daughter but rather the mother's right to supervise the daughter's behavior:

> It's not that I'm a real slob—my mother is just too neat. Everything has a place. I'm the type of person if I didn't feel like doing the dishes right away, just go in the living room and relax, I'd do it. But she—the dishes get done right away after supper.

Is that a problem?

It used to be, but now I just get up and do them—usually I'm headed for a class at night and I have to get up and do them in a hurry anyway . . . That was a source of conflict . . . If I come home from work and I put my jacket and books on the kitchen table, she'll say those don't belong there—go put those where they belong. I'll think, Ma, I'll pick them up later. I'm not going to leave them there forever.

Do you say that or just think that?

I do say that—that's where we have little disagreements. I just moved up the hall into my sister's room. She hated the fact that my room could be seen as soon as you came in the front door. It tends to be a mess. When I take clothes off at night and I'm tired they just go on the chair. She's the opposite. Everything is neat. And I just have a lot of clutter. If it gets too cluttered I'll clean everything out. But I'm not the type of person to put everything where it belongs and she is.

In this family, the daughter's position in the household creates a context for supervision and belies her status as adult. This situation may closely resemble families with younger adolescent daughters in the home—where the boundaries of independence and responsibility are subject to negotiation.

The hierarchical nature of these relationships was revealed in different ways in the course of the interviews. In a few of the interviews, the mothers specifically commented on the daughters' immaturity—implying that they were not quite ready for independence. In other families, it was clear that the daughter relied on the mother for both instrumental and emotional support and the sense of responsibility and concern was very one-sided. In all of these relationships, the focus of concern, for both the daughter and the mother, was on the daughter.

One of the interview questions was, "Can you tell when your mother is upset?" Most of the daughters, when asked this question, indicated concern about their mothers' feelings and well-being. But the following response from one of the "dependent" daughters (this was the married daughter, described above, who was doing laundry in her mother's house) illustrates a continuation of a hierarchical relationship:

Yah I can. Sometimes when she comes back from work and if

it's been a bad day, you know just by the way she comes in—
it's been a bad day so don't say anything, don't ask her if you
want to borrow something, or take this or that. It's the wrong
day.

This daughter focuses on her own needs—so that, if she is able to
understand her mother's viewpoint, her motivation for doing so
relates to her orientation to her mother as a parent.

Responsible Daughters/Dependent Mothers So far, I have
discussed asymmetry in mother-daughter relationships in terms of
a continuity of mother parenting daughter. But a reverse form of
asymmetry also can occur—with mothers dependent on daughters.
In five of the relationships, there is a striking pattern of dependent
mothers and responsible daughters. The most salient characteristic
of families with this type of relationship is emotional instability—
cither of the mother or of the father. In all of these families one of
the parents exhibits severe emotional problems and, whichever parent has the symptoms, these daughters have developed highly protective relationships with their mothers. In all of these families, the
daughters are geographically distant from their mothers. Possibly,
their physical distance provides some boundary to their feeling of
responsibility for their mothers.

The lack of reciprocity in these relationships is seen in Table
4. These relationships are the mirror image of Type I relationships,
in the sense that these daughters are much more likely to give than
to receive help from their mothers. In these five relationships, there
is a lack of reciprocity because the daughters are far more likely to
see themselves as responsible for their mothers than the other way
around. One of the dependent mothers is widowed and has physical
and mental problems. She is supported financially as well as emotionally by her daughter and son. The daughter said:

I try to make an effort to call her so that she'll know that somebody's there [both she and her brother also send money]. The
way we feel is—her parents are going to die soon. Well, one's
dead and the other's as good as dead. And soon she's going to
have to say, Now what? So we're making an effort to show her
that we're there. If we say we care we really mean it. It's not
the same kind of care that her mother showed her.

The last sentence suggests an explicit sense of role reversal—the adult children are trying to care for their mother to substitute for the mother's mother (both because the grandmother is going to die and because she never was very nurturant). When asked if her mother helped her, this daughter replied: "Well, she helps me in the sense that I know I'm helping her . . ." This mother, during her interview, bemoaned her dependence on her children. She also seemed to fear the limitations of such dependence. She worried: "Something may have to be done. I may have to live close enough to someone [to be cared for] or be put away. I can't even get to the hospital in a taxi by myself. I don't know what I'm heading for. That's my situation—if I don't become strong enough to tend to myself."

With responsible daughters the issues of supervision and concern are more ambiguous than with responsible mothers. The daughter just cited indicates that, over the years, she has given her mother a considerable amount of advice—particularly concerning the mother's parents. It is apparently a source of frustration to the daughter that her mother, in her passivity, does not take her advice—"she's rejecting my help." In terms of the mothers' supervision of the daughters, all of these mothers were highly permissive, from the daughter's childhood onward. In most of these families, the fathers appeared to be autocratic, the mothers passive. Thus, the dependency of these mothers seems to have early roots.

These daughters, unlike the other daughters, tend *not* to ask for their mothers' advice. This can be seen from responses in questionnaires that the daughters filled out. The daughters were given a question about advice that they asked from their mothers and advice that their mothers offered. These daughters ask for advice even less than the noninvolved daughters (in Type X relationships). In every other category of relationship the daughters ask for more advice than their mothers spontaneously offer—suggesting that they look to their mothers for at least some measure of help and supervision. These daughters ask for even less advice than their mothers offer; and these mothers offer less advice than most of the other mothers. The implication is that these responsible daughters neither expect nor receive supervision from their mothers.

All of these daughters exhibited a high level of concern about their mothers and they described their mothers' problems at great length. It is striking, however, that none of their mothers, in their separate interviews, presented comparable pictures of their "problems." In the relationship just referred to, the daughter talked in detail about her mother's difficulties with her own parents; the mother in portraying her many troubles in life never mentioned her parents. In other relationships, the daughters gave highly negative portrayals of the mothers' relationships with the fathers; the mothers mentioned almost nothing about such problems. Possibly, the overconcern displayed by these daughters reflects their entanglement in their families' emotional problems. In any case, these role-reversed daughters indicated a sense of confusion about who is mothering whom. The mothers' concern about their daughters also seemed to be distorted. They tended to project onto their daughters fears that they have had in their own lives. The mothers who were divorced or widowed viewed their daughters' life chances with trepidation. One mother who has a retarded child projected onto her daughter her own (the mother's) preoccupation with that child. These mothers, because of their emotional and family problems, tended to be preoccupied with themselves—and this ego focus interfered with their ability to understand their daughters as separate individuals.

Mothers and Daughters with Peerlike Friendships Genuine peerlike friendships between mothers and daughters appear to be somewhat uncommon; only six of the forty-three relationships approximate this type. These six relationships all have a conjunction of two characteristics: (1) high involvement in each others' lives and (2) a strong norm for independence—for both daughter and mother. It is this combination that makes these relationships look like peer friendships. In four of these relationships, the daughters are married with children and live near to their mothers. But even for nearby married daughters, this pattern of peerlike friendship represents a minority of mothers and daughters.

In several ways, these mother-daughter relationships are very different from the relationships with dependent daughters or dependent mothers. First of all, in these Type III relationships both mother and daughter are careful not to exercise control over each other's lives. The effort not to exercise control is illustrated by an incident related by a mother and daughter who live in the same town. The daughter described her most recent argument with her mother, which took place "over a year ago." This daughter said that when her mother gets overtired (the mother has a chronic disability) she gets "bossy":

> She had pushed herself to the limit . . . And she didn't like the way I decorated the house or anything else. So I finally said, "Mom, it's none of your business anymore." I said, "I'll decorate the way I want and I'm going to lead my life the way I see fit."
> *Was she hurt?*
> No she wasn't. She didn't realize she was getting that bossy and all of a sudden she realized she was, and she said, "I'm doing it again, aren't I?" And that was the end. Now all I have to say if I see she's getting tired, I say, "Mom, you're doing it again." So we don't argue about it anymore.

The mother seemed to refer to the same incident when asked about arguments:

> . . . when we painted our kitchen in the spring we had a gallon of paint left and I said to Aileen, "Maybe you'd like this bright yellow paint for your kitchen?" And Aileen said, "No thanks, I want blue in my kitchen."
> *Did you feel hurt?*
> No, it doesn't bother me. She feels very free to say, "Mom, get off my back." That's fine because I know I am that kind of person. I'm much more aggressive than she is. So it's very good that she can do that. And I don't feel hurt by it simply because I know it's right.
> *Do you ever do that to her—tell her to get off your back?*
> Well, I would . . . but she's not that kind of person really.

In this context, the choice of a color of paint or a decorating style becomes symbolic of the daughter's independence. The confrontation described here suggests that relinquishing the parent-child hierarchy requires effort on the part of both daughter and mother. Whether or not the mother actually felt hurt, it is clear that she was trying very hard to sustain her daughter's sense of independence. In contrast, the mothers with dependent daughters tend to assume that the daughters need help in making decisions. Indeed it is likely that this daughter, at younger ages, relied on her mother's supervision. She mentioned, for instance, her indecision about college majors and her mother's advice and involvement in her decision. Her confrontation with her mother may represent a marker of her independence as a married adult with her own home.

This family also illustrates another difference from the relationships with dependent daughters or mothers—a reciprocated concern for the other. Even while resisting her mother's domination (her "bossiness"), the daughter is concerned about her mother's underlying feelings—perceiving her mother as "overtired." Similarly, the mother also tries to understand how the situation looks from the daughter's viewpoint. What is somewhat unusual about this relationship, and about the few relationships that appear to have peerlike friendships, is the ability to maintain some sense of objectivity about the other.

Finally, in contrast to the relationships with dependent daughters or mothers, most of these mothers and daughters express overt concern for reciprocity—with neither mother nor daughter wanting to be too dependent or to overburden the other. This does not necessarily mean that the exchanges of goods or services are actually balanced. In the case of the mother and daughter I have just been discussing there is ostensibly considerable imbalance. The daughter is heavily involved in providing services, not only for her mother but also for her maternal grandmother and her paternal aunt. The mother has been disabled since her early adulthood; the daughter has been more of a helper than is found in any of my other family cases. The intimacy of this helping relationship is suggested by the fact that, from an early age, the daughter had to help her mother put on her stockings. The daughter nonetheless characterizes her helping relationship with her mother as a "two-way street." The mother, though she does some baby-sitting, expresses concern that her daughter may become "burdened with everybody's burden." Most of the mothers who seem to have peerlike friendships with their daughters said that their daughters helped them more than the other way around. (This is corroborated by the balance between help given versus received, from the daughter questionnaires, as seen in Table 4 on page 50.) Nonetheless, there is a quality of interdependence in these relationships that makes these mothers very different from the dependent mothers. Unlike the dependent mothers, the peerlike mothers express a desire not to burden their daughters; and the daughters, whatever services they provide, portray their mothers as having a clear sense of autonomy.

Mutual Mothering Symmetrical mother-daughter relationships are much more likely to be characterized by mutual dependence than independence. Fifteen of the relationships fit into a pattern of "mutual mothering." The hallmark of these relationships is a sense of mutual responsibility or "protectiveness." This is the most common pattern found among the relationships. What distinguishes these relationships from those with dependent daughters or mothers is the mutuality or balance of responsibility.

These relationships are, more or less, symmetrical in terms of reciprocity, control, and concern—but in a much more complex way than the peerlike friendships just described. Whereas peerlike mothers and daughters try to minimize their debt to each other, these daughters and mothers draw each other into an amorphous set of commitments. Peerlike mothers and daughters endeavor to support each other's autonomy; the mutual motherers supervise each other's activities and behavior. The cases of mutual mothering vary in how much they accept each other's advice; what they have in common is their mutual propensity to supervise each other's lives. Finally these mothers and daughters are highly attuned to each other's feelings, but their perspectives on each other tend to become entangled with their own needs and emotions.

The reciprocity in these relationships emerges from their sense of responsibility for one another. Two of the invested mother-daughter pairs illustrate the process of reciprocal caring. Both daughters are married and live near to their mothers; one of them has a two-year-old son. They are both nurturant toward their mothers. They telephone and/or visit daily to make sure the mothers are okay; they do errands for their mothers; and they make their homes accessible to their parents. These daughters are somewhat unusual in their willingness to invite their parents to join them when they are with their age peers. At the same time, they want and receive "mothering" from their mothers. Their mothers give them a considerable amount of advice and tend to be freer in offering advice than some of the other mothers. These daughters also "listen" to their mothers' advice more than most of the other daughters. In fact, they attribute a kind of magical power to their mothers. One of them notes that her mother is always right: "I'd ask my mother and whatever she said always seemed to happen." The other daughter makes a comparable statement about the ability of her mother to take care of her: "I get peace of mind. You know how some people talk about church—that's how I feel. When something is bothering me I can go and talk to her about it. For instance—the house—I wanted to have her say, 'Well, you'll be all right; you can make the payments.' I knew in my heart that we could do it—but I needed to have her say that."

Mutual mothering does not necessarily mean that relationships are harmonious or loving. One daughter depicted her mother as remote and unaffectionate and expressed anguish at being dominated by her mother: "All my life I've been under her thumb." (This was one of the families with remote relationships when the daughters were adolescents.) This daughter, nonetheless, expressed a strong sense of responsibility for her mother. She noted that despite her mother's financial difficulties, she has given various kinds of help, such as outfitting the daughter's kitchen, lending money to the daughter and her husband, and taking the daughter for her weekly grocery shopping. In spite of her negative feelings about her mother, she expressed a sense of being in her mother's debt: She said that they (she and her husband) should do things for her mother because "my mother has done so much for us."

These mothers and daughters seem to switch back and forth between mothering and being mothered. The propensity for mutual supervision is illustrated by one daughter's depiction of recent arguments with her mother (the daughter is married, childless, and geographically distant from her mother):

> I mean she does annoy me a couple of times a year—which is usually because she won't take time off from her job to do something, or something involving spending money.
> *What is it that annoys you?*

Sometimes it's something she doesn't do for herself. And sometimes she doesn't understand my aspirations—why I can't be content with certain things she is perfectly content with. That's a source of conflict when it comes up.

This daughter points to two issues of conflict—the daughter's supervision of her mother (that is, the daughter wanting the mother to do certain things for herself) *and* her mother's supervision of her. The mother, in her interview, indicated a strong concern for her daughter's future because "she's still searching" and "she's not practical." The mother said, "I try not to tell her what to do." She noted that this particular daughter does not give her advice (though her other daughters do). What is perhaps most striking about the issue of supervision is that neither particularly wants to listen to the other. We might wonder: *Does* this daughter tell her mother to do things "for herself"—advice that the mother simply does not take seriously enough to recall? Conversely, it is clear that the daughter does not really listen to her mother's suggestions for her future.

This situation also illustrates a mother and daughter systematically misreading each other—based on their overlapping concerns with "mothering" and being "mothered." When the daughter tells her mother to do something "for herself," it is not at all clear that the daughter's advice is without self-interest. For instance, the daughter expressed a strong sense of disappointment that her mother had never visited her—in *her* home. She noted feeling "aggravated . . . furious . . . very upset" when, the previous summer, her mother had canceled a visit and chosen to attend a cousin's wedding. But she decided not to push her mother further, and (switching to the protective daughter role) she said that she did not want to get her mother "upset." The mother, in her interview, indicated no awareness of the daughter's discomfort with their visiting arrangements but just said she hoped her daughter would soon come to Georgia to visit in her (the mother's) home.

Beyond the Typology The pattern of mutual mothering goes beyond these fifteen relationships. Most of the mothers and daughters displayed some evidence of mutual responsibility. Daughters expressed responsibility for their mothers in several ways. First, most of the daughters, including the dependent daughters, made statements indicating a general concern about their mothers' well-being. Daughters worried about their mother's health, family relationships, or social activities. A number of the daughters talked about their mothers' experiences as a child or young woman and indicated that they were "sorry" for their mothers. Second, most of the daughters indicated that they wanted their mothers' approval and they wanted to be viewed as "good" daughters. Several daughters described situations about which they felt guilty—because they were not being good daughters. The underlying theme in all of these breaches is a failure to do something for the mother—so that, by inference, being "good" means being responsible for the mother. For example, one daughter (in the Type I—responsible mother/dependent daughter—category) expressed guilt and remorse that she once refused to type a paper for her mother.[4] Finally, although there is great variability in the amount of help given and received, most of the adult daughters in this sample provided at least minimal services for their mothers. Other studies have reported that adult children have a sense of filial responsibility—that is, that they recognize the obligation to provide care and support to their parents when or if needed.[5]

Despite the fact that all the daughters defined themselves and were viewed by their mothers as adults, in most of the relationships there was evidence of mothers' retaining a mothering role vis-à-vis their daughters. Two indicators illustrate the continuity of a parent-child hierarchy: (1) sibling rivalry and (2) daughters' "homesickness." Although some of the daughters portrayed close friendships with their siblings, especially sisters from large families, comments on siblings were more likely to be negative than positive. The most frequent criticism was that their siblings were too dependent—not "breaking the tie," being "spoiled," or demanding too much from their parents. This criticism of siblings' dependency may signify a rivalry over parenting—suggesting that the sibling, by being spoiled, etc., is receiving an unfairly large share of parental love and care. One of the mothers, while she was being interviewed long-distance over the telephone, noted the continuity of sibling rivalry. At the time of the interview, another adult daughter was living temporarily in her household and, apparently, was listening to the interview. The mother, in answering one of the questions, praised Molly (the daughter in this study), while in the background I could overhear her other daughter making some remark. The mother said: "My daughter says that's because Molly's my favorite. You know that feeling never ends!" Research has shown that sibling rivalry can survive long after the death of parents.[6]

A feeling of homesickness—or missing their mothers—was expressed by over two-thirds of the daughters who lived at a distance from their mothers. When asked, "Do you ever feel lonely"—many of the geographically distant daughters talked about feeling lonely "here"—that is, far from "home." One daughter, who is married, has one child, and lives a hundred or so miles from her mother, stated:

> . . . I don't feel lonely for other people but I feel lonely for my family. It's not a great distance but it's a long-distance call. I wish that my mother was nearby. I wish that I could talk to her. I wish if the time comes up that I need a sitter or questions come up, I want to talk to someone close . . .

Her mother described a recent incident:

> . . . two weeks ago Judy called up crying: "I want to see you. Can't you come down and spend the weekend?" Well, it wasn't so convenient. I tried to arrange it, but it didn't seem to work out. But she said, Please come. She had a friend whose mother was with her and she felt she wanted her own mother. Well, my son drove me up there and we spent two days there . . . As I was driving up there I started to think this is quite a hassle going all this way for two days just because she wants me to. And then I thought it really isn't a hassle at all. She misses her family. But she doesn't want to live in Salem [same town as mother]. She likes living in Hatfield and they like their house . . .

Although several mothers said that they missed their daughters or that they would miss them if they lived far away, it was far more likely for the daughters to express an emotional need for their mothers than the other way around. This may seem counterintuitive—given the stereotypical image of lonely empty-nest mothers who are devastated by the departure of their children. But there are several reasons why the daughters might be more likely to express feelings of homesickness than the mothers. First, the mothers may be denying such feelings—aware that it is "normal" and expected for their children to leave. Second, the mothers may not miss having their daughters around. Other studies have reported that mothers are likely to feel relief, an increase in self-esteem, and a decrease in anxiety when their children "empty the nest".[7] Third, the daughters are the ones who literally leave home and need to adjust to new surroundings. Finally, and the central point here, the homesickness may indicate a continued need to be mothered. Even daughters who place a high value on their independence talk about occasionally wanting to "go home to Mom." A number of daughters described their mothers as lonely without children in the household, while their mothers did not admit such feelings. The daughters may be projecting onto their mothers their own feelings of loneliness and homesickness. Possibly, these daughters may want their mothers still to need to mother them.

Type X—"Uninvolved" Daughters   Six relationships were not included in any of the other four types. In these relationships, the daughters are considerably less involved with their mothers than in the other families. At one extreme is a daughter who has not talked with her mother for several years. With the exception of that relationship, the lack of involvement appears to be primarily from the daughters' perspective. In all of these relationships, the emotional distance between mother and daughter did *not* develop suddenly with the daughter's emergence into adulthood but rather was part of the long-term history of their relationship. Despite their negative feelings, most of these daughters said they *wished* they were closer and indicated, in various ways, that they were searching for "mothering." These daughters expressed a sense of wistfulness about not having family to "lean on" or, unlike some of their friends, not having a large close family nearby. Although they were not included in any of the four types, these daughters described feelings and behaviors similar to other mother-daughter relationships. For

Table 5. Cross-tabulation of Mother-Daughter
Relationships by Daughter's Marital/Parental Status

TYPES OF MOTHER-DAUGHTER RELATIONSHIPS	SINGLE	MARRIED, CHILDLESS	MARRIED WITH CHILDREN
I. Responsible mothers/ dependent daughters	5	3	3
II. Responsible daughters/ dependent mothers	1	2	2
III. Peerlike	1	1	4
IV. Mutual mothering	1	4	10
Total	8	10	19

example, one single daughter, who spends little time with her mother and who views herself as very independent, mentioned that until recently she had had long hair and when she would go home for a visit her mother "would always come by me and brush it [the hair] out of my face." This epitomizes the mothering posture: By her touch the mother demonstrates her intimate access to and supervision of her daughter.

MARRIED DAUGHTERS VERSUS SINGLE DAUGHTERS

Under what circumstances do mothers and daughters develop each of these types of relationships? Type III (peerlike) and Type IV (mutual mothering) are both symmetrical relationships in that these mothers and daughters respond to each other in approximately equivalent ways.[8] Table 5 shows the distribution of relational types by the daughters' marital/parental status. This table suggests that there may be developmental changes in the mother-daughter relationship associated with the daughter's marriage and motherhood. Daughters who are married with children are considerably more likely than the other daughters to have both peerlike and mutual-mothering relationships. Conversely, the single daughters are two or three times as likely as the other daughters to have Type I—

Table 6. Cross-tabulation of Mother-Daughter
Relationships by Daughter's Age

TYPES OF MOTHER-DAUGHTER RELATIONSHIPS	DAUGHTER 25 OR YOUNGER	DAUGHTER OVER 25
I. Responsible mothers/dependent daughters	11	0
II. Responsible daughters/dependent mothers	1	4
III. Peerlike	2	4
IV. Mutual mothering	4	11
Total	18	19

responsible mother/dependent daughter relationships.[9]

The daughter's age is another developmental factor that seems to affect the nature of the mother-daughter relationship. Table 6 divides the sample in about half between daughters who are twenty-five and younger and daughters who are older than twenty-five. This table shows sharp differences between the younger and older daughters in terms of the types of mother-daughter relationships. In fact, *none* of the older daughters have responsible mother/dependent daughter relationships. Conversely, more than three-quarters of the older daughters have "symmetrical" relationships with their mothers (peerlike or mutual mothering), compared to a third of the younger daughters.

Age and family roles (wife and mother) appear to be correlated with each other. The mean age of the married-with-children daughters is twenty-seven; whereas the mean ages for the childless-married and the single daughters are twenty-six and twenty-four, respectively. If we think of the cross-sectional design as mimicking a developmental profile, we would expect to have daughters be somewhat older at "later" developmental stages. Given the small size of my sample, I cannot sort out the effects of age and marital/parental role statistically. Clearly, the daughter's age—an indicator of maturity—is one factor that affects the mother-daughter relationship.

Nonetheless, differences between married daughters and single daughters are not necessarily attributable solely to age. There are systematic differences in the "life structures" of single and married daughters. These differing life structures create different backgrounds for interaction between mothers and daughters. I am using the term "life structure" to mean the *subjective definition of self now and into the future.* In a very general way, the life structures of the single, married-childless, and married-with-children daughters can be described, respectively, as "unsettled," "newly settled," and "settled-in."

A notable characteristic of the life structures of most of the single daughters is a sense of being unsettled. Conversely, being settled means having a sense of doing and having done what they want, having concrete plans for the future and being able to envision what their life course will be like. To a large extent both the single daughters and their mothers see the daughters' future as beyond their control. The shaping of the future is contingent on what may or may not happen to them—such as marriage. Since most of the single daughters see marriage as desirable, they find it difficult to envision concrete plans for the future—especially if they do not yet have a boyfriend. The haziness of the future is illustrated by the following comments from one of the single daughters who fits into the Type I relational category:

> Sometimes I look at friends who are married and think that would be good—some choices would be over. Sometimes I think I've just got too many choices and I can't make them . . .
> *To what extent do you think your life will turn out like your mother's life?*
> I really have no idea if it will be different . . . or even the question about getting married and having children—I don't know. That doesn't look that good to me, not such a good alternative. I don't have anybody in mind either.

Her mother, asked if her daughter is doing what she wants with her life, said:

> She doesn't know what she wants. Anything she's doing she decided on herself [that is, her major at college, her living situation

in an apartment, etc.]. But it's not what she wants now.

While this mother asserted that the daughter had made her own decisions, the daughter's uncertainty created a context for supervision and dependence. There are constraints, of course, on the mother's supervisory role—even more so than during the daughter's adolescent years in her mother's household. Thus, all the daughters, in fact, do make decisions for themselves about their future lives. But pragmatically, a daughter's decisions about the future can involve her mother. At times, the daughter may become temporarily dependent on her mother (or her parents). There were a number of examples of single daughters moving out and then back into their parents' (or mothers') homes.

During the interviews, I asked about the similarity of the daughters' lives to their mothers' lives—"now" and in the future, "ten years from now." Most of the daughters both saw their lives as different now from their mothers' lives and wanted in the future to have lives substantially different. But the single daughters were the most likely to have difficulty with this question—because they did *not know* what their mothers' lives were like. Therefore, they had no frame of reference with which to make the comparison. For example, one single daughter (geographically near), when asked if her life will turn out in the future to be like her mother's life, said:

> I don't know. To tell you the truth I don't really know what my mother's life is like. She goes out to work and she comes home and they go out to eat a lot. They seem to have a lot of freedom. I can't answer that.

Only one married daughter answered in terms of not knowing what the mother's life was like—compared to half of the single daughters.

Some of the mothers of single daughters also had difficulty projecting their daughters into lives like their own. The mothers were asked to rate both their daughters and themselves on mothering ability. *All* of the mothers of married daughters rated their daughters as better than or equal to themselves; most, in fact, saw their daughters as better. In contrast, over a third of the mothers of single daughters gave their daughters lower ratings than themselves in mothering ability. One mother of a single daughter, asked how her daughter would be as a mother, stated:

> Lousy. She has to look beautiful. It takes her all morning to get
> ready. You can't do that when you are a mother. She's not like
> me. Well, she loves kids, but she dresses by the hour. With kids
> you can't do that. I went days without leaving my kids. I had no
> sitters. All the time they were little, I never had a sitter. My
> mother wouldn't come. She was just down the block but she
> wouldn't baby-sit.

Another mother, whose daughter now has two small children, commented:

> She's an excellent mother. You know, I was surprised. You see
> your children as teenagers. She was extremely attractive and
> she was very interested in clothes. She wouldn't mind spending
> $100 on an outfit but wouldn't care if she went without food.
> But I am pleased that she's turned out to be a marvelous mother.

The implication of relief in this mother's statement reflects a background of nervous anxiety and frustration—with a mother not
knowing how the daughter will "turn out" and not being able to
control the outcome of the daughter's development. A mother of a
single daughter noted:

> I think she might be like me after a while. She has a little adjusting
> to do in her values. Right now what she thinks isn't important,
> I think will become important to her.
> *Like what?*
> Home hours. Schedule. Linda has no schedule and I think she'd
> find herself when she became a mother adhering to a schedule.

A number of the mothers of single daughters, like the mother just
cited, made specific comments on their daughters' lack of maturity.
Although mothers of married daughters sometimes criticized aspects
of their daughters' life-style or personality, none of them depicted
their daughters as immature. It seems that mothers of single daughters are much more likely than other mothers to see their daughters
as focused on their own needs—such as clothes, their creative im-
pulses, and decisions about their futures. In fact, some of these
mothers tend to foster this ego focus by catering to them and thereby
indicating that the daughters' interests come first. Conversely, the

daughter's marriage may symbolize a sense of responsibility to another person and a moving away from focus on self.

The childless married daughters are newly settled in the sense that they are in the "establishment" phase of their families. These newly settled daughters are in the process of developing their marital relationships as well as reorienting relationships with others—including their mothers.[10] For mothers and daughters, the daughter's wedding symbolizes a break in the structure of their family life. A sense of this discontinuity is conveyed by one mother in her description of the day of her daughter's wedding:

> It was a big wedding, a humongous wedding. After the bride and groom came downstairs and had some pictures taken . . . she did some [packing] and she cried the whole day like I have never seen her cry in my life . . . cried and cried . . . It was time for them to go and friends were taking them to the airport. She could not leave. I am not kidding when I say they physically forced her in the car. "We've got to go. We're going to miss the plane." "I know . . . I know. Where's Jimmy?" [her brother]. And then she had to come to me first. And then she went to her father. She went to Jimmy, who she adores. She's out in the car and I hear her scream: "I didn't say good-bye to Mummy!" But she's a beautiful young woman—a good mother and a good homemaker.

In some ways, this case is an "ideal type." As an adolescent, the daughter rejected her mother and did everything she could to shut her mother out of her life. But as a young mother herself, she established a new closeness with her own mother. This mother said, "The fact that we have this beautiful relationship is the high point of my life 'cause it was pretty bad."

This daughter was only seventeen when she married and her marriage coincided with her first real experience of leaving home (other than one brief vacation). Most of the other daughters moved away from their parents' homes at least several years before marriage. Nonetheless, for most daughters, marriage brings an important shift in position in two senses: first, having a "home" of her own, with a separate residence, which is likely to be more permanent than during the single years (often with the prospect of home ownership), and second, establishing a new family, with a more-or-less permanent relationship with a husband.

For the daughters, part of the symbolic value of their marriages may be that they now have a way to demonstrate concretely their adult status via their domestic skills. A number of the childless married daughters indicated in various ways that they wanted to "show" their mothers that they were good housekeepers. Several of the childless married daughters talked of keeping their homes neat just in case their mothers should drop in. But a common complaint from these daughters was that their mothers did not visit them in their homes often enough. In their own homes the daughters are surrounded by the material proofs of their marital status. That the daughters' skills as wives and mothers are important in their mothers' evaluations of them is evident in the fact that during the interviews, most mothers of married daughters spontaneously praised their daughters' domestic (including maternal) abilities.

For the mothers, a central issue may be the need to respect the barriers around the daughter's marriage. The daughter's home is also the son-in-law's home. The mothers tend to visit during the daytime, since evening hours are reserved as time to spend with the husband. A few mothers or daughters related uncomfortable incidents when a son-in-law was home (sometimes in his bathrobe) and the mother felt herself to be an intruder.

Mothers and married daughters maintain an unequal access to each other's households. Many of the nearby daughters described going "home" at times when no one else was there—implying that they retained keys to their mothers' homes. The mothers, however, never described their daughters' households as "home" and it seemed rare for a mother to have a key or ready access to her daughter's house or apartment. Mothers of childless married daughters, particularly, seem to have low access to their daughters' homes. The mothers spend more time visiting and are more likely to "drop in" for unannounced visits at the homes of their daughters with children than of their childless married daughters.[11]

For the childless married daughters, being newly settled does not mean that they have a clear sense of their future. These daughters are pretransitional—in the sense that, sometime in the near future, they probably will become parents. For many of these daughters, the issue of children constitutes a source of confusion— with decisions about when and how many children still in the future and, for many, a concern about how to balance working and motherhood. For instance, one daughter reflected: "I want to continue working after I have kids but I don't know how to go about doing it . . ." The sense of self-in-the-future tended to be very different for the daughters with children than for the married childless daughters. We can get a sense of these differences when we compare statements about the future from the daughters with children versus the childless married daughters. The daughters with children tended to talk about their lives ten years in the future as extensions of today and tomorrow, as illustrated by the following responses from two daughters who are married with children.

> I think that I will have a part-time job and still be home for the family and I have a lot of hobbies and friends.
>
> *What will you be doing in ten years?*
> Working probably.
> *Doing what?*
> Probably go into some form of teaching. I am thinking of taking some courses in the fall.

Notice that having friends and hobbies *now* and taking courses in the fall become merged with the sense of the distant future. By contrast, the married daughters without children convey a much vaguer sense of the future; and much of the ambiguity emerges from the issue of having children. One childless married daughter answered about what she would be doing in ten years:

> I don't know. Our lives are very unsettled right now as to our immediate future . . . In ten years I would hope to have a child. But economic circumstances might dictate our lives . . . it's taken me two years to get this second degree and I might want to do an internship in a hospital and I want to work for a while. I'm very unclear . . .
> *Would you take off time with a child—from your job?*
> At least for the first. I say this now. But I don't really know what it will be like.

Like many young married couples, this daughter[12] and her husband
are students. Her husband was completing his degree and had taken
a job in another city at the time of the interview. She describes
their lives as "unsettled" because of uncertainty about both her
professional training and having children. But this daughter is set
or settled, at least temporarily, in the sense that her plans for her
future are both shaped and constricted by her commitment to her
husband. Thus, although she does not know precisely what she will
be doing, even in the near future, she assumes that she will follow
her husband.

Their daughters' marriages place constraints around the
mothers' ability or willingness to influence the daughters. A major
issue in the daughters' future concerns when they will have children
and how many they will have. None of the mothers tried to exert
positive, direct, and specific influence on their daughters concerning
having children. A few of the mothers, and only a few, talked a little
with their daughters about having children in general. One mother,
for instance, argued that it is "selfish" for young people nowadays
to want not to have children. Two mothers and a few fathers joked
about having grandchildren. Three mothers tried to discourage their
daughters from having a child at a particular time (negative influence). The closest attempt at pressure came from one mother who
hinted that she "would make a good grandmother." But more than
three-quarters of the mothers said absolutely nothing to their
daughters that could be construed as an attempt at influence. There
was much evidence that most of the mothers viewed the birth of
grandchildren as highly desirable. Both mothers and daughters reported that mothers became excited at the "good news" of pregnancy. One daughter was amused when her mother became flustered
with delight because she thought, inaccurately as it turned out, that
one of her daughters was pregnant. But mothers do not choose
when or if to become grandmothers.

This noninterference might seem counterintuitive, given the
stereotypes of mothers and mothers-in-law. But, in some ways, the
lack of attempted influence by mothers is not really surprising. First
of all, decisions about pregnancy are made, ostensibly, jointly by
husbands and wives. Mothers who would like to exert influence

would have to be supervising their sons-in-law, not just their daughters. Second, the impact of having a child is far greater on parents than on grandparents. This means that potential grandparents have minimal legitimacy in pressing for grandchildren because they have a minimal stake. Finally, a mother obviously would be powerless in enforcing any sort of compliance to a demand that her daughter become pregnant.

The daughter's future as a mother both excludes and affects her mother. On the one hand, the mother (potential grandmother) exerts virtually no direct influence on family planning. On the other hand, the daughter's motherhood does have a potential impact on her mother—both in terms of creating an emotional tie with a grandchild and, to varying degrees, entailing an instrumental role with both the daughter and her child.

DAUGHTERS WITH CHILDREN

Daughters who are married with children can be described as "settled in" in the sense that having children places constraints around both their current and future lives. Under most circumstances, daughters cannot and do not divorce their children.[13] Despite changes in divorce laws, it is still very rare for mothers to give up custody of their children. In terms of relationships with their mothers, the daughters with children differ from the childless daughters in several ways. First, their perspectives on their mothers seem to shift as they move from being role complements (as mother-daughter) to role colleagues (as mother-mother). Second, having a child changes the rhythm of their lives—so that, particularly for geographically near daughters, there are more opportunities for interaction and involvement with their mothers. Finally, the parent-child hierarchy takes on a new meaning with the birth of the daughter's child.

The shift in the daughter's perspective is illustrated by the fact that the daughters with children were somewhat more likely than the single and childless daughters to rate their mothers as better in "mothering ability" than themselves: Three-fifths of the daughters with children rated their mothers as better, compared to two-fifths of the other daughters. Conversely, they were half as likely to give themselves higher ratings than their mothers: Only three of the daughters with children, compared to a third of the other daughters, rated themselves as better. Perhaps, in part, this demonstrates a tendency on the part of young mothers to elevate their own mothers as role models. These young mothers, with their oldest children at the toddler stage, were still rather new at mothering. But the differences in evaluations of mothers also may reflect a changing role perspective. In a pilot study for this research,[14] young mothers (with children between six months and seven years) said that they revised their feelings about their own mothers when they became mothers themselves:

> Now that I had children I realized what she had been through. Before that . . . it just didn't dawn on me what kind of responsibility she had.
> *In what specific ways?*
> Well, her patience—she really understood. I never realized how much she did understand—what we were going through when we were teenagers and when we were younger. She was really almost I consider almost a saint now . . . Now that I realize what she had to go through, especially with younger children. And I have five brothers and sisters and that's really quite a responsibility, raising six children.

> I understand how hard it was for her—like, to cook a meal and not have everybody like the meal. And have them complaining, "Oh, this again," or "I don't like this," but you can't satisfy everyone. You know—things like that. You understand what they went through more.

> I guess I understood more why she did things and wouldn't let me do things. I guess you don't realize it until you really have your own and want to protect them.

The women in these interviews were viewing themselves from the dual role perspectives of mother and daughter. They saw themselves in the position of a mother confronting some of the same problems that their own mothers faced. The woman in the first quote, who called her mother a "saint," had a son and twin daughters at the time of the interview—all toddlers; she could easily appreciate that motherhood is "quite a responsibility." The daughters with children are settled in in the sense that they have little choice about their role. Until all their children are grown (and even beyond) they will continue to have the responsibility of motherhood.

These daughters also saw themselves with a different hindsight. In the last quote, the daughter justified her mother's behavior as a parent by recognizing how her mother must have felt—that is, wanting to protect her children. Interestingly, these daughters adopted their mother's viewpoint as much toward adolescence as toward early childhood, although their actual experience as mothers was only with young children. In part, this may be so because the adolescent years were more recent and therefore came to mind more easily. But adolescence was also the period when the daughter's attitude toward her mother was likely to be the most negative. It must come as something of a shock to the daughter-mothers to see their own past—their adolescent relationships with their mothers—potentially echoed in their future with children of their own. Thus, the daughter's own sense of herself is at stake as she reassesses her mother's role as a mother.

In two senses, motherhood transforms the life structure more than marriage. First, the mother role entails a more permanent and obligatory commitment (although the nature of that commitment changes as the child grows). And second, the amount of work and level of responsibility for a dependent child are much greater than for an ostensibly independent adult.[15] The implication of the shift in life structure is that, for mothers of young children in particular, their daily lives are likely to revolve around their children. When daughters become mothers, their involvement with their own mothers reflects this child-centered orientation.

Geographical distance is likely to be a determining factor in how much mothers and daughters can be involved in each other's lives.[16] Taking only the near mothers and daughters, I found that the daughters with children were considerably more involved with their mothers than the daughters without children. Half of the childless married daughters saw their mothers less than once a week, compared to only one of the ten daughters with children. All of the childless daughters worked during the day or were full-time students—limiting the possibility of daytime visiting with mothers. Of the daughters with children who lived near to their mothers, only two worked during the daytime. Although some of the mothers worked, they seemed to have flexible hours; so that most were able to visit each other at least occasionally during the daytime.

Married daughters with children also talk on the telephone with their mothers much more frequently than do childless daughters. When daughters become mothers there is often a pattern of daily "checking in" between mother and daughter. More than three-quarters of the nearby mothers said that they spoke on the telephone daily to their daughters with children. None of the mothers talked daily to their daughters without children.

The geographically near daughters with children also had started to be service providers to their mothers. The daughters with children tended to provide more types of services to their mothers than they received (excluding baby-sitting). Services to mothers included helping with cleaning and cooking and running errands. Four-fifths of the daughters with children, compared to two-fifths of the childless daughters, provided more types of help to their mothers than they received.

For geographically distant mothers and daughters, there is no opportunity to change the pattern of their involvement on a daily or weekly basis. For them, telephoning may serve as a substitute for face-to-face contact. Distant daughters with children tended to talk on the telephone to their mothers more frequently than distant daughters without children: Three-fifths of the daughters with children talked to their mothers at least once a week, compared to one-fifth of the childless married daughters. But for daughters with children and their mothers, telephone contact does not seem to be an adequate substitute for face-to-face visiting. Three of the five single daughters who lived at a distance from their mothers said that it was "not very important" to see their mothers frequently; if they spoke with them on the phone every now and then, that was sufficient to keep up contact. In contrast, all of the eleven "far" married daughters with children said that it was very important to see their mothers—if not for themselves, at least for their children. (Seven of the distant young mothers said it was very important both for themselves and their children; four said it was very important just for their children.)

> *How important is it for you to see her?*
> What do you mean to see her? I don't see her that often. I think it's very important to see her at least once a year or so. A friend of mine that has parents in Texas said it was expensive but she didn't look on it as a luxury to go back home and see her family— it was a necessity. I look on it that way.
> *How important is it for Annie to see your parents?*
> I would like them to see her. I would like to show her off and have them see how she's grown and everything.
>
> *How important is it for you to see your mother?*
> It used to be that I felt that I was doing it for her, that I was doing her a favor but I don't feel like that anymore.
> *What changed it?*
> I think that some of the feeling wasn't true . . . Also there was tension between us that I don't feel now. Especially since I am a mother I want to see her.
>
> *How important is it for you to see your mother?*
> Not important enough. I feel that I should want to see her more but I don't.
> *How important is it for your children?*
> I want them to know their grandparents 'cause I feel it's a special relationship and as a result I never say anything negative about them in front of the kids. I want them to get to know her. She's not the type to come up on a Saturday and get the kids and spend the day with them.
> *Do you wish she would?*
> Yes. I have friends that have family in the area and there are benefits.

For geographically distant daughters, there is often a sense of wistfulness about the lack of involvement with their families. In the last quote above, the daughter referred to the "benefits" she is missing by not having family nearby. By not having a mother in the area, most of these distant daughters did not have a backup support system on which to rely for baby-sitting and other types of respite from the work of mothering.

For the distant daughters, fewer than half of the mothers baby-sat even during a visit. Since the visits with the daughters were rare, the mother may have wanted to spend the time with the daughter rather than in providing a service for the daughter. By contrast, all but one of the near mothers did at least some baby-sitting for their daughters. Near daughters rarely relied exclusively on their mothers as baby-sitters. But their mothers provided a standby sort of help. They were willing to do some of the baby-sitting; often arrangements could be made in the last minute; and they were "right there" in an emergency.

Possibly mothers and daughters who live near each other have an opportunity to develop peerlike relationships just because of their greater involvement in each other's lives. Indeed, of the six pairs that approximate peer friendships, four are between mothers and *near* daughters with children. Geographical proximity allows access to each other and thus facilitates the development and maturation of their relationship. Nonetheless, the majority of the near daughters with children do not have peerlike friendships with their mothers.

What is perhaps most significant is not that the asymmetry disappears when the daughter becomes a mother herself but rather that the hierarchical nature of their relationship becomes less of a problem. With the birth of the daughter's child, the mother-daughter hierarchy becomes legitimated in several ways. First of all, in comparison to the child, the mother and daughter are both adults. Throughout the interviews there were a number of references to daughters' attempts at confirming their status as adults (for instance, by trying to have mothers not interfere in their lives and by "showing" mothers that they were competent housekeepers). These symbolic gestures of independence were found almost exclusively with the single and childless daughters and not the daughters with children. The young mother in the quote above who acknowledged that it really "wasn't true" that she was doing her mother a "favor" by visiting her was implying that in previous years she had placed a great effort on establishing her independence. Now, however, it seemed that her status as an adult was inherent in her role as a mother and no longer had to be proven.

Second, the mother's "mothering" has been reoriented and refocused onto the daughter's child. The daughter could ask for her mother's advice and help for the sake of the child—without having the mother's nurturance jeopardize the daughter's sense of independence. Thus, if the daughter is recognized as an adult, the mother can shift her "mothering" to her grandchild.

But the mother-daughter hierarchy also becomes legitimated in a third and seemingly opposite way: Particularly during the early period of first motherhood, daughters are likely to have a renewed dependence on their mothers. Several psychologists have portrayed new mothers, just after childbirth, as needing nurturance and expecting to be "mothered" by both their husbands and their mothers.[17] In this sample, almost all of the near daughters relied on their mothers' help after they gave birth. Two of the near daughters went to their mothers' homes after leaving the hospital. Four of the distant daughters had their mothers stay with them for a period of time after the birth. All of the distant daughters at least considered the possibility of having their mothers come to help.

It is not only during the emotionally charged postpartum period that daughters need their mothers' help. The birth of a child brings rising costs and a drop in income, since most new mothers drop out of the labor force at least temporarily. At the same time, the "work" of mothering entails continuous and often heavy responsibilities. Daughters with children are much more likely both to need and to receive help from their mothers than are married daughters without children. This does not mean that all or most daughters are given a lot of help by their mothers. To the contrary, not all daughters receive baby-sitting or other kinds of help; only one daughter relied on her mother as a full-time baby-sitter. But at least for some of the daughters, both living near to and far from their mothers, there were occasional opportunities to go "home"— to become a daughter again, letting their mothers provide a temporary respite from the responsibilities of adulthood.

PEERSHIP AND PARENTING

I am wary of typologies. Combining cases into certain types means summarizing a lot of information into these categories and probably ignoring differences within each type. Nonetheless, I decided to create the typology with which I began this chapter for two reasons.

First of all, this typology emphasizes a simple, but nonetheless important, point—that not all mother-daughter relationships are alike! Second, with this typology, we can begin to understand how mother-daughter relationships change as a result of the daughters' maturation and transitions to marriage and motherhood.

How do mother-daughter relationships change when daughters become mothers? The picture is complex. On the one hand, daughters as mothers seem to develop relationships with their own mothers that are more nearly equal. The daughters are givers as well as receivers in these relationships. Moreover, their roles as mothers give them a new insight—reflecting a sense of their peership in motherhood. On the other hand, daughters in some ways seem to become more dependent on their own mothers.

Is it possible that when daughters become mothers they become *both* more equal and more unequal in their relationships with their mothers? In the next chapter, I will discuss how their shared gender brings together generations of mothers and daughters. One of the consequences of the daughter's motherhood is that daughters and mothers become more involved in each other's lives. Their greater involvement accentuates the contradictions in their relationships.

4

GENDER AND GENERATION

When I was growing up, I thought my mother's life was a waste of time. What she was most interested in, it seemed to me, was playing bridge. One afternoon a week, she played with her women friends (she called them "girls"). Then there was duplicate bridge every Tuesday night with my father at a bridge club in a neighboring town. And, on the weekends, they would often get together with another couple and spend an evening playing bridge. Thus my father played bridge too; but he was also consumed by his work. When I decided that I never wanted to be a bridge player, it was clear to me, even then, what I meant—I did not want my life to be anything like my mother's life!

Several years ago, while I was doing my interviews with young adult daughters and their mothers, I was taken aback when I heard one of the daughters in my sample echoing my own feelings and experiences: This daughter told me that she was determined never to learn to play bridge and join bridge clubs because that was what her mother had done and she felt that bridge clubs just "kill time." For this daughter, as for me, not being a bridge player had become a symbolic component of her identity—which was shaped in counterpoint to her image of her mother.

The specific issues varied. But, in various ways, most of the adult daughters in my interviews said that they wanted to be different from their mothers. At the same time, most of these daughters described close and emotionally positive relationships with their mothers. What does it mean when daughters both acknowledge their bond with their mothers and, at the same time, reject their identity with their mothers?

As females in the family, mothers and daughters appear to share a "natural" identity. To the extent that the two genders are not equal, however, a daughter's "natural" identity with her mother is a negative affiliation—that is, a tie with the less powerful parent.[1] Ann Oakley, who has written extensively on women's roles as housewives and mothers, suggests that the mother-daughter relationship is important precisely because of the priority of men in women's lives:

> The preservation of bonds between adult daughters and their mothers gives women in their economically dependent position the protection of a valuable "trade union": a source of help in troubled times, financial protection in the event of marital breakdown and, perhaps most importantly, a common basis for self-esteem.[2]

I am not sure, however, that the mother-daughter bond necessarily provides a "basis for self-esteem." The daughter who insists that she wants to be "just like" her mother may enhance her mother's self-concept and also, implicitly, grant her mother a position as role model, teacher, or adviser. Conversely, the daughter who overtly rejects her mother as a model is suggesting that she wants to detach herself from a negative image and therefore is implying negative feelings or judgments about her mother.

The social changes that have occurred over the last two decades create further complications in daughters' identification with their mothers. These changes include the rising participation of women in the paid labor force, the liberalization of sexual codes, and the increasing acceptability of feminist ideology. All of these changes mean that daughters can anticipate adult roles that are different from their mothers'. However, the magnitude of social change is not easy to measure. In some ways, feminism and the ideology of gender equality are very new. But some form of feminism has been around for a long time. Throughout much of western history there have been people who have espoused a more-or-less feminist ideology.[3] Moreover, it is not clear how fundamental and permanent the recent changes are, especially since there seems to be one central feature of gender roles that has not changed much yet: the social arrangement of motherhood.

This chapter addresses several questions about gender roles and about changes across generations: To what extent are daughters attached to their mothers as role models? In what ways is mother-daughter attachment defined through relationships with men? To what degree has there been change or continuity between these generations of mothers and daughters?

MOTHERS AS ROLE MODELS

The concept of identification potentially has multiple meanings: To identify can refer to the way people think about each other—that is, their subjective sense of similarity in personality or role. Identification also can mean a set of behaviors—a conscious or unconscious modeling on the other. Finally, the process of identification may include an emotional response—through a desire to accentuate and reinforce the similarity with the other or to negate this identity and differentiate from the other.

I used several indicators to measure daughters' identification with their mothers, with data from both interviews and questionnaires. Taken together, these indicators showed that most daughters could point to similarities between themselves and their mothers—in terms of personality, life-style, and/or family roles. Daughters with children and daughters with relatively less education were the most likely to identify with their mothers. This pattern conforms to other research on married daughters and their mothers in working-class families.[4] I also found, however, that, in various ways, *most daughters either view themselves as different from their mothers and/or they want to be different.*

Role Models in Adolescence The interviews began with a series of questions about the daughters' childhood and adolescent years. One of the questions addressed to the daughters was, "Were there any adults whom you saw as models—people you wanted to be like?" After being asked this general question, they were then asked specifically if they wanted to be like their mothers, fathers, or other adults—so that there are three categories of role models.

About half of the daughters said they saw their mothers as role models, at least to some degree. Most of the daughters who said that their mothers were role models seemed to merge together the mother role and the personality qualifications for that role. Most of these daughters said that they wanted to emulate their mothers' "nurturant" or "mothering" qualities. Only four daughters (or about one-tenth of the sample) said they wanted to be "assertive" or "independent" like their mothers. Only one daughter specifically mentioned her mother's success in her career as a characteristic that she would like to emulate. The daughters seemed to be just slightly more likely to say that they saw their fathers as role models than their mothers (three-fifths vs. a half).[5] Of those daughters who saw their fathers as role models, about half pointed to general personality characteristics—suggesting that they wanted to emulate their fathers because they liked them. The other half pointed to characteristics of their fathers that attracted their respect—that is, power, intelligence, and career success.

I used educational attainment as an indicator of social class, and I divided the sample into two groups—(a) daughters who either had completed or were currently enrolled in a four-year college program and (b) daughters with less education (generally, high school, junior college, or technical school). I then compared the college-educated with the less-educated daughters in terms of the three types of role models. In terms of mothers as role models, there was no difference by educational level; the daughters with and without college educations were equally likely to say that they saw their mothers as models. The college-educated daughters were a little more likely to look back on their fathers as role models than less-educated daughters (two-thirds vs. a half).

The social-class variable (measured by college education) was most evident in the likelihood of having "other adults" as role models: College-educated daughters were four times more likely to say that they had other adults as role models than the less-educated daughters. It is probably a mistake to imply that having role models "caused" these respondents to pursue a college education. Rather, the difference in the availability of role models is likely to reflect environmental factors associated with the family of origin: The educated daughters tended to come from middle-class families and neighborhoods where they had friends, neighbors, and relatives with professions and life-styles that seemed attractive and worthy of modeling on. In contrast, in working-class families there may be few people accessible who can serve as models of success.[6]

The "role model" variable raises a number of issues about daughters' identification with their mothers: First, when daughters say their mothers are role models, it is difficult to distinguish between liking their mothers and identifying with them or modeling on their behavior. Second, it is not clear in what ways characteristics of mothers actually are modeled on and transmitted across generations. Finally, the implications of social class need to be explored. For example—why is it that social class does not seem to affect the likelihood of adolescent daughters viewing their mothers as role models?

Young Adult Daughters Identifying with Their Mothers

One of my research instruments was a paper-and-pencil questionnaire. As part of that questionnaire, the daughters were given a list of possible areas of resemblance with their mothers and they were asked to check the column on the right if they and their mothers were "very much alike" and to check the left column if they were "very different" from each other. Thus, for each item on the list, there were three possible responses: "very much alike," "very different," or neither; that is, respondents who did not check either the left or the right column on any particular item were giving a neutral response. Although the topics ranged from "facial features" to "how we feel about spending money," there were three items on this list that correspond to three roles: "How we discipline children" is an indicator of the mother role. "How we clean the house" refers to the housewife role. And "How we relate to men" alludes to the spousal role (or heterosexual relationships in general).

Table 7 shows that the daughters are most likely to feel identified with their mothers in terms of the mothering or child care role: Two-thirds of the twenty-one young mothers said they are

Table 7. Daughters' Rating of Themselves as Being
Very Similar to or Very Different from Their Mothers*

	VERY SIMILAR	NEITHER	VERY DIFFERENT	TOTAL
"How we discipline children"	14	5	2	21
"How we clean house"	26	2	15	43
"How we relate to men"	15	7	21	43

* Based on responses to selected questions in the daughter questionnaires.

"very much alike"; only two rated themselves as very different (for this item only the daughters who were mothers were included). Three-fifths of the daughters also rated themselves as very similar to their mothers on housecleaning.[7] The area about which the daughters were most likely to rate themselves as very different is "How we relate to men." This does not mean that all daughters see themselves as different from their mothers in this way; but they were five times as likely to consider themselves "very different" in relations to men as very different in disciplining children.

One interpretation of the findings in Table 7 is that a large proportion (most) of the daughters sense a strong similarity between themselves and their mothers—especially in terms of their mothering and housewife roles. But most of the daughters do not see themselves as similar in terms of their marital (or cross-sex) relationships.[8] There are a number of reasons why daughters might tend to view themselves as different in terms of relationships with men. First, they may not really understand their mothers' relationships with men. Because of norms of privacy, most mothers tend to say little about their marital relationships. Thus, the daughters may be guessing that their mothers may be very different and cannot have the same kinds of experiences as themselves. A second explanation is that there is a cohort effect—that is, because of a trend toward more egalitarian relationships with men, it is possible that daughters actually may be very different from their mothers. Finally, it is also possible that daughters view their mothers' relationships with men as negative and therefore want to be different.

Table 8. Awareness of Daughter's "Saying or Doing Something that Seems Just Like" Her Mother—from the Perspectives of the Daughter and Her Husband*

AWARENESS OF SIMILARITY	SINGLE DAUGHTERS	MARRIED DAUGHTERS	DAUGHTERS' HUSBANDS
Daughter does *not* say or do things like her mother	6	10	15
Positive similarity	0	1	1
Neutral similarity	2	9	4
Negative similarity	2	13	13
Total	10	33	33

* From daughter interviews.

Her Mother, Herself In their interviews, the daughters were asked: "Do you ever find yourself doing or saying something that seems just like something your mother would do or say?" They also were asked if their husbands ever point out ways in which they seem similar to their mothers. This question evokes daughters' awareness of identification with their mothers. Table 8 shows that most of the married daughters appeared to be self-conscious about mirroring their mothers' behavior. The single daughters, however, were less likely to recall saying or doing things like their mothers. To a large extent daughters "know" their mothers primarily through their role as mothers, secondarily as wives, and probably only minimally within the context of other role relationships. Most of the similarities mentioned by the daughters, especially those with children, concerned their roles either as mothers or wives. Thus, it is not surprising that single daughters tend to lack the experience of seeing their mothers' reflection in their own behavior.

Table 8 also indicates that both daughters and their husbands tend to portray the daughters' similarity to their mothers as negative and rarely as positive. The husbands seem especially likely to define their wives' similarity to their mothers as a negative factor.

I'll hear myself saying, for example, as I was never allowed to get dirty as a child and Christine will come and I will say, "Oh look at you, you're so dirty." And I feel like a parrot.

Do you say and do things like your mother?
Yes—as far as disciplining the children—the standard things—
"If you do that one more time, I'll do such and such."
Does your husband ever point out similarities?
Once in a while as far as holding things in—he'll say, "Your
mother does that too." He knows it's not good.
*How does it make you feel—doing something similar to your
mother?*
Mostly terrible. 'Cause it's always the negative things that I
remember and associate with her . . . Of course, there are positive
things but they don't come to mind . . .

I think I pick up a lot of her qualities. She repeats a lot of things
and I think she goes on a lot like I do. I kinda ramble at the
mouth a lot . . .

Only one daughter in the whole sample described a positive similarity
to her mother and only one married daughter said that her husband
pointed out a positive resemblance.

There are a number of reasons to explain why daughters'
resemblance to their mothers might be viewed negatively, or at
best neutrally, and not positively. First of all, if a daughter is still
in the process of disengagement from parents, this awareness of
similarity to her mother might serve to undermine her sense of her
individuality. One of the single daughters said, "It upsets me greatly"
when she realizes she is doing something like her mother or someone
points out a resemblance to her mother because "I don't want to
be my mother. I want to be me." The daughter quoted above who
said she feels like a "parrot" when she finds herself mimicking her
mother, also implies that her similarity to her mother is beyond her
control. When her resemblance to her mother is brought into
awareness, the implication is that she is still her mother's child.

A second interpretation of the negative evaluation is that the
daughter's bond of identity with her mother competes with her tie
with her husband. To the husband, his wife's attachment to her
mother represents that part of her that derives from a family and
gender culture different from his own. The birth of a child emphasizes the reproductive divergence between males and females. The

daughters tended to swap stories with their mothers about pregnancy and birth; and many of the daughters told of wanting their mothers around when they brought their babies home from the hospital. Especially in the initial adjustment to the birth of a child, then, the husband may find himself excluded from his wife's experience of motherhood.

Finally, there is a third interpretation of the daughters' negative identification with their mothers—that is, that their mothers have a problematic status in their families and in society.[9] Research on humans and animals in groups has shown that individuals of high status tend to be emulated much more than individuals of low status.[10] Most of the daughters' families of origin are characterized by a sharp gender division of labor and differentiation of power. The fact that the daughters almost never portray their resemblance to their mothers in positive terms suggests that they do not necessarily admire or look up to their mothers. If the mothers' status is problematic and the daughters as young adults find themselves in similar roles, they may be motivated to differentiate themselves as much as possible.

Daughters Wanting to Be Different Throughout the interviews, there were examples of both positive and negative identification with mothers. Daughters often spoke warmly and affectionately about their mothers; and most daughters saw their mothers, at least in some ways, as models in personality and/or role. Overwhelmingly, however, the interview material contained numerous examples of negative identification—that is, daughters wanting to be different. Their negative identity suggested not simply that daughters were neutral about their mothers as models. Rather, they portrayed specific ways in which they wanted their own identity to be diametrically opposite to the way they saw their mothers.

Most of the daughters saw the course of their lives, in the present and future, as different from their mothers' lives. When the daughters were asked to compare their own lives to their mothers' lives at the same age, less than a third of the daughters saw their lives as similar to their mothers'. The daughters with children, however, were more than twice as likely to see their lives as replicating their mothers' as the other daughters. Even so, when projecting their lives into the future, hardly any of the daughters—even those with children—anticipated that their lives would be similar to their mothers'.

The daughters' negative identity—or rejecting identification with their mothers—may reflect their need to differentiate themselves from their parents at this stage in their lives. Bengtson and Kuypers,[11] who have interviewed college students and their parents, found that young adults tend to exaggerate their differences from their parents. They theorized that during the stage of early adulthood, sons and daughters have a "developmental stake" in pushing away from their parents and establishing their separate identity.

A negative identity with mothers was especially characteristic of geographically distant daughters. A third of the near daughters mentioned a sense of negative identification, compared to most (nineteen out of twenty-two) of the distant daughters. Possibly, some daughters may move because they *want* to live at a distance from their mothers. But geographical distance is associated with social class.[12] College-educated daughters and sons tend to leave "home" both to receive their advanced education and to match their training with specific jobs. Thus, they tend to be more geographically mobile than blue-collar workers.

The evidence for daughters' negative identification with their mothers can be grouped into three categories: personality, role, and life-style. Several of the daughters said that they had inherited negative personality traits from their mothers—with "nervousness" the most common characteristic. In terms of family roles, about a quarter of the daughters portrayed their mothers as "too submissive" or "not selfish enough." For example, one daughter said that her mother was always

> very submissive to my father and I always looked down on her for that. I thought she should stand up for herself and tell him where to go once in a while. She keeps things inside her. She has colitis . . .

Another daughter, explaining why she did not want to be like her mother, noted:

. . . It always bothered me that she never did anything for herself and she never had any friends. I didn't want that. I wanted to be independent and my own person.

Similarly, another daughter portrayed her mother as "very unselfish" and said "I'd probably be more selfish." One daughter said she wanted to be like her mother in the sense that her mother was "sure of herself professionally and she seemed to enjoy her work." But she did not want to be like her mother in that "I didn't want to be catering to a man as dependent as my father is." All of these comments directly reflect an awareness of the problems of women's roles and the negative status of females in the family.

In a similar way, the third category of comments—the most common—also relates to gender. Nearly half of the daughters *rejected* their mothers' life-style in both general and specific ways. These daughters tended to view their mothers' lives as "stagnant" or "uninteresting," while they themselves wanted more personal freedom, better marriages, and/or more opportunities for jobs and careers.

The emphasis on negative identity suggests that young adult daughters do use their mothers as role models—but largely through negation. The use of a mother as a negative model is illustrated by the daughter who decided *not* to learn to play bridge. There is an inherent paradox: On the one hand, most daughters both maintain an intimate tie with their mothers and are aware of their similarities to their mothers, especially in their maternal and domestic roles. On the other hand, daughters also tend to view their mothers as negative role models and these negative images motivate daughters to want to be different. For many daughters, this combination of identification and rejection suggests that their shared gender both sustains their attachment to their mothers and devalues their relationship.

THE IMPORTANCE OF HUSBANDS

A mother of one of the single daughters said that she looked forward to her daughter's getting married because a husband is a "friend for life." In our culture, the most frequently given reason for marriage is "love" or "companionship." Just as a parent might want a child to have financial security, marriage potentially provides an emotional investment—with a lifetime "payoff." None of the daughters or mothers talked explicitly about marrying for money. However, among those mothers who expressed dissatisfaction about their sons-in-law or future sons-in-law, the most frequent complaint related to the lack of adequate earning power.

Almost all of the mothers in this study said that they wanted their daughters to marry. The mothers did not always approve of their daughters' choice of mates; and they did not necessarily push their daughters to marry at particular ages. The daughters in this sample have tended to marry at somewhat older ages than their mothers—most of whom married in the "familism era" of the post–World War II years. Nonetheless, although women today may remain single for more years, over 90% eventually marry.

When a daughter marries, her life is transformed by the presence of a husband. Her relationships with others, including her mother, need to be adapted to the new structure of her life—particularly when her marital relationship is viewed as her primary commitment. Daughters' relationships with their husbands may affect their bonds with their mothers in contradictory ways. On the one hand, the allocation of family responsibilities by gender means that mothers and daughters share a similar set of domestic tasks. Thus, mothers and daughters may participate together in certain joint "domestic" chores (e.g., preparing for holiday meals with the "extended" family); they may help each other with their separate chores; and mothers may serve as advisers when daughters are acquiring household and maternal skills. On the other hand, both married daughters and sons are expected to place priority on their marital commitment. Moreover, to the extent that women are economically dependent on men, their relationships with other women (including their mothers) are likely to revolve around and be contingent on their marital obligations.[13]

Women's Work Despite the increasing participation of women in the paid labor force and a growing ideological commitment in our society to some measure of feminism, the notion of "women's

Table 9. Participation of Daughter's Husband in "Female" Household Chores by Parental and Work Status*

| | | WITH CHILDREN | |
HUSBAND'S PARTICIPATION	CHILDLESS†	*Working wives*	*Nonworking wives*
Little or none	2	4	7
Some	8	4	4
Substantial	1	1	0
Total	11	9	11

* These data are from the husband questionnaires. Seven "female" chores are used as indicators for this scale: housecleaning, cooking, washing dishes, laundry, sewing, ironing, and shopping. Each item was scored from 0 (no participation) to 4 (prime responsibility), with a total possible score of 28. The category "little or no participation" is based on a score of 0 to 7, where the top score is equivalent to a response of "helps rarely" on all seven chores. The category "some participation" includes scores 8 to 14; the top score is equivalent to a response of "helps often" on all seven chores. A rating of "substantial participation" was given to scores of 15 or over, with a score of 15 equivalent to a response of "shares equally" in at least five chores. This means that husbands are rated high in household participation even if they do not do all the above chores. This leeway in the scale is necessary because some chores, especially sewing and ironing, might not be done by either husband or wife. There was 90% agreement between husbands and wives in terms of score categories. Only two wives' scores would put husbands in a lower category of participation, and two wives would put husbands in a higher category (but even these scores were very close).

† All of the childless wives were either working or were full-time students.

work" and "men's work" has persisted. In my research on mothers and daughters, I asked the daughters' husbands to fill out questionnaires. Table 9 summarizes husbands' ratings of their participation in certain household chores that traditionally would be designated as "female jobs"—housecleaning, cooking, washing dishes, laundry, sewing, ironing, and shopping. (I have not included child care in this list.) Only two husbands who filled in the questionnaire reported substantial participation in these "female" tasks. Their wives (the "daughters" in the sample) also were asked to rate the husbands' participation in household chores. For these tasks, there is very high agreement between husbands and wives in terms of the three categories listed in Table 9.

The husbands are most likely to have some participation in housework before the birth of children and when their wives work outside the home. All of the childless wives (the daughter generation)

Table 10. Husband's Participation
in Child Care by Wife's Work
Status*

HUSBAND'S PARTICIPATION	WIFE'S WORK STATUS	
	Working	*Not working*
Some	3	10
Substantial	6	1
Total	9	11

* From perspectives of husbands.

either work or are full-time students; and their husbands have the highest rate of participation in household chores. Conversely, the husbands of nonworking wives who have small children are the least likely to participate in "female" household chores. When the wife works and when there are no children, the gender divisions are less sharply drawn; but even in these couples a traditional division of labor is maintained. Although the young husbands may "help" with household chores more than their fathers did, only two of the thirty-three couples indicated a significant attempt at an egalitarian division of labor.

This does not mean, however, that husbands do not contribute their labor to their families, for two reasons. First of all, the one traditionally female job that husbands are most likely to participate in is child care. All of the husbands with children were rated by either husband or wife as having at least some participation in child care—as Table 10 shows. Table 10 also shows that husbands are considerably more likely to say that they share substantially in child care when their wives work.[14] Secondly, when the wives rate their husbands' participation in "male" chores (financial support, car repair, fixing things, and taking out the garbage), the husbands' scores are very high: Nearly all of the husbands carry major responsibility for these chores; all of the husbands were rated as having at least some participation in this set of "male" family chores. The basic point is that among almost all of these young couples, family jobs are allocated by gender. All other studies that I have read on family work rôles have reported similar findings.

The allocation of work by gender facilitates relationships between adult daughters and their mothers in two related ways. First of all, most daughters look to their mothers, at least to some extent, as experts in women's work—that is, household and child care. At the very least, their mothers are sources of information. The daughters and mothers, in their questionnaires, were given a list of items on each of which the daughter may have "asked for" or been "offered" advice by the mother. In analyzing these data, I grouped the items into three categories: (1) general household issues (twelve questions); (2) child care (two questions); and (3) issues related to marriage or relationships with husbands (three questions). (The child care questions were given only to the daughters with children; the marriage questions only to the married daughters). While there was some variability in how much daughters relied on their mothers for advice, almost all of the married daughters asked their mothers for some kind of advice concerning general household care. Only one daughter said that she asked for no advice from her mother—and this was a daughter who had not spoken with her mother for several years.

The single most common item was advice on cooking; four-fifths of the married daughters had asked for advice on "how to cook a particular dish." The geographically near daughters are a little more likely to ask for their mothers' advice, but the differences are not large. Most of the daughters with children had asked for at least some advice from their mothers on child rearing ("how to toilet train a child" and/or "what to feed a child"). Even daughters who have conflictful or problematic relationships with their mothers tend occasionally to ask their mothers' advice about such issues as recipes or toilet training. These findings may not be particularly surprising. But the fact that these patterns are expectable does not diminish the importance of gender-based expertise in providing one context for mother-daughter interaction.

In addition to expertise and information, a second, and related, context for mother-daughter interaction entails help on child care and household chores. Myra Leifer[15] in her study of pregnancy and new motherhood found that young women received more help in caring for their new infants from their mothers, who came for a week or two after the birth, than from their husbands, who quickly returned to their work and study. In my study, most of the near daughters and some of the distant daughters had received substantial help from their mothers after childbirth.

In addition to help after childbirth, almost all of the mothers and daughters in this sample noted helping each other in a variety of ways. Most of the mothers did at least some baby-sitting and provided occasional loans. The daughters, particularly the geographically near daughters with children, helped their mothers by running errands, occasionally doing some household chores, and working with their mothers on family get-togethers. The point is that "female" jobs bring together women in the family—particularly mothers and daughters.

Power and Priority   The position of husband as family bread-winner is central to control over resources in the family. Previous research has shown that wives who work outside the home and earn their own incomes tend to exercise greater power in their marriages than nonworking wives.[16] An important point to make, however, is that working wives generally earn less than their husbands. In my study, because the focus was not on marriage, there were no direct indicators of marital "power" included in the design. Nonetheless, throughout the interviews there were a number of references to husbands' making economic decisions. For example, a number of daughters talked about the purchase and use of a car. One daughter (who works in a factory and has a two-year-old son) noted that she did not want to be stuck at home like her mother. She said that she is able to go places because "my husband bought me a car." The implication of this phrase and similar statements is that husbands tend to make decisions about major purchases.

Particularly in cases with geographically distant mothers and daughters, the daughters' husbands are likely to have an impact on mother-daughter access to one another. A central issue is the right to make decisions about the allocation of money and time. For instance, in one case, a distant mother noted that her daughter visits rarely because she "has her own life. And anyway it's Dick who decides when they come down here. He makes the rules. Karen is very submissive." In contrast, a number of the respondents implied that the husbands were "lenient" or "good." For example, one daughter, who lives about fifteen hundred miles from her mother, noted about her husband: "He's been good about sending me home for visits." Another daughter, who lives about a hundred miles away, said: "My husband is good. He says take the car and go for a few days. [*How often do you do that?*] Once a month, just the two of us [she and her two-year old son]. Or sometimes he'll bring us for a weekend. When I was single, he drove me down and said stay as long as you want." This last daughter, just quoted, seemed to attribute to her husband a benign form of control over her whole life. In describing her hobbies (sewing, quilting, and decorating), she stated: "My husband lets me do creative things like that." The implicit language in these statements is suggestive of underlying power factors. Whether the husbands are "lenient" or "good" or overtly dominant, it is the husbands who tend to purchase and determine the use of, for example, the family car. Thus, they maintain, to a large degree, decision-making power over the use of economic and material resources. The access to a car is particularly important in determining how often mothers and daughters can spend time with each other.

Husbands and Mothers as Confidants Several researchers have suggested that women's relationships with other women constitute an important source of emotional support.[17] These researchers have reported that wives are better "confidantes" for their husbands than husbands are for their wives. One implication might be that mothers and daughters need each other as "friends" and confidantes—to supplement the emotional support in their marriages.

As part of my study, the daughters, their husbands, and their mothers all were asked about their sources of emotional support. The daughters and mothers, during their interviews, were given the question: "Most of us have times when we feel down or depressed. What do you do at such times?" The major purpose of this question was to see if mothers and daughters would mention talking

Table 11. Confidants for Daughter's
Husband by Parental Status

HUSBAND CONFIDES IN:	PARENTAL STATUS		
	Childless	*With Children*	TOTAL
Wife first	9	15	24
Wife second	1	2	3
Husband's mother	4	8	12
Husband's father	4	2	6
Other relatives/friends	6	12	18
No one	1	2	3
Total*	11	19	30

* Does not add up because more than one answer given by each respondent.

with each other in response to an open-ended question. Later in the interview, they were asked explicitly if they talk to their mother/ daughter when they feel "down." With the open-ended question, the respondents also could mention other sources of emotional support, including husbands.

In the questionnaire that the daughters' husbands filled out, one item read: "Most people have times when they feel 'down' or depressed. Check the people whom you would talk to when you are feeling 'down.' Put a double check (✓✓) by the person whom you would be likely to speak to first." Then they were given a list of relationship categories to check off. We need to be cautious about comparing the information from husbands and wives, since the questions were slightly different. But, at the very least, the comparison can be suggestive.

Table 11 shows that four-fifths of the husbands, with and without children, noted that they talk to their wives first when looking for emotional support. Indeed, virtually all of the husbands, if they talk to anyone at all, talk to their wives. Data from the daughter interviews also show that most daughters rely on their husbands as confidants. (See Table 12.) Almost two-thirds of the daughters mentioned talking with their husbands when they feel "down." However, there were two ways that the daughters depicted

Table 12. Confidants for Married Daughter
by Parental Status*

DAUGHTER CONFIDES IN IF FEELING "DOWN":	PARENTAL STATUS		
	Childless	*With Children*	TOTAL
Husband—no limitations stated	4	11	15
Husband—with limitations	1	5	6
Mother—no limitations stated	2	5	7
Mother—with limitations	5	9	14
Other friends/relatives	7	5	12
No one	2	2	4
Total*	12	21	33

* Does not add up because more than one answer given by each respondent.

their husbands as confidants—with and without qualifiers. Many of the daughters made qualifying statements. Although they mentioned their husbands as confidants, they described limitations in their confiding in them. For instance, a number of the daughters said that "sometimes" they can talk to their husbands. Work schedules constitute a major barrier. One daughter who works during hours when her husband is home, and vice versa, noted that "we don't see each other 'til the weekend." Another daughter, asked if she can talk to anyone when she feels down, said "Tim [husband] sometimes, but sometimes he is so busy I just keep it to myself." In contrast, a daughter, who did not place qualifiers or limitations on her husband's role as confidant, said that when she is depressed she talks to "Bert—he's my best friend—and it works the other way around." As Table 12 shows, less than half of the married daughters mentioned their husbands as confidants without any qualifiers.

The same proportions of the wives and husbands say they talk to "no one" when they feel "down." When we take away those individuals and use as our baseline those spouses who talk with confidants, we find that all but three of the husbands but only about half of the wives pointed to their spouse as the primary source of emotional support.[18]

When we compare the social supports of married daughters

and mothers, we find that the mothers were considerably less likely than the daughters to rely on their husbands to support them when they feel "down." Only five mothers (out of twenty-nine mothers who were currently married) said that they generally turn to their husbands when they feel down. But eight of these mothers (compared to only four of thirty-three daughters) said that they talk to "no one" when they feel "down." Many of the mothers, when asked directly about talking to their husbands when depressed, noted the difficulty of approaching their husbands with emotional problems. For instance, one mother said that she might talk to her husband "if he's willing to listen." Another mother, who said that usually she did not talk to anyone when she was feeling depressed, said that she might talk to her husband; but when she was asked directly, "Is he a good person to talk to?" she answered "No." Another mother reflected:

> I don't seek out anyone necessarily when I'm feeling down, except my husband, and he doesn't know how to deal with that sort of thing. He's a very different human being—a super guy—but, like I tell him, he seems to have missed certain things. For instance, he says he has never been lonely. He doesn't know what I'm talking about. He has never experienced homesickness; he doesn't know what it is. Either that or he doesn't know what label to put on the feeling he's got and I don't know which it is.

This quote is consistent with Lillian Rubin's depiction of married couples as emotional "strangers" to one another. Rubin, in her recent book *Intimate Strangers,* asserted that husbands and wives tend to have divergent emotional needs and different ways of expressing their feelings.

The daughters were much less likely than their mothers to make such direct statements about their husbands' inability or unwillingness to listen to their feelings. The daughters who remarked on the limitations of confiding in their husbands tended to say that they did not have sufficient time together. It is difficult here to distinguish between "life stage" and "cohort" effects. Possibly, there may be less "companionship" in the mothers' marriages because of a process of "disenchantment," or a diminishing emotional bond over the years.[19] But the difference between daughters and mothers in their emotional relationships with their husbands also may reflect a cohort or generational effect. The daughters and their husbands tend to be more educated, are likely to have somewhat better communication skills, and may be more aware of popular psychology. The greater likelihood of daughters' confiding in their husbands may be associated with a trend toward more egalitarian marriages.[20]

The daughters were about equally likely to say that they confide in their mothers as in their husbands. However, there is a major difference: They were much more likely to suggest that there were limitations or restrictions in confiding in mothers than in husbands. Table 11 shows that, while more than three-fifths of daughters said they can talk to their mothers when they are feeling "down," most of these daughters placed limitations on confiding with their mothers. Thus, it does *not* appear to be the case that mothers substitute for husbands as confidants. For most of the daughters, their husbands were much more likely to be close confidants than their mothers.

The Confidentiality of Husbands   The daughter's intimacy with her husband is private and exclusive of her mother. The confidentiality of daughters' relationships with their husbands is illustrated by the fact that daughters are more than twice as likely to ask advice from their mothers about child care than about their marriage and the mothers are almost three times more likely to offer advice about child care than about marriage. The implication is that daughters' relationships with husbands place constraints around their relationships with their mothers by imposing boundaries around mother-daughter intimacy.

When the daughters were asked explicitly if they talked to their mothers about their husbands, most indicated that they talked only in "superficial" or "general" ways about their husbands. In the sample of thirty-three married daughters, there are only five exceptions—that is, daughters who said they talk with their mothers openly and freely about their husbands. In two of these cases, according to the daughters, the mothers make a point of taking the "side" of the daughter's husband in any argument. In the other three cases, the daughters' marriages were unstable and the daugh-

ters were subjected to their mothers' negative comments about
their husbands. For example, in one of these cases, the mother
stated:

> I think sometimes perhaps she'd be happier with someone else.
> I don't think it's good for a wife to earn more than her husband.
> I think Marge wouldn't want to just stay home and it would be
> nice if she could work part-time. But now she has to work. He
> isn't the type I would have picked for Marge.

Those daughters who do not protect the confidentiality of their
relationships with their husbands may be implicitly acknowledging
the lack of future commitment in their marriages.

For the other daughters, if their mothers do not completely
approve of their husbands, there is automatically a source of strain
in the mother-daughter bond. A third of the mothers had negative
reactions to their daughters' husbands—at least initially.[21] In these
cases, the mother was confronted by a barrier in her intimacy with
her daughter, as is illustrated by the following responses from one
of the mothers:

> *How did you feel about Susan getting married?*
> I was happy about her getting married—period.
> *What does that mean?*
> Because of Joe.
> *Did you tell her how you felt?*
> Yes.
> *Did it create a strain between you?*
> I thought it did.
> *How do you get along with him now?*
> I get along with him all right. But I still don't know him. He's
> very closed. Especially it seems that he's closed to me. But he
> does something to her. She's happy and that's good . . .
> *How much confiding do you and Susan do now?*
> It depends on what area we're talking about—her marriage—
> not at all . . .

In another family, a daughter (married with children) stated:

> I think my mother was disappointed that I didn't marry this other
> guy and to this day every time I see her she brings his name up.
> He's not married yet and she's always telling me what he's doing.

I don't want to talk about him. I have no interest in him. She does it in front of Peter. I know it bothers him. I don't think it's right.

This was one of the families in which the daughter decided that she did not want her mother to come after she had her baby. She believed that it would be too stressful to have her mother and her husband in the same household. Several of the distant daughters made similar statements about difficulties when their mothers came to visit.

Even in families where daughters and mothers are very close and openly confide in each other, when mothers criticize their daughters' husbands, daughters tend to become defensive. A daughter's protectiveness toward her marital relationship is illustrated by a daughter who is very close with her mother and confides in her freely. (This was one of the invested adolescent daughter-mother relationships, where the daughter claimed that she did not censor what she said to her mother.) But she does not feel comfortable when her mother makes comments about her (the daughter's) husband. She remarked about her mother's reaction to her husband:

> She doesn't live with him and she doesn't understand him. There are some things that I can understand well that can disturb her— like on Friday night if he wants to go with his friends for a few hours or on Saturday he wants to go out, something like that. She looks at it that I am stuck in the house and doesn't see both sides of it.

This daughter implied, in fact, that her husband's Friday night activities were a source of annoyance to her. But what is striking is that, despite her intimacy with her mother, she quickly experienced a sense of conflicting loyalties when her mother criticized her husband. The daughter's alliance with her mother would challenge her husband's right to use his leisure time as he pleases. As a nonworking mother with a small child, possibly she felt wary about being pushed by her mother to try to change her husband's behavior.

I found that daughters who have children and live near their mothers are more likely than other daughters to have mutually confiding relationships. Nonetheless, even among these daughters, the presence of the daughter's husband operates as a constraint in mother-daughter intimacy. The daughters know that their mothers do not "love" their (the daughters') husbands with the same kind of intimacy; and therefore they cannot assume their mothers' loyalty. Daughters who confide "too much" about their husbands to their mothers (or to others) not only feel emotionally torn between conflicting loyalties but also risk jeopardizing the exclusivity of their marriages.

BETWEEN GENERATIONS

How much has changed in women's roles between these generations of mothers and daughters? This is a critical question in trying to understand mother-daughter relationships. When there is little change between generations, mothers are the transmitters of gender and family roles to their daughters. Conversely, if there should be rapid change, the process of intergenerational transmission either is nonexistent or is reversed.

The sociologist Gunhilde Hagestad[22] has pointed out that generations in a family and generations in society, or "birth cohorts," are *not* the same. The term "birth cohort" comes from demographers and social historians and refers to people who are born around the same time. The mothers and daughters in my study represent different "generations" within their family lineages. The daughters also might be viewed as belonging to a ten-year birth cohort, since they were all been born between 1948 and 1958. However, their mothers' ages vary by over twenty years, with the mothers having been born between 1913 and 1935. One implication of these differences in age span is that the mothers' experiences growing up reflect more historical variability than the daughters' early years.

Nonetheless, there is another way, based on the ages of their daughters, to depict the mothers as a cohort: These mothers were all rearing children during the 1950s. Conversely, their daughters belong to a mothering cohort of the late 1970s to early 1980s. Sociologists have called the 1950s "the era of the family"—when marriage and birth rates were unusually high. Women had given their factory jobs back to the men returning from war. In the movies, radio, television, and magazines of the fifties there was an emphasis on traditional wife/mother roles for women. It was in response to the mothering cohort of the 1950s that Betty Friedan published *The Feminine Mystique* and Alice Rossi wrote "Equality between the Sexes: An Immodest Proposal."[23] Two decades later, by the time the daughters had reached young adulthood, the ideology of feminism was familiar, if not universally accepted, throughout American society. By comparing these two mothering cohorts, we can begin to assess the impact of social change between generations.

Cohort and Generation Many of the mothers and a number of the daughters (even some who saw their lives as similar) made the point that the daughters were better off. Both mothers and daughters noted advantages for the younger generation—in terms of material resources and marital/family relationships. In terms of material resources, the married children tended to buy houses earlier in their lives and, in general, enjoyed a higher standard of living than their parents had during their early years of marriage.[24] In terms of marital relationships, the married daughters were described both by themselves and by their mothers as "freer," more "independent," and having more "open" relationships with their husbands. Their husbands were said to spend more time with their wives and children than their fathers had. Also, some of the daughters noted that, unlike many of their mothers, they were able to drive their own cars so that they could be physically mobile on a daily basis. Two aspects of social change account for the greater advantages of the daughters: First, there is the increased prosperity of the society as a whole. The greater well-being of the society is the result, in large part, of advances in technology—bringing material goods, such as cars, washing machines, dishwashers, processed foods, etc., to ever larger portions of the population.[25] The second aspect of social change that accounts for differences in life-style patterns between mothers and daughters entails the changing roles of women and the impact of the feminist movement.

One major difference between cohorts over the last century has been the increasing level of education for each succeeding cohort. This is very clear when we compare the educational attainment of the daughters and their mothers. The daughters are considerably more likely to be college educated than their mothers: eighteen of the daughters, compared to only five of the mothers, have completed at least four years of college. The daughters also appear to be a little more likely to be college educated than their fathers—a third of whom attained at least a four-year college degree. The difference in education between daughters and mothers may reflect both the increasing prosperity of society—with more people able to afford education—and the changes in women's roles—with a greater likelihood that family resources will be used for the education of daughters.

The lack of priority that had been placed on education for girls in the past became clear in the interviews with the mothers. The mothers were asked about their own plans when they were growing up. Only one-tenth of the mothers (four out of thirty-nine mothers interviewed) said that they had career plans which they had actually fulfilled in their lives. About a quarter of the mothers noted that they had had "no plans," other than marriage and motherhood. Most of the mothers—almost two-thirds—described *unfulfilled aspirations*. Several of the mothers said that they had wanted to be nurses: "I always wanted to be a nurse, but I never made it . . . I just never got to it. My family couldn't afford it." Most of the mothers with unfulfilled aspirations made similar comments—that they lacked economic resources for pursuing career goals. A number of the mothers noted specifically that education was not available to daughters in their families. For instance, one mother stated:

> I would have loved to go to college but my mother was from the old school—a woman is going to diaper a baby, what does she need college for? My first job was in an office. I realize now that I have tremendous potential for learning. I learned typesetting very quickly.

Another mother in the sample told a similar story about unfulfilled hopes:

> I wanted to be a fashion designer as a teenager.
> *What happened?*

I wasn't able to. My father died and my stepfather didn't have the funds to educate me. He didn't believe girls needed education anyway. In those days we didn't think of educating ourselves. Now the kids can work and put themselves through college. There's more opportunity and it's easier to get started. But then we didn't think of it. Now kids are encouraged to work part-time.

In all of the families just cited, the daughters have had college educations and the mothers are clearly aware that their daughters' life chances, in terms of educational and career opportunities, have been very different from their own. However, although nearly two-thirds of the mothers describe unfulfilled aspirations, most of them also say that they have "no regrets" about how their lives have turned out. For instance, the second mother quoted above, who said that her mother was from the "old school," said that she was not disappointed about how things have turned out and she insisted: "No, I think I'm lucky—making the best out of something. I could learn whatever came to me; I have that ability."

The lack of regret might be explained by the theory of "cognitive dissonance."[26] According to this theory, individuals have a need to reconcile discrepancies ("dissonance") between their values and their experiences. People are especially likely to rationalize or validate choices that are made voluntarily, because when they have made their own choices they cannot blame others if they subsequently have negative experiences. The unfulfilled aspirations of these mothers might be viewed as sources of dissonance in several ways: First, in a general way, at middle age if they view their adult years as wasted, there is no way to recoup those lost years. Second, their life choices have been "free" choices in the sense that they were not forced into particular jobs or marriages. Thus, if these roles are chosen, they need to be rationalized. Finally, specifically for wives and mothers, regret over life choices has a very personal meaning: Their limited career opportunities have been justified, by others and by themselves, on the basis of their family roles. Virtually all of the mothers affirm that having children was "very important" to them. Only some of the mothers who are currently divorced expressed regret about their marriages. For the generation of

Table 13. Types of Careers for Mothers and Daughters

TYPES OF CAREERS	MOTHERS	DAUGHTERS
"Male" professional-managerial careers	4	3
"Female" professional careers	5	10
"Female" nonprofessional jobs	17	13
Student	0	5
Nonworkers	17	12
Total	43	43

mothers, their lack of educational opportunities may well have reinforced their commitment to motherhood as a domestic career. Certainly motherhood was a more attractive and available option than most other kinds of jobs or careers. Thus, motherhood became their choice and, along with marriage, the central commitment in their lives.

When we compare the daughters' career lives with their mothers', we find some marked differences as well as some striking similarities. Between these two generations of mothers and daughters, educational opportunities had suddenly become much more available to women. The educational gap between the mothers and daughters has been noted above: The daughters were almost four times as likely to complete a four-year college degree. Similarly, there are differences in aspirations and career attainments. The mothers were nearly three times as likely to have "no plans" for careers, other than marriage and motherhood—a quarter of the mothers but only a tenth of the daughters had "no plans." Conversely, the daughters were over four times as likely to have attained or even exceeded their career goals (almost a half versus one in ten).

However, a comparison of the career lives of the mothers and daughters is complicated by the differences in age. For instance, Table 13 shows that five of the daughters but none of the mothers are currently students. Clearly, this reflects the fact that the daughters are in the establishment phase of their careers—with some of them still in training. But this is not the only complication. For example, the fact that more mothers than daughters are "nonworkers" is difficult to interpret for several reasons. First of all, the statistic on the daughters is misleading, because all of the non-working daughters have small children, while all of the other daughters are either workers or students. Second, most of the nonworking mothers did work, at least for some time, during young adulthood. Finally, we do not know about the future labor force participation of the daughters. Some of the daughters with children may return to the labor force; a number of those who are currently working are likely to drop out, at least temporarily, when they have children. In short, any conclusions about differences between career paths of mothers versus daughters need to be tentative.

Nonetheless, one difference between the career paths of daughters versus mothers is that the daughters are more likely to have entered "women's" professional careers. This category is comprised of careers that require college-level training and that are filled mostly by women. Such careers include teachers (primary and secondary), nurses (RNs), and occupational and physical therapists. When we include students who are training for these careers, these daughters are more than twice as likely as their mothers to enter "female" professional careers. However, the daughters are not more likely than their mothers to have "male" professional-managerial careers.[27] Thus, most of the daughters who attained their career goals planned for careers in "women's" professions—particularly teaching and nursing.

When we look at career aspirations, daughters were less likely than their mothers to have unfulfilled career aspirations. Nonetheless, nearly half of the daughters did have plans that they did not accomplish (versus two-thirds of the mothers). But there tends to be a difference between the unfulfilled aspirations of the daughters and their mothers: The mothers wished for "female" professions but lacked the educational opportunities to embark on such careers. Their daughters were much more likely to become trained professionals, as teachers and nurses; but many of the daughters aspired to "male" professions. When asked what they hoped to be as teenagers, a quarter of the daughters envisioned "male" professional careers—wanting to be doctors, engineers, veterinarians, architects, etc.

One implication of these generational differences is that, in a number of families, the daughters have fulfilled career ambitions that the mothers had had for themselves. A number of theorists of human development[28] have argued that parents in middle age have a need for generational continuity—with their own accomplishments measured, in part, through their success in establishing the next generation. For women, particularly women who are now middle-aged and older, the need for generational continuity has a special meaning. Having limited opportunities for careers on their own, their "success" in the world outside their families was based largely on the accomplishments of their husbands and children. But over the last two decades there appears to be a change in the investment of mothers in their children: Until very recently, intergenerational mobility meant educating sons and preparing daughters for good marriages. But, as the participation of women in the labor force has risen steadily, the education of daughters has become increasingly significant. The daughters who had thought about "male" professional careers tended to say that at some point they "realized" that these careers did not seem "practical" or "realistic." But we are confronted with an intriguing speculation: *If this generation of daughters fulfilled their mothers' ambitions, will their own daughters in turn fulfill theirs?*

The Meaning of Motherhood   There is a famous quotation: "Plus ça change, plus c'est la même chose"—"The more things change, the more they remain the same."[29] This might also be said about motherhood and gender. Despite cultural change that creates technological and ideological changes between generations, there is nonetheless a sense of continuity in "family culture" over time. In numerous idiosyncratic ways, daughters replicate their mothers' style of mothering—even though they do not necessarily like doing so.

More significant, the priority of motherhood seems to be reproduced across generations of mothers and daughters. The daughters varied in terms of their career goals, plans, and achievements. But despite this variability, in virtually all of the families there was evidence for the pull of a "traditional" ideology about motherhood. According to this ideology, it is preferable for women not to work, or not to work full-time, when they have small children. Most daughters, with and without children, and most of their mothers expressed this preference. Of course, in those cases where daughters with children were full-time homemakers, this ideology should hardly be surprising. But there was also at least implicit evidence of this traditional ideology about motherhood among the most career-oriented women in the sample. For these women, the issue of working and motherhood has been an ongoing dilemma.

Some of the daughters were pressed by their mothers to espouse the traditional motherhood ideology. One mother, whose daughter is a teacher and has a two-year-old son, quipped: "I wish she'd spend more time with him—be at home. I'm old-fashioned. I'd like her not to work when the kids are small." The mother of a childless married daughter also is clear about the priority of child care: "If you're a mother, it's your responsibility to be home all the time that your husband isn't. We never went out without the children—never went on vacations without them."

The following situation seems somewhat unusual in that the mother encouraged the daughter to continue working full-time. This daughter was a teacher, had a two-year-old daughter, and was trying to decide whether or not to continue working full-time. She described the social pressure she faced when she returned to work after her daughter was born. She felt isolated from peers because "a lot of the people with kids her age were home full-time and were either disapproving or didn't understand." She expressed surprise that her parents encouraged her "to get a job when we move rather than stay home with her. I felt they would want me to stay home with their grandchild. But I think they're more concerned about us financially, and it worked out this past year." Later in the interview, she reflected on why her mother was encouraging her to work:

> In some ways it was different for her because attitudes have changed. I don't think she had a choice about going back to work when I was young . . . I think she really would have liked to have a career now. I think she sees it as—if I don't get back in now I may never.

This family presents an interesting counterpoint to most of the other families. In this family, the mother had only one child and,

although she had no career, in many ways her life was focused more
on her husband's professional career than on her mothering role.
Both mother and daughter described this only daughter as very
adultlike from an early age and fitting into the company of adults.
Clearly this daughter saw her mother as identifying with her—
expecting the daughter to fulfill the mother's ambitions. When the
other mothers identified with their daughters, they were likely to
view motherhood as an all-consuming role and a total responsibility.
In contrast, this mother expected her daughter to fit her mothering
role around her other activities and responsibilities—just as she
had. Her daughter, however, saw her life-style now and in the future
as different from her mother's. (This was the daughter who insisted
on becoming a non–bridge player.) Unlike her mother, she expected
to have more than one child:

> At this point I think I would like to have several children but not
> necessarily very close together—so that would stretch it out
> over a long time. But I can see with friends the more you have—
> you get tired and you don't want any more kids. But I only have
> one and I haven't been home with her. Maybe if I'm home full-
> time I might say "enough" sooner than I think.

Despite this daughter's commitment to her career, she was uncertain about how many children she wanted and whether or not she
wanted to work.

Only a few of the mothers pursued careers for most of their
lives. But even those few who had successful careers still tended
to espouse the "traditional" ideology of motherhood. Among the
mothers, the one who had the most education and appears to be
the most successful professionally is a clinical psychologist. Her
daughter was one of the few who saw her mother as a role model
in terms of career possibilities, in that the mother was "sure of
herself professionally" and "seemed to enjoy her work." But the
mother also noted that she has a "traditional marriage. Working or
not—I do all the cooking, cleaning . . ."

Thus, even for those few daughters who had professionally
involved mothers, their mothers tended to see their family roles as
their central commitment. This daughter was working part-time

and both mother and daughter expressed ambivalence about the choice to work. The mother commented: "I think the fact that she's working has to have an effect. That is, it's good for Judy to be working but I think a two-year-old misses some mothering." Her daughter also expressed ambivalence about her balance between motherhood and work: "I work two and a half days a week and I'm not away more than that, but I feel that I'm pushing it a little. I didn't want to do any more than that."

Many of the daughters seemed to be trapped between two ideologies—"traditional mother" and "modern woman." They wanted to be both, but their attempts at reconciling these ideologies often seemed awkward and tentative. One daughter/mother was a registered nurse and was committed to working "in order to have the things we want and it's a joint type of thing . . ." Thus, as a "modern woman" she accepted partial financial responsibility for her family. However, later in the interview, she said that, next time, if she has another child, she would like to be home most of the time. "I feel I miss a lot with Joanie. I went back to work when she was five weeks old. The first word or whatever—she always did it with a baby-sitter."

Another daughter/mother, a teacher, said that because of her working, her son was late in learning certain skills. She blamed herself—saying that she would always be doing things for him: "We are in a hurry. We have a schedule where we get up at six and leave the house at seven and if anything gets in the way we are all late."

Daughters who are not yet mothers also wrestle with the dilemma of careers or babies—suggesting different solutions to this dilemma. One single daughter said that she does not know if she will ever marry because "I can't find anyone who's untraditionally oriented—who'd want to have a wife who worked and not have kids." But when asked if she would want both a career and children if she found the right person, she replied, "Very much." One married childless daughter, a teacher, said she would leave the work force and return after her children are older. She insisted that she would like to be home because "I think it's important, especially when they are very young." Another childless married daughter, who was currently a student, said: "I do think about that [being "home or away" when she has children]. I would like to be home. There's a chance that I would be working and Arnold would be home. But I would like to be home for about the first two years." Still another, who currently had a managerial position, had thought of a compromise solution for the career-motherhood dilemma:

> My idea—theoretical, of course—I'd like to have a job in the home. I don't know what I could do. I'd like to set up a doll shop. I have an interest in dolls and doll clothes—both making and sewing dolls. I have a doll collection and I have sewn doll clothes for many years.

Of course, we cannot predict whether or not this daughter someday will own a doll shop or how any of the other solutions to the career-motherhood dilemma will be actualized. But all of these solutions are based on the assumption that the woman will be the primary parent. Studies of dual-career families have shown that, except in very rare cases, women continue to assume both physical and psychological responsibility for their children. Moreover, there is a distinction between "physical" versus "psychic" allocation of tasks—that is, who carries in their head the management for all the jobs that need doing.[30] A third of the young fathers said that they shared "equally" in parenting; these were mostly young couples where the wives worked full-time. However, for half these couples where the husbands claimed equal sharing in child care, their wives said the husbands had "some participation." In any case, none of these fathers said that they had prime responsibility for their children. In effect, although some of the new generation of men may participate in child rearing more than their fathers did, nonetheless their wives are likely to assume prime responsibility for child care.

One of the tenets of the traditional ideology is that mothering is an all-consuming role. One respondent, in the mother generation, used a striking phrase in describing good mothering: She praised her daughter because, like herself, her daughter had the capability of anticipating her child's needs. In other words, motherhood entails an intense cognitive and emotional involvement—a total commitment, at least during the child's early years of development. Although this is just a phrase used by one mother, the notion of motherhood as an all-consuming role is the underlying rationale for the traditional ideology of motherhood. When mothers of preschool children stay home, they can immerse themselves in the mothering role and they become "experts" in the idiosyncratic needs of their own children.

HOW MUCH HAS CHANGED?

How much has really changed in women's roles? Education has become an equalizer between females and males; and there is a little more flexibility in terms of jobs and careers. There are changes in family roles too. Women, as well as men, are expected to be providers; young husbands today do more household chores and young fathers have more involvement in child care than in past generations.

Certainly my mother did not have the opportunities that I have enjoyed. When I think of my mother's life and my own, the differences seem to be prodigious. My husband, son, and I share the work around the house. For example, my husband does the laundry; for the first five years that we lived in our current house, I never used the washer or dryer. In contrast, my mother did all the household chores; my father's job was to earn a living for the family. Once, when I was visiting my parents—after my father had retired—I asked my father if he would help me make up their bed. He looked at me in astonishment and exclaimed: "A man make beds?!"

I realize that my mother's family life and my own experiences lie at the extremes in terms of traditional versus modern-egalitarian family roles. Each of us is unusual, even taking into account differences in generation or birth cohort. It is because my mother and I represent such extreme differences in our gender roles that I have been so puzzled by the one way in which we seem to be very much alike—that is, in our experience of motherhood.

The priority of motherhood, with the traditional ideology, provides a source of continuity between generations of mothers and daughters, despite the impact of cultural change. This continuity means that daughters as mothers have a powerful bond of identity with their own mothers. But most daughters—particularly educated daughters—seem to experience a sense of strain in their attachment to their mothers. Daughters maintain their affection for and attachment to their mothers, while they insist that they do not want to become like them. But, in fact, most daughters do share life experiences with their mothers—particularly when they become mothers themselves. Like their mothers before them, they find their lives both enriched and constrained by the "all-consuming" role of motherhood.

5

HER MOTHER
VERSUS HIS

When a woman marries, she acquires a new set of close kin. She is likely to have more involvement with her husband's mother than with his father or other relatives, for the same gender-based reasons that account for the continuity of her bond with her own mother. The mother-daughter and mother-in-law/daughter-in-law relationships are strikingly similar in a number of ways: They are both female-female bonds; they are both parent-child relationships; and they are both ties of kinship. Moreover, both women in the older generation are mothers and mothers-in-law; and both, at least potentially, are grandmothers. One of the major differences between these relationships concerns their history: The lives of mothers and daughters are linked from the time of the daughter's birth. In contrast, daughters-in-law and mothers-in-law meet as strangers when the daughter is already an adult, and the continuity of their relationship depends on the endurance of the daughter's marriage.

In my interviews with young married daughters, I included a number of questions about their mothers-in-law. I asked about their relationships with their mothers-in-law for two reasons. First, a comparison of these relationships reveals some of the unique features of the mother-daughter bond. Specifically, the contrast with the in-law relationship underscores the continuity of the bond between adult daughters and their mothers. And second, I wanted to understand how having a mother-in-law—another "mother"—affects a daughter's relationship with her mother. Many of the daughters were sensitive to the mother/mother-in-law comparison as a factor in their interactions with their families. A few daughters, for instance, insisted that they could talk more openly with their mothers-in-law than they could with their own mothers. For some daughters, their attachment to their new mothers-in-law seemed to help them distance themselves from their mothers. But for many other daughters, the contrast between their mothers and their mothers-in-law seemed to have an opposite effect; it seemed to reinforce their attachment to their mothers. In almost all of these families, the daughters' adolescent "rebellion" against (or pulling away from) their own mothers had been muted when they became mothers themselves. At the same time, however, many of the daughters seemed to be struggling for their independence all over again in their reactions to their mothers-in-law.

"WHY MOTHERS-IN-LAW ARE WONDERFUL PEOPLE"

Despite many jokes and anecdotes, there has been little research on mothers-in-law. In one of the few systematic studies of in-law relationships, Evelyn Duvall[1] reported that the negative image of in-law relationships is largely a myth. Most of her book is based on a content analysis of responses to a national radio contest on "Why Mothers-in-law Are Wonderful People." She found that about half of the five thousand or so respondents to the radio contest said that they "love their mothers-in-law as a mother" or as "the best friend I ever had." She noted, in fact, that women are more likely than men to have strong and positive emotional attachments to their mothers-in-law.

There is, of course, a serious flaw in Duvall's research: Although her sample is "national," it is by no means a random sample. The people in that radio contest chose to respond to a particular question about mothers-in-law and therefore this group of in-laws is not representative of the population as a whole. Nonetheless, her study is useful both because it calls attention to an important topic— in-law relationships—and because it points out a fallacy. The negative stereotype about mothers-in-law does not necessarily mean that individuals have negative feelings about their own particular mothers-in-law.

My findings, in some ways, agree with Duvall's. Most of the daughters that I interviewed said that they got along well with their mothers-in-law. As part of my study, I sent questionnaires to the mothers-in-law. In their written comments at the end of these questionnaires, many of the mothers-in-law described their daughters-in-law in glowingly positive terms. Several noted that their friends "envy" them for having such good relationships with their daughters-in-law.

The relationships varied, of course. One daughter-in-law was not on speaking terms with her mother-in-law. One mother-in-law (who died shortly after her son's marriage) apparently had refused to accept her daughter-in-law. But such cases of overt breaks were rare. More commonly, many of the daughters complained about their mothers-in-law during the interviews, but they also indicated that they did not share their negative feelings directly with their mothers-in-law.

Although Duvall asserted that the negative image of mothers-in-law is a "myth," she also noted that people are more likely to report negative feelings about mothers-in-law than about other relatives. Similar findings of problematic relationships with in-laws have been reported in other research as well.[2] In my study, the daughters were considerably more likely to express negative feelings about their mothers-in-law than about their mothers—or fathers or fathers-in-law. This did *not* mean that all daughters-in-law had negative things to say about their mothers-in-law or that those daughters-in-law with difficult relationships had *only* negative feelings about their mothers-in-law.

Tension with in-laws is not inevitable, but it is more likely than with other relatives. Strain in in-law relationships emerges from the structure of kinship—whereby in-laws are simultaneously "strangers" and "kinfolk." In my daughter interviews, I was struck by the hostility with which some of the daughters spoke about their mothers-in-law. For these young women, it was as if there were two mothers in the family—a "good mother" (their own mother) and a "bad mother" (their mother-in-law).

INTERACTIONS WITH MOTHERS-IN-LAW

I found three patterns of daughter-in-law/mother-in-law interactions: friendships; minimal involvement; and quasi–mother-daughter bonds. All of the mother-in-law/daughter-in-law relationships seem to fall primarily into one of these patterns—although most of the daughters-in-law described some mixture of these ways of interacting with their mothers-in-law. None of these patterns corresponds exactly to the types of mother-daughter relationships in Chapter Three. In-law relationships are different from mother-daughter relationships in one fundamental way: They lack the intimacy and familiarity that has emerged from the lifelong, childhood through adulthood involvement of mothers and daughters.

In-law Friendships The "friendship" pattern is characterized by friendly "chatting" in an adult-to-adult context. Daughters-in-law are adult women when they meet their mothers-in-law, so that we might expect this to be a common pattern for in-law relationships. In fact, however, this is the least common type—including only six cases, or a fifth of the sample with mothers-in-law (half as likely as either of the other types of in-law relationships). These daughters-in-law report sharing personal/professional interests with their mothers-in-law, so that their interactions do not focus exclusively on family topics.

There are several obvious reasons for the rarity of friendship relationships between in-laws. First, most of the daughters-in-law do not know their mothers-in-law very well. By the time of the interview, they had been connected by marriage for just a few years. Second, mothers-in-law and daughters-in-law, although both "adults," are not age peers. Finally, their relationship is defined as a family rather than a friendship bond. The in-law bond is an automatic, nonvoluntary consequence of marriage; a friendship between a mother-in-law and daughter-in-law is *optional.*

For most of the daughters-in-law with in-law friendships, their friendly relations with their mothers-in-law sharply contrasted with the difficulties that they experienced with their own mothers. Four of the six daughters with friendship in-law relationships had "problem" mothers. These daughters described emotionally entangling or conflict-ridden interactions with their own mothers. In contrast, they portrayed their mothers-in-law as "normal" individuals with whom they could carry on conversations that were not emotionally laden.

The contrast between a problematic mother-daughter bond and an in-law friendship can be illustrated by the case of Clara. In the sample as a whole, the daughters tended to say that they talked about pregnancy and childbirth more with their mothers than with their mothers-in-law. Clara, however, said that her ideas about pregnancy and childbirth were much more similar to her mother-in-law's perspective than to her own mother's:

> *Did you talk with your mother about childbirth?*
> No. I was always told what a terrible time I gave her when I was born.
> *Did you talk with your mother-in-law about childbirth?*
> I talked with her a lot. She was very good. She's more natural a person than my mother. I don't think my mother ever enjoyed her pregnancy. She can't understand why I wanted to breastfeed. My mother wanted to be completely out of it. My mother-in-law had done all these things and she was a big help.

This daughter interpreted her mother's childbirth stories as an expression of her mother's rejection—the "terrible time I gave her." In contrast, her relationship with her mother-in-law is much less emotionally entangled. Moreover, she indicates that her mother-in-law is more modern in her perspective (implied by the term "natural," which had become in vogue by the late 1970s)—so that her mother-in-law's opinions are compatible with her own. At various points in the interview, Clara portrayed herself as more "comfortable" in talking with her mother-in-law than with her mother. However, we can infer also that her relationship with her mother-in-law was more casual than intimate. For example, except for a limited period of time when her mother-in-law was helping regularly with baby-sitting, she saw her mother-in-law infrequently, had no particular desire to see her more often, and she rarely confided in her mother-in-law—even though she viewed her mother-in-law as an understanding person. The in-law friendships in some ways resemble "peerlike" (Type III) mother-daughter relationships. The main difference is that in the in-law relationships there is almost always much less emotional involvement.

Minimally Involved In-law Relationships Twelve cases (of the twenty-nine daughters with mothers-in-law) can be described as minimally involved in the sense that these daughters-in-law and their mothers-in-law see each other infrequently, spend little time alone together, and appear to have minimal emotional involvement. All of the daughters had been married for no more than a few years and almost none of them knew their mothers-in-law for a long time before their marriages. Most of the daughters-in-law who have minimally involved relationships with their mothers-in-law also engage in friendly interchanges with them from time to time, but their relationships are not sufficiently developed to be called friendships.

Most of these minimally involved daughters-in-law (two-thirds) live geographically distant from their mothers-in-law, and distance has been both a cause of and a mechanism for their lack of involvement. Visits with distant parents and parents-in-law tend to be both formal and intense. They are formal in that they are prearranged (distant relatives almost never "drop in") and they require special arrangements—such as extra-careful housecleaning, preparing holiday dinners, and planning activities for a particular time frame. They are intense because they entail continual contact, though generally for a short period of time. The combination of formality and intensity is illustrated by one daughter's depiction of visits with her husband's parents:

> *Do you ever sit and talk with your mother-in-law?*
> It happens sometimes when we're together when there's nothing special going on—we sit down and talk, but it's not the same as with my mother.
> *Do you share feelings?*
> I try but I don't feel that she particularly hears what I am saying.
> *How do you feel about the visits?*
> They are hard on me, but in some ways I think that if we saw them more it would be less hard and more casual. She has so

much invested in her little grandchild. Maybe if she were more casual . . .

How important is it for you to see her?

I don't feel it's that important. It's important in the sense of keeping in touch and [having] some kind of contact—not that I have to see her.

Substitute Mothers The comparison of a mother-in-law with a mother is a natural one and is implied by the very kinship term. Duvall[3] reported that many of the respondents to the national radio contest had asserted that they "love their mother-in-law as a mother." In my sample, eleven of the daughters portrayed their interactions with their mothers-in-law as quasi–mother-daughter relationships. But almost all of these young women resisted or resented their role as substitute daughters. In fact, of these eleven daughters-in-law, *only one* insisted that she wanted her mother-in-law to substitute for her mother—and this was the daughter who had severed her relationship with her own mother!

It is possible that some daughters-in-law who have lost their own mothers may come to appreciate their mothers-in-law as mothering substitutes. But the daughters that I interviewed all had living mothers; that was one of the criteria by which I chose my sample— so that I could study the mother-daughter relationship. However, their mothers-in-law did not necessarily have daughters. In all of the cases where the daughter-in-law reported explicitly resisting her mother-in-law as a substitute mother, the mother-in-law either had no daughter of her own or no daughter living nearby. When daughters-in-law explicitly reject their mothers-in-law as quasi-mothers, they suggest that they are weighing off relationships— as if an emotional investment in the mother-in-law would have to be "stolen" from the mother.[4]

Many of these daughters explicitly said that their mothers-in-law were treating them as if they were their daughters and they did not like this. One young woman described herself as not as "grateful" to her mother-in-law as perhaps she ought to be—considering her mother-in-law's generosity:

Well, they'll have a roast and they'll have too much left over for the two of them so they'll say, "Why don't you take the roast," and I'll take it and I probably wouldn't be as grateful as for little things that my mother does.

Why is that?

I guess the thing behind all this is that my mother-in-law is treating me like her daughter. Her daughter has had lots of problems with operations and that sort of thing, doesn't want to get married, isn't interested in a family, a house, all that sort of thing—doesn't even like coming home. So I am the daughter in their family. So she would be giving advice or talking to me like a daughter. And a lot of times I feel like telling her: "I'm not your daughter! I have a mother and I want to tell my mother things. So don't do that to me." Whereas if I wanted I could open myself up completely . . . If my mother was not living—maybe I could take Bob's mother as my mother. But sometimes I feel like saying: "Back off. I have a mother and you're not my mother . . ." I don't think it's something everybody is aware of. I think it's just in me, that I'm not as grateful as I should be. But I don't think they're aware of it.

This mother-in-law has had a tense relationship with her own daughter who is single, lives nearly a hundred miles away and rarely comes home for a visit.

The quote from the daughter-in-law who is not "grateful" reveals a number of common themes in in-law relationships: First, the gift of the roast symbolizes a problematic exchange for the daughter-in-law; accepting the gift reinforces her obligations to her in-laws. Second, her insistence that no one else (most especially her mother-in-law) is aware of her feelings is suggestive of the barriers that tend to exist between in-laws. In this quote, she tells us what she wishes she could say to her mother-in-law—but it is clear that she has not said these things directly. Finally, her discomfort with her mother-in-law's attempts to treat her as a substitute daughter reflects the ambiguous nature of kinship bonds. She both is and is not a "daughter" to her husband's parents.

NOT QUITE DAUGHTERS

The terms "mother-in-law" and "father-in-law" are terms of reference—that is, they are useful for talking about someone but not to someone. What do in-laws call each other? For parents-in-law, there is no particular problem: Parents-in-law almost always address their children-in-law by their first names. It is sons- and daughters-in-law who need to choose a name—or to be left with the "no-naming" pattern described in the following quote from a daughter-in-law (who has been married about a year and does not yet have children):

> I don't call them anything. I avoid calling them when their backs are turned so I don't have to call them to attention—'cause I don't know what to call them. In talking about them I say Mr. and Mrs. Moss, but I feel funny calling them that to their face. I don't want to call them Mom and Dad and Mother Moss sounds so stupid.
> *Could you use their first names?*
> I can't do that either.
> *What does George call your parents?*
> He doesn't call my parents anything either.

A number of the mothers and daughters whom I interviewed spoke of decisions that had to be made—or were avoided—regarding what to call parents-in-law. A number of the mothers expressed delight when their sons-in-law called them "Mom" or "Mother." In some families the naming decision appeared to be a source of strain. One daughter-in-law reported:

> She wanted me to call her Mom. I kind of felt like she was pushing too much. I told her that I really have only one mother. I couldn't find it in my capacity to call her Mom.
> *Was she hurt?*
> A little bit, but it was okay. I call her by her first name. Sometimes if I really do feel close to her I'll call her Mom.

The fact that the choice is made by the son- or daughter-in-law gives a "reward power"[5] to the younger generation. In the above quote, the daughter-in-law suggests that she uses the term "Mom" as a kind of reward which she can give to her mother-in-law. But it is not clear what the mother-in-law has to do to gain this reward—since the use of this kin term depends on the *daughter-in-law's feelings.*

Conflict about Children   Many of the daughters spoke about feeling annoyed or irritated toward their mothers and/or their mothers-in-law. They often resented specific behaviors or personality traits; and many of the daughters told angry or amusing stories about problems that they had experienced with one or both of them. But there were two striking differences in the problems that these daughters reported with their mothers versus their mothers-in-law. First, having children seemed to lead to more conflict with mothers-in-law but less conflict with mothers. The daughters with children were considerably more likely to express irritation with their mothers-in-law than those without children. Conversely, the daughters with children were less likely to report feeling irritated with their own mothers than were the childless daughters. And, second, the sources of irritation tended to be very different for mothers than for mothers-in-law. Most particularly, the daughters-in-law often felt irritated about something their mothers-in-law had said or done concerning their children. In contrast, only a few of the daughters made comparable complaints about their own mothers.

We might suppose that the birth of a grandchild would create closer, more harmonious relationships with both mothers and mothers-in-law. After all, both mothers and mothers-in-law are likely to have an interest in their grandchildren. Moreover, both have had experiences with pregnancy, childbirth, and child rearing. We might anticipate that the daughters would perceive both their mothers and their mothers-in-law as role colleagues who are sources of empathy and expertise.

Many daughters said that when they became pregnant for the first time, they wanted to talk with "anyone" about the experiences they were undergoing and they were anxious to compare notes with other women—including their mothers and mothers-in-law. Not surprisingly, the daughters with children were considerably more likely than the childless daughters to have talked about pregnancy with both their mothers and their mothers-in-law.[6] All but a few of the daughters with children said that they had discussed their pregnancy experiences with their mothers. But nearly half had not discussed their pregnancies with their mothers-in-law. These daughters-in-law tended to have minimally involved relationships with their mothers-in-law. Perhaps more important, almost half of the young women who said that they did talk about pregnancy and birth with their mothers-in-law noted that their mothers-in-law told them *too much*—that is, that the amount of information exceeded their interests. The daughters-in-law who complained that their mothers-in-law told them "too much" had quasi–mother-daughter relationships, which they resented and resisted. One daughter-in-law, for instance, commented: "Well, my mother-in-law loves to talk about things like that so she would go on and on about her four pregnancies—almost to the point that you get sick of hearing about it." In contrast, none of the daughters made comparable comments about their own mothers. The implication is that virtually all of the daughters were interested in their mothers' pregnancy and birth experiences.

The issue of child care is considerably more likely to be a source of strain with mothers-in-law than with mothers. The daughters were far more likely to be upset with their mothers-in-law than their mothers for giving their children a cookie before a meal or complaining that the daughter-in-law spanks the child too much. Three-fifths of the daughters-in-law with children mentioned feeling irritated with something their mothers-in-law had said or done concerning their children. Only two daughters (of twenty-one with children) talked of their annoyance with their mothers on issues concerning their children. Thus, when the daughters have children, it is mothers-in-law, rather than mothers, who tend to be seen as subverting the daughter's right to manage her own child.

Even many of the young women who have generally good relationships with their mothers-in-law said that they were bothered by something their mothers-in-law would say or do concerning their children. For example, one daughter-in-law commented: "It sounds awful, but when David was first born, she used to call practically every day or at least two or three times a week. After the newness

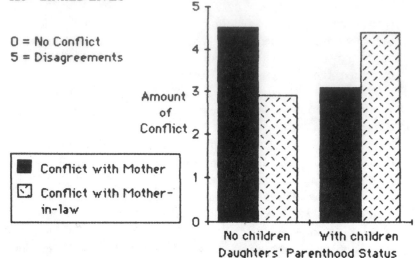

Figure 1. Conflict with Mothers and Mothers-in-law, by Daughters' Parenthood Status

wore off she didn't. . . ." This daughter-in-law sees her mother-in-law fairly frequently (they go shopping together) and, from each of their comments, they appear to have warm feelings for each other. She also has a close relationship with her mother—whom she talks to daily on the telephone and sees several times a week. For this daughter, daily contact is acceptable and desirable in her relationship with her mother. But such frequent involvement with her mother-in-law does not seem quite appropriate; she notes that it "sounds awful."

One of the questionnaire items that the daughters filled out was a "harmony-conflict" scale—where "one" meant "no conflict at all," a "five" meant that they had disagreements, and a "nine" indicated "arguing all the time." The daughters were asked to use this scale to rate their relationships with their mothers and mothers-in-law (and also their fathers and fathers-in-law). Hardly any said they argued all the time; most scores were between 1 and 5. As Figure 1 shows, the impact of the daughters' having children appears to have an opposite effect on mothers versus mothers-in-law: There seems to be *less* conflict with mothers but *more* conflict with mothers-in-law for daughters who are married with children, compared with married but childless daughters.

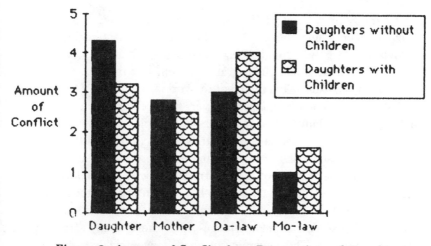

Figure 2. **Amount of Conflict from Perspectives of Daughters, Mothers, Daughters-in-law and Mothers-in-law**

When the mothers and mothers-in-law were given the same scale in their questionnaires, their responses showed the same trend: When the daughters have children there appears to be less conflict with mothers and more conflict with mothers-in-law. (See Figure 2). A comparison of responses from the two generations also shows that the daughters tend to indicate more conflict in these relationships than either their mothers or their mothers-in-law.[7] However, there is much more divergence from mothers-in-law. All but two of the daughters-in-law rated their relationships as more conflictful than did their mothers-in-law. When we take into account the daughters' parental status, we find that the mothers and their daughters with children have the most convergence in the way they assess their relationships, while the mothers-in-law and their daughters-in-law with children have the most divergent perspectives. In other words, mothers and their married daughters with children tend to agree that there is little conflict in their relationships. In contrast, the in-laws tend to have differing perspectives on their relationships: Most of the daughters-in-law indicate that they have disagreements with their mothers-in-law; most of their mothers-in-law say that they have no conflict at all in these relationships.

There are two underlying reasons why daughters-in-law report considerably more conflict: First, mothers-in-law have a greater stake in maintaining these relationships because, as I shall show below, it is largely through these relationships that they sustain ties with their sons and their grandchildren. For mothers-in-law, then, it may be especially important to overlook evidence of tension and strain. A second reason, moreover, may be that the strain is not expressed. Many of the daughters-in-law told of purposely *not telling* their mothers-in-law when they felt irritated with them. Possibly the issues that are problems for the daughter-in-law— especially her perception of being intruded on with her children— are not problems for the mother-in-law. When a daughter-in-law chooses to "hold in, keep quiet," her mother-in-law may not know— and may choose not to acknowledge—that there is any strain in their relationship. The dynamics of conflict over children can be seen in the following example.

Alice: The Unhappy Daughter-in-law Alice depicted un-happy relationships with both her mother, whom she saw several times a week, and her mother-in-law, whom she saw several times a month. She portrayed her mother as overly strict and unaffectionate as she grew up. Alice described her mother-in-law's feelings about her as "she just doesn't care." Asked if her mother-in-law called her on the telephone, this daughter-in-law replied:

> To tell the truth, there's usually some kind of remark—"I wanted to see how Ted and Emily [child] were." She calls me to find out how they are. Am I taking care of them or not—that's what it feels like she's calling me to find out.

Recalling her own upbringing, Alice complained bitterly about her mother's strictness; she said that her mother yelled at and spanked her too much. And yet later in the interview, she commented:

> I was brought up to spank—that's the way you teach 'em not to touch things. His mother has the view that you don't ever hit a kid. You change their mind; hand 'em a toy or something. And yet I feel—all right it's a good idea to change their minds, I'd rather if I didn't have to hit her, but that's not teaching her not to play with the TV. It's teaching her to play with something

else. She's still going to go back and do it. . . .
Does your mother-in-law say things to you about that?
Yeah, I'm still holding that in . . .
Do you talk to your husband about what she says?
Oh, yeah. I don't let it out with her. I wait till we get in the car.
Then I kind of just dump on him. I feel terrible but I've got to
let it out. Even if he doesn't listen—I just yell in the car.

Alice's in-law relationship illustrates three potential sources of strain
between in-laws: First, Alice indicates that she remains an outsider
in her in-laws' family—considerably less important than her husband
(her mother-in-law's son) and her child (the granddaughter). But
because of the gender structure of family relations (women being
in charge of home and children), for a mother-in-law to maintain a
bond with a son and grandchild means sustaining a relationship with
the daughter-in-law. Second, Alice also feels estranged from her
mother-in-law in terms of family culture. It is striking in this case
that despite her negative identification with her own mother (that
is, her specifically wanting to be different from her mother), she
regards her mother-in-law as representing an alien form of family
interactions ("I was brought up to spank"). Finally, the estrangement between in-laws is vividly illustrated by Alice's insistence that
she cannot tell her mother-in-law when she feels annoyed with her
advice (so—she yells at her husband in the car on the way home!).
Although this relationship is unusual in the extent of the antagonism,
the underlying theme of caution is found, in various ways, in almost
all of the mother-in-law/daughter-in-law relationships in my sample.

The Caution of In-laws The mothers-in-law were given an
open-ended question at the end of their questionnaires: "Please
describe your relationship to your daughter-in-law in your own
words. (You may write as much or as little as you would like.)" The
comments varied in length from just a few words to almost two
pages. All but two of the comments from the mothers-in-law were
positive—and most were glowingly positive. Mothers-in-law described their daughters-in-law as "sweet," "wonderful," "loving,"
etc. and several noted that "I would help her in any way I can." In
most of their comments, the mothers-in-law emphasized one com-

mon theme: They do not interfere. One mother-in-law remarked, for example, that ". . . I have tried to continue our relationship as it started—friendly, warm, loving, but not overbearing, inquisitive, or possessive." Another mother-in-law stated: ". . . I don't want her to feel because she lives close that I am going to bother her all the time." (This daughter-in-law, however, complained about her mother-in-law's help with housework—which she interpreted as an implicit criticism and as an attempt to "take over" her homemaking role.)

Another mother-in-law said:

> I am extremely fond of my daughter-in-law. We live close to each other and I make it a point never to drop in unexpectedly or interfere with their lives in any way. However, I feel they know that we are willing to help if needed. My daughter-in-law frequently stops to visit me in the evening. I try not to pry into any of their affairs.

The mother-in-law's caution—her endeavor not to "pry"—implies a form of self-censorship—so that she carefully limits what feelings she reveals. During her interview, this daughter-in-law wondered if her mother-in-law regards her as a "pest" because of her frequent visits. The mutual censorship between mothers-in-law and daughters-in-law means that even when they see each other frequently they are likely to sustain distorted perceptions of one another. Thus, neither mother-in-law nor daughter-in-law is likely to tell the other if she is visiting "too much" and both may wonder (but not be able to ask) if she is overstepping her welcome.

The following family case study provides another illustration of the theme of caution in in-law relationships. Alice was cautious with her mother-in-law against a background of hostility in her family relationships. But another daughter-in-law, Linda, had warm and affectionate relationships in her family. It is all the more striking to find a similar sense of caution expressed by both of these daughters-in-law.

Linda: The "Good" Daughter-in-law   As a teenager, Linda was a rebellious daughter—particularly toward her mother. She was sixteen when she began dating her husband-to-be and she quickly established a close relationship with his mother. In fact, for a while, before her marriage, she seemed to spend more time with and to be closer to his mother than her own. She married right after high school, had her first child within a year or so, and settled into close and comfortable relationships with both her mother and her new mother-in-law. Both her mother and her mother-in-law noted their pleasure in their current relationships with her. Her mother-in-law's affection for Linda is evident in the statement that she included at the end of her questionnaire:

> I couldn't love Linda any more if she was my own daughter. We don't use in-law terms when referring to each other. I think of her as my daughter and when she introduces me to people she says, "This is my other mother." Before Linda and Donald got married she told me, "I'm not taking your son away from you, we will share him." She is a wonderful wife, mother and a truly giving person . . . All of my friends envy me for our wonderful relationship.

Linda lives near to both her mother and her mother-in-law, she sees them both at least every other day, and she is involved in two-way help exchanges with both of them. As the above quote suggests, she is very much invested in being a "good" daughter and daughter-in-law. For Linda, being a "good" daughter-in-law entails two priorities. First, it means establishing a close personal relationship with her mother-in-law. Second, it means facilitating her mother-in-law's tie with her family—that is, her husband and children.

Two stories that Linda told about her relationship with her mother-in-law illustrate the repercussions of these priorities. The first story is about her childbirth experience when her second child, Suzie, was born:

> My mother-in-law was with us in the labor room when Suzie was born. I wasn't too pleased about the whole thing. I wanted Donald there and I wanted to say things to Don that I didn't want to say in front of his mother. She's just very involved in everything. She's a great woman; she's here a lot. She takes Michael [older son] for a few hours in the afternoon. We never have a baby-sitter. We never go anywhere, but whenever we do we usually call his mom or my mom. And it's not that often, so I don't feel that we're pawning the grandchild off on them either.

> . . . The doctor asked her to come in. She said, "I won't
> stay," and I knew if I said so she was just going to go out and
> sit in the other room . . . I said, "That's all right," when I was
> thinking—why don't you persist a little more. I did want her
> there rather than having her on the other side of the door. I
> thought that was being very selfish of me if I'd said that. In some
> ways I'm glad. But she was there when they checked me and I
> thought—uh oh—she wasn't my mother. I was embarrassed. If
> it had been my mother I might have said something.

One might interpret this story as reflecting Linda's dependence on
her mother-in-law—that is, her need for her mother-in-law's baby-
sitting services. But if this is so, it is striking that Linda is careful
not to impose on her mother-in-law. Indeed, particularly in this
case, it is not clear that the baby-sitting is entirely a service provided
to the daughter-in-law. An opposite interpretation might be more
accurate—that Linda is accepting the offer of baby-sitting for her
mother-in-law's sake, to facilitate access to her grandchild.

Linda's "good" daughter-in-law role is suggestive of stereotypical femininity—caring for others at the expense of self. A second
story further illustrates these efforts to be a "good" daughter-in-
law: She describes her mother-in-law as being "too good to us" but
she indicates that this generosity can sometimes be a problem.
Linda's son Michael was about two when Suzie was born and, shortly
thereafter, she decided that Michael could be moved out of the crib
and into a real bed. Linda described what happened as a "little
thing"; she said:

> I had picked out—at a tag sale—a really nice wicker headboard
> for Michael's bed when he was going to have his bed. I loved it.
> And Donald's mother had gone and bought Michael a bed which
> was a beautiful gift and very expensive. But I was heartbroken
> because I really wanted this bed. I couldn't tell her because she
> was so happy to be buying this bed for Michael. It was almost
> worth it to let her be happy and me not . . . little things like
> that—I don't want to hurt her.

Asked if she was likely to encounter a similar situation with her
own mother, Linda commented:

> Your mother's always your mother. Growing up you shit on your

mother—but she's always your mother. You can tell things to your mother that would not hurt her. She knows me. She might not like things but they wouldn't exactly go to heart.

These two stories together illustrate the paradoxical qualities of Linda's "good" relationship with her mother-in-law. She clearly has a warm and caring relationship with her mother-in-law; but the sense of self-sacrifice implies anger and resentment. She is intimately involved with her mother-in-law—but she is particularly careful in what she says to her. She is like a daughter to her mother-in-law—but she is acutely aware of the distinction between these two "mothers."

Mothers versus Mothers-in-law There are a number of similarities between Alice and Linda: They both were married around age eighteen, had two children within three years (Alice was pregnant with her second child at the time of the interview), and lived near both sides of kin. They differ in the types of feelings expressed both about their family relationships and about themselves. Alice indicates that there is an underlying sense of hostility in her relationship with her mother-in-law; Linda portrays her tie with her in-laws largely in positive terms. Alice and Linda also differ in their presentations of themselves. Alice appears to be a young woman with rather low self-esteem. In contrast, Linda presents herself as having high self-esteem; and her roles as a "good" daughter and daughter-in-law contribute to her positive feelings about herself.

In some ways these families represent extremes in terms of types of in-law relationships—with Alice's in-law relationship especially hostile and Linda's exceptionally close. But in spite of the fact that they have opposite types of mother-in-law/daughter-in-law relationships, there are some striking similarities in the underlying themes. First, both portray themselves as compliant daughters-in-law. They may not like what their mothers-in-law do and say but they do not directly oppose them. Possibly their compliance reflects a family ethic found particularly in working-class families—that is, an emphasis on family cohesion and respect from younger to older family members. The gender structure of working-class families is also likely to be a factor here. The overt passivity of both of these young women is not typical of the more educated daughters.

A second similarity is that both Linda and Alice acknowledge the right of their mothers-in-law to sustain relationships with their sons and grandchildren. Linda, of course, was explicit in this acknowledgment when she told her mother-in-law that they would "share" Donald—the son/husband. Moreover, she accepts the gift of the bed—indicating that this gift is part of her mother-in-law's relationship with her grandchild. For a similar reason, Alice does not refuse to visit her in-laws because this contact is necessary for continuing the grandparent-grandchild relationship.

Finally, an important similarity between Alice and Linda is that both are sensitive to the contrast between their mothers and mothers-in-law. What is vividly illustrated in these stories is the sense of boundaries that exist in in-law relationships. Both Linda and Alice note their endeavors to remain silent toward their mothers-in-law. Of course, in previous chapters, I have discussed the fact that daughters also do not fully confide in their mothers. But the issues that require silence in these two relationships tend to be different. With mothers, daughters are particularly likely to censor what they say about their relationships with others—girl friends, boyfriends, and husbands. This silence concerning other relationships both facilitates the daughter's development away from her mother and protects the exclusivity of her other relationships. But silence toward mothers-in-law, as described by Linda, Alice, and most of the other daughters-in-law, is not about issues extraneous to these in-law relationships. On the contrary, daughters-in-law are silent toward their mothers-in-law specifically about the behavior of their mothers-in-law.

The issue of "silence" is suggestive of an underlying distinction between the daughters' relationships with mothers and mothers-in-law: A potential danger in relationships with mothers is that mothers may be too "familiar" and "overly involved" in their daughters' lives. The inherent source of difficulty in relationships with mothers-in-law is in a sense an opposite problem—that mothers-in-law may be "estranged" and underinvolved.

When the daughters in my study expressed irritation with

their own mothers, the single most frequent issue was that their mothers *criticized* them too much. Over a fifth of the daughters suggested that their mothers were overly critical; less than half as many portrayed their mothers-in-law as too critical. Moreover, criticism from mothers-in-law tended to be different in tone from criticism from mothers. Critical mothers-in-law seemed to reject their daughters-in-law entirely. In these families, the mother-in-law was never pleased with her son's choice of a wife. Criticism from mothers was not necessarily viewed as a rejection of the daughter, but rather as an extension of the mother role. Mothers who were critical tended to focus on issues such as their daughters' weight, temper, and past and present behavior—all based on an intimate knowledge of and access to their daughters. Criticism from mothers thus indicates their familiarity with or "overinvolvement" in their daughters' lives.

Six of the daughters-in-law were irritated with their mothers-in-law for being "underinvolved"—that is, "not being interested" or "not being understanding." Only two daughters made comparable statements about their mothers. One daughter-in-law noted that she does "not really" talk with her mother-in-law who is "very involved with her own kids and it runs bare. The youngest is eighteen . . . She talks about things like politics—things like that, not really raising kids and what's going on in *my* daily life." Another daughter-in-law described her disappointment with her mother-in-law's lack of empathy:

What do you talk about with your mother-in-law?
She'll talk mainly about the children and her other grandchildren. She likes to talk about their daily life, down to the tiniest detail—what they ate for a certain meal.
Do you share your feelings with her?
Some of them she can't relate to, she can't respond. When Jonathan was born I was feeling very depressed—postpartum. I told her and she was shocked, almost in disgust. "Here you have this beautiful child—how can you feel depressed about it?" To try to explain that this was a natural bodily reaction—she wouldn't even want to listen to that.
Did you share those feelings with your mother?
Yes. [She was] sympathetic. No real advice—just I know what

it's like. I know it's not pleasant. She understood how I felt and that there was nothing wrong in feeling that way.

What is particularly striking about this example is that the daughter had described her mother as generally *not* empathic—especially when she was growing up. But she makes a distinction between her mother and mother-in-law in terms of their focus of concern. Her statement about her mother-in-law is similar to Alice's comment—that her mother-in-law "just doesn't care" about her and is mainly interested in her son and grandchildren.

I have already noted that the daughters are most likely to be irritated with mothers-in-law over issues concerning their children (three-fifths of the daughters with children report at least some annoyance with mothers-in-law over some child-rearing issue, compared to less than a tenth who are irritated with their own mothers over this issue). The second most frequent source of irritation with mothers-in-law concerns housekeeping issues. Over a fifth of the daughters noted this as a problem with mothers-in-law. Only two daughters were irritated with their mothers about homemaking. Both child rearing and home management represent women's roles as mothers and wives. It is these roles that bring together both mothers and daughters and mothers-in-law and daughters-in-law. But these domestic roles also differentiate their family cultures.

A mother-in-law's comments or help with housecleaning often seem to be interpreted as the intrusion of a stranger. One daughter-in-law, for instance, lives in a house that was built on her in-laws' property. She said that when she was first married, she noticed that her mother-in-law's kitchen cabinets seemed to be a "real mess." Her mother-in-law is partially crippled, so she thought she would help her by putting these cabinets in order. She said: "I always wanted to clean up over there, and after about a year—I started to put things in the cupboards and she got very upset." The mother-in-law apparently resented this help, which she interpreted (accurately, in a sense) as a criticism of her housekeeping. Later, when the mother-in-law came and tried to help her daughter-in-law with housecleaning, her help was resented in a similar way. The daughter-in-law noted: "She's getting back at me for cleaning her house so she comes and cleans mine."

In contrast, a number of daughters and mothers reported their pleasure at help that they received from one another with housework and related errands. Linda, for example, noted about her mother: "... if she comes down and the dishes are there—which many, many times they are—she insists on doing them." And her mother said:

> If she's up for a meal and I'm doing something she'll set the table. I never have to say, "Will you do such and such?" I've been wanting to wash the kitchen curtains so she said, "Don't you dare do that 'cause you can't stand to iron. Wait till I come up next week. You can wash them but I'll iron them." Anything she can do. Or she'll be up and she'll see my hair looks a mess and she'll say, "Mom, go wash your hair; I'll roll it up."

The sociologist Erving Goffman[8] has made a distinction between "front stage" and "backstage" behavior—that is, activities that are set up for view by the public ("strangers") and behavior that is behind the scenes, meant to be seen only by family and other intimates. What is particularly noticeable about these quotes from Linda and her mother is the ease and familiarity with which they address one another. Their dialogue reflects a "backstage" atmosphere— where dirty hair and dirty dishes can be seen and even commented on. In contrast, the next-door daughter-in-law who does not want her mother-in-law's help with housecleaning is implying that her mother-in-law does not belong with her in those behind-the-scenes housekeeping arrangements.

At the same time, however, the nature of women's roles means that not only mothers and daughters but also mothers-in-law and daughters-in-law do participate together in "backstage" house-keeping arrangements. At the very least, at holiday celebrations, they are likely to work together in the kitchen. This does not mean that most mothers-in-law and daughters-in-law have difficulty with home management issues—only a fifth of the daughters-in-law complained about such issues. But the sense of estrangement between in-laws is a potential problem for mothers-in-law precisely because they are brought together in doing women's work.

WHAT CAN GRANDMOTHERS DO?

Most grandmothers[9] describe being a grandparent as a positive—even a wonderful—emotional experience:

> It puts you on cloud nine. It is very different from having your own. I love all my own kids but the love for a grandchild is almost deeper I think. It is like doubling Judy's [daughter's] love with little Debby [granddaughter] running around. . . . It's a terrific feeling.

> I think it's the most wonderful thing that has ever happened to myself. Other than having my son, and I think, well it's so different. It's like you relive your own children and they're just about the most precious thing in the world to me—you know with the family, the whole family. But grandchildren—that's something else. They're just—I'd say, they're the essence of crown and glory in life.

> It's a good feeling; she's a plus. And it's really fun seeing her and I don't feel as though I have any responsibility because her parents are very responsible. It's been a plus, we thoroughly enjoy seeing her; she's a lot of fun. But see, I don't expect her to fill my life or that kind of thing. It's a plus—but it's not a motive for being here.

> It's a nice feeling—to see your children have their children. It's kind of fun to see them growing, changes as they get older. You're out and, even though you aren't seeing them much, you show pictures and your other friends are bragging now, they have a new one, maybe a first grandchild. And you had that eight years ago. And you know what they're feeling, because you went around and everybody had to look at the picture whether they wanted to or not . . .

There is considerable variability in the extent to which grandmothers see and do things with their grandchildren. Not surprisingly, grandparents who live nearby see their grandchildren much more frequently than distant grandparents. Also, maternal grandmothers tend to have more contact with their grandchildren than paternal grandmothers.[10] But in one sense, there is remarkable universality in grandmothers' depictions of relationships with grandchildren:

Virtually all grandmothers describe grandparenthood as an emotional investment. Despite the fact that many grandparents rarely see their grandchildren and some do little with them, they almost always say that they feel a strong emotional attachment to them.

How Grandmothers Help Most married daughters receive help from both sides of kin; but they do not rely extensively on either side of kin. Daughters whom I interviewed commented either that their parents and parents-in-law have limited resources and/or that they believed that young adults ought to be independent from their parents. The daughters tended to list more types of help received from their mothers than from their mothers-in-law, and there were some differences in kinds of help: Mothers-in-law were listed more often as giving money; mothers were more likely to help with errands. But the similarity between mothers and mothers-in-law as sources of help is more striking than the difference. Maternal and paternal grandmothers appear to be about equally likely to be occasional baby-sitters. The most important factor in determining whether or not grandmothers baby-sit is geographical distance.

I noted, above, that the daughters were much more likely to say they felt irritated with their mothers-in-law than with their mothers over issues concerning their children. A major source of this irritation relates to the help they receive from their mothers-in-law—in terms of gifts for their children and help with baby-sitting. Although daughters may receive comparable amounts of help from mothers and mothers-in-law, they are considerably more likely to say negative things about help from mothers-in-law. Many of the daughters-in-law said that their mothers-in-law gave "too much" and that their gifts were not really wanted or needed.

> My mother-in-law goes overboard. Like at Christmas she buys him things and she tries to outdo my mother. And my mother sees this as childish. She does what she can and she's happy with it . . .
>
> *Does your mother-in-law give you things?*
> Yeah, she does give things, especially to Bobby [child]. She goes

way overboard. The birthdays are like Christmases and Christmas
is like something else. Like for Easter she went out and got a
three-piece suit which he'll never put on his back again.
How did you feel about that?
I thought it was ridiculous and my husband did. People don't
dress like they used to for Easter. But she wanted him to have
a suit so he has a suit. I would rather her buy him a summer
outfit or something. You couldn't tell her. She wanted him to
have a suit and that was that.
Does your mother buy him things like that?
No, my mother doesn't buy him so much. She bought him some
colors to crayon with—more practical things. Besides that, my
mother-in-law got him a whole basket of candy, which was a bit
too much, I thought.

My mother-in-law goes overboard. You dare not say, "Oh, I
couldn't afford groceries this week," 'cause she'll turn around
and give you the money to buy groceries. Always buying clothes
for the children. Supergenerous—she'd give her last nickel away.
And I wasn't raised that way. My mother was almost on the
stingy side. My father made a very good salary but you would
never have known it the way we lived. So that carried over. She
doesn't have the money now and she wouldn't give anything
away. So I'd sort of like a balance somewhere between the two
of them . . .

More than a third of the daughters-in-law with children made negative comments about material gifts from their mothers-in-law. Almost none of the daughters expressed irritation with their mothers
for gifts they had given or for being too generous. It is notable that,
despite the differences in family situations, many of these daughters-
in-law use the same word in describing help from their mothers-in-
law—"overboard."

A number of the daughters-in-law also expressed annoyance
or discomfort with having their mothers-in-law baby-sit. The attitude
of these daughters-in-law toward baby-sitting help from their
mothers-in-law can best be described as ambivalence—as is illustrated by the following quote:

*How satisfied are you with the amount of help from your mother-
in-law?*

I would like more help with Johnny—not just things. When we go to my mother's house she gives him his bath and changes his clothes and my mother-in-law doesn't do that at all. . . . Recently she offered to watch him some time but then I'm uncomfortable leaving him with her.

About a third of the daughters-in-law indicated some sense of discomfort in having their mothers-in-law baby-sit. Of course, this means that a majority do not express any negative feelings about this. But *none* of the daughters made comparable statements about their mothers' baby-sitting. The only complaint that a few daughters made is that their mothers did not baby-sit and they wished they would.

These negative feelings need to be understood in terms of both the perspectives of the daughters-in-law and the behavior of the mothers-in-law. From their perspective, many of the daughters-in-law appeared to distrust the motivation of their mothers-in-law— in two senses. First, they implied that gifts from mothers-in-law created obligations that they would not otherwise have. One daughter-in-law who had an overt break with her mother-in-law stated this most bluntly: "I feel if she does too much, I owe her." Second, a number of the daughters-in-law appeared to view help from their mothers-in-law as being essentially nonaltruistic. Many of the daughters-in-law seemed to be saying that the help was not to them but through them—that is, that they were not really concerned about the daughters-in-law's needs. A number of daughters-in-law complained about the "help" they received from their mothers-in-law when they first came home from the hospital after delivering their babies. They asserted that their mothers-in-law needed to be "entertained"—thus preventing them from getting needed rest. They implied that their mothers-in-law offered to help primarily because they wanted to be involved with the baby. Conversely, many of the daughters and their mothers stressed that when the mothers helped after the birth and when they baby-sat, they did so specifically intending to provide a service *to* their daughters.

But are the helping behaviors of mothers-in-law and mothers substantially different? One difference is that mothers-in-law do seem to give somewhat more in terms of goods and money gifts. Potentially, paternal grandmothers believe that they need to "woo" their grandchildren in order to compensate for lesser access than maternal grandmothers. But the difference in amounts given by the two sides of grandmothers is rarely very large. Moreover, when maternal grandmothers give more than paternal grandmothers, the responses of the daughters are not likely to be negative. What is perhaps more significant is that the amount given by the mother-in-law seems to increase when the daughter-in-law has a child.

In their questionnaires, the daughters were asked to check off a number of types of help that they received and gave to their mothers and mothers-in-law. To give a rough index of help received and given, I grouped the amounts of help into three categories: "little" (0 to 1 type of help); "some" (2 to 3 types of help); and "much" (4+ types of help given or received). Table 14 shows that daughters with children receive somewhat more help from both sides of kin than childless daughters. But the biggest change in amount of help received is in terms of help from mothers-in-law. When daughters have children, it appears that they receive a little more help from their mothers. They receive substantially more help from their mothers-in-law. One implication is that before the daughters have children, they are likely to receive more help from their own than their husbands' mothers. But, after the birth of grandchildren, there is nearly equal help from the two sides of kin. In a sense, the mothers-in-law "catch up" to the mothers as help givers. Thus, help from mothers represents a continuation of their previous relationship; help from mothers-in-law is more likely to mean a substantial change in their relationship.

Most daughters are givers as well as receivers of help in their relationships with both their mothers and mothers-in-law. Some types of exchanges are considerably more likely to flow from the older to the younger generation. For example, it is only the daughters with children, and almost never their mothers or mothers-in-law, who require baby-sitting services. Furthermore, most of the daughters (over two-thirds) receive gifts of money from the mothers and/or their mothers-in-law. Only a few of the daughters give money gifts to them.

Table 14. Amount of Help Exchanged between
Mothers and Daughters and between Mothers-in-law
and Daughters-in-law

PARENTAL STATUS OF DAUGHTERS	AMOUNT OF HELP*			TOTAL
	Little	*Some*	*Much*	
Help from Mothers				
No children	2	6	4	12
With children	2	10	9	21
Help from Mothers-in-law				
No children	5	4	1	10
With children	3	10	6	19
Help to Mothers				
No children	5	4	3	12
With children	4	4	13	21
Help to Mothers-in-law				
No children	5	3	2	10
With children	6	7	6	19

* "Amount of help" refers to number of types of help indicated by daughters in their questionnaires: "Little" = 0 to 1 type of help; "Some" = 2 to 3 types of help; "Much" = 4+ types of help.

Table 14 shows that, compared with the childless daughters, the daughters with children both give and receive more help in their relationships with both their mothers and their mothers-in-law. When we look specifically at help given to mothers and mothers-in-law, we see that daughters with children are considerably more likely to be givers of substantial amounts of help to their mothers than daughters without children (more than three-fifths versus a quarter). But the daughters-in-law with children seem to be only a little more likely than the childless daughters-in-law to be substantial help givers to their mothers-in-law. When we consider only daughters who live near to their mothers or mothers-in-law (not shown in Table 14), the pattern of daughters with children as help givers to their mothers is even more striking: four-fifths of these near daughters with children are substantial help givers to their mothers! (Only about a third of the near daughters-in-law with children are substantial help givers to their mothers-in-law.)

Daughters' obligations to their own mothers have emerged from their long-term relationships. There are probably several reasons why daughters with children increasingly become help givers to their mothers. First, the daughters with children are more likely to be out of the labor force; they therefore have more time than other daughters to help their families. Second, when daughters become mothers themselves they may become more mature and therefore more sensitive to their filial responsibilities. Third, the daughters with children have more need for help from their mothers, so that there is increasing interdependence. Finally, the birth of children leads to greater involvement between mother and daughter and their families; the help that they give to one another is both a cause and a result of their increased interaction.

Daughters-in-law and mothers-in-law also may be interdependent. The question is one of degree. The propensity for daughters-in-law to view help from mothers-in-law with suspicion needs to be understood within the context of help given as well as received. When daughters-in-law resist becoming "like daughters" toward their mothers-in-law, they are retreating from a complex set of obligations and emotional commitments.

Grandmothers as Experts Both mothers and mothers-in-law have had considerable experience in "parenting," while the daughters are likely to be novices. To what extent do these young mothers ask the grandmothers for advice? I asked questions about advice from grandmothers in two studies: my mother-daughter study (in Massachusetts) and another study of mothers and grandmothers, which I did in Minneapolis. Although the questions asked were somewhat different, the findings were similar: First, daughters ask for and grandmothers on both sides offer at least some advice— particularly on selected issues. Second, not surprisingly, daughters are more likely to ask advice from their mothers than their mothers-in-law. Third, grandmothers (particularly mothers-in-law) express caution about their role as advice givers. Finally, there tends to be considerable divergence of opinion on the extent to which advice from mothers-in-law is solicited.

In my Minneapolis grandmotherhood study,[11] I gave my subjects (thirty young mothers, twenty local maternal grandmothers, and twenty-four local paternal grandmothers) a set of scenarios concerning potential interactions between mothers and grandmothers. I also asked, in general, if they could describe actual interactions that were similar. One of the scenarios concerned what would happen if the grandmother had information about a "new kind of teething ring" that "might not be safe." In this kind of situation, which concerned the grandchild's well-being, only two grandmothers (one maternal and one paternal) said that they would say nothing at all. Seven of the maternal grandmothers but only one of the paternal grandmothers said that they would try to persuade the mother not to use the teething ring. Most said that they would just give the information.

The open-ended responses of the daughters/daughters-in-law were coded into three categories: listening to advice and changing; listening and considering changing; and not listening to the advice. *All* of the young mothers in this sample said that they would take their mother's viewpoint seriously—that is, they would stop using that kind of pacifier, based on their mother's advice. In contrast, only a quarter said that they would follow advice from their mothers-in-law; a quarter said that they would listen and consider the possibility of changing; and half of the young mothers would not listen at all to and they would not change the type of pacifier based on advice from their mothers-in-law.

What was particularly striking about the responses of the grandmothers was their tendency to express a sense of caution about "interfering." Half of the maternal grandmothers and more than three-quarters of the paternal grandmothers spontaneously and explicitly mentioned their caution in giving advice. One paternal grandmother quipped: "I'm very careful how I say things to my daughter-in-law because I know the reputation of a mother-in-law." Another mother-in-law commented that there are things that she

> would like to discuss but don't because I don't care to interfere
> . . . One thing—I don't believe in a pacifier for a baby. I never
> did and I never will. But she believes in them because they keep
> the baby quiet or whatever . . . I told them I didn't like them but

that was the end of it. The baby continues having a pacifier. I believe in early potty training, she does not . . . That would be something I would change also. I mean I raised four kids of my own and I mean I'm still familiar with raising children. But somehow they think as you get older you forget what you're doing.

The exasperation of this grandmother (her sense of powerlessness) and the caution expressed by so many of the mothers-in-law might be viewed as warranted, given the responses of the young mothers to this scenario.

In my grandmotherhood study in Minneapolis, when I asked the young mothers and the grandmothers to indicate if advice was asked for or given, and on what issues, there appeared to be one topic about which the young mothers are especially likely to call on grandmothers for advice—their children's health. About one-third of paternal grandmothers and two-thirds of maternal grandmothers had been asked for advice in dealing with a child's sickness or accident. In the area of health advice, the interaction lies on the boundary between family and non-family relationships. A grandmother serves as a screen—often being asked for her opinion before a paid professional is called upon. That grandmothers are asked, and may have somewhat more freedom to give, advice about health implies that they are utilized for their parenting expertise. But if the parameters of advice giving are fuzzy, grandmothers continually need to be cautious about overstepping boundaries.

In my mother-daughter study in Massachusetts, I found similar themes—that is, that the daughters were more likely to ask for and listen to advice from their mothers than their mothers-in-law and that the mothers-in-law were particularly likely to express caution about interfering. When I looked at advice about child-rearing issues specifically, I found that the daughters were four or five times as likely to ask advice from their mothers as their mothers-in-law.

One set of questions on the questionnaire allowed me to compare perspectives on advice giving across generations. Each of the subjects was given a list of issues (such as "tips on cleaning the house," "what car to buy," "how to toilet train a child," and "how to cook a particular dish") and they were asked to put a check in the right-hand column if the daughter asked for advice and a check

Table 15. Comparison of Advice Asking and Advice
Offering, by the Paired Perspectives of Daughters and
Mothers and Daughters-in-law and Mothers-in-law

PAIRED PERSPECTIVE ON BALANCE BETWEEN	RELATIONSHIP	
ASKING AND OFFERING ADVICE	*Mother*	*Mother-in-law*
Mother (in-law) seen by daughter (in-law) as *less* intrusive than mother (in-law) thinks she is	5	3
Perceptions agree	19	6
Mother (in-law) seen by daughter (in-law) as *more* intrusive than mother (in-law) thinks she is	4	14
Total	28	23

in the left-hand column if the mother/mother-in-law offered advice
on each item. For each individual, I then subtracted the number of
checks in the right column (daughter asking for advice) from the
number of checks in the left column (mother/mother-in-law offering
advice). I grouped the responses of each pair of mothers and daughters and mothers-in-law and daughters-in-law into three categories:
(a) mother is perceived by daughter as offering less advice, on balance, than mother reports offering (mother is "less intrusive"); (b)
perceptions of mothers and daughters agree; and (c) mother is perceived by daughter as offering more advice than mother reports
offering (mother is "more intrusive").

Table 15 shows that more than two-thirds of mothers and
daughters but only one quarter of mothers-in-law and daughters-
in-law agree about how much advice is asked versus offered. Specifically (not shown in this table) most of the mothers and daughters
agree that the daughters ask for more advice than the mothers
offer. Conversely, in three-fifths of the in-law relationships, the
mother-in-law asserted that the daughter-in-law asked for more
advice than was offered, while the daughters-in-law claimed that
more advice was offered than asked for. The inference from Table
15 is clear: *Mothers-in-law are perceived as intrusive; mothers
are not.*

The mothers-in-law confront the ambiguity of their grand-

parental position in two ways: First, they monitor their own behavior—so that they approach their daughters-in-law with an overt
sense of caution. This means that they *try* not to give advice. Second,
they maintain a subjective perception that is consistent with their
own needs. Thus, they perceive their daughters-in-law as treating
them as mothers and as asking for their advice. What Table 15
suggests is that mothers-in-law tend to view themselves as similar
to the daughters' mothers—that is, both grandmothers perceive
themselves as "experts" who are called on for advice. It is the
daughters (the young mothers) who differentiate between the
grandmothers on the two sides. In the mother-daughter relationship,
the mother's role as advice giver constitutes both a continuation
and a clarification of the mother-daughter bond. Advice to the
daughter becomes legitimated in terms of the child's needs. Advice
to daughters-in-law also, in a sense, is legitimated on the basis of
grandmotherhood. But grandparents on both sides have only constricted rights to "parent" their grandchildren. Some daughters-
in-law ask some advice from their mothers-in-law—especially about
certain topics, such as health care for their children. But most of
the daughters rely much more on the expertise of their own mothers
than their mothers-in-law.

MARRIED DAUGHTERS AS MEDIATORS

There is a folk saying about mothers' relationships with daughters
versus sons: "A daughter is a daughter the rest of her life; a son is
a son until he takes a wife." This is, of course, an exaggeration.
Although many studies have found that married couples tend to
have greater involvement with "her" kin, most families maintain
relationships with both sides.[12] Nonetheless, this saying reflects the
gender structure of family relationships.

Relationships with in-laws always involve triangles, with a potential competition between in-laws around the child/spouse. The
folk saying "a son is a son 'til he takes a wife" suggests that bonds
with a wife and a mother are particularly likely to be viewed as
mutually incompatible. The potential competition between wives
and married sons was described by Lillian Rubin in her book *Worlds*

of Pain: Life in Working Class Families. Rubin wrote that young working-class husbands (often still in their teens) tended to "drop off" at their mothers' homes—sometimes continuing to have regular meals there. Their wives were furious—both because they did not want their husbands to remain dependent sons and because they wanted them to be established as *their* husbands, in their own homes. In a similar way, several of the daughters in my mother-daughter study complained that their husbands' mothers competed for their husbands' time:

> The minute we got over there—it's Bill do this and that. He knows his father can't do everything but he's got his own life. We have only two days out of the week and I think she was taking him off and having him do their things . . .

> [Before the husband's mother sold her home] no sooner he'd get home, and maybe even before he'd get his supper down, she'd be on the phone: "Dick, bring the snowblower." There were other things—nothing I begrudge her, but sometimes it just got under my skin. I felt he was paying more attention to his mother than he was to me. And when they had the pool they would always ask Dick to clean it.

But the linkage through the son/husband is not just a source of competition. It is also a reason for bonding between mother-in-law and daughter-in-law. I noted, above, that, on most issues, the daughters are considerably more likely to ask for advice from their mothers than their mothers-in-law. But in the questionnaire there was one issue on which daughters-in-law turned more frequently for advice to mothers-in-law than mothers—"a habit of your husband's you dislike." In their interviews, also, the daughters mentioned that they had had discussions with their in-laws about their husbands. In Chapter Four, I discussed the reluctance of daughters to discuss their husbands with their own mothers. But a number of daughters mentioned talking about their husbands with their mothers-in-law and sometimes their fathers-in-law. One daughter-in-law, for instance, confided in her in-laws when her husband was out of work:

> If there is a difference between Doug and I or if I find something

very frustrating I can discuss it with them . . . We did have a period when Doug was out of work for a while and I was the only one working and we did have some problems and I found it easy to talk to them.
Were you and your husband arguing a lot?
Yes. He was having difficulty finding a job, got to the point that he was so depressed about not finding a job that he would have been happy to stay home and take care of [the baby] and let me work. I didn't want him to. We wanted a home and we wanted things.
Were your in-laws supportive?
I talked to them mostly to talk and 'cause my father-in-law would say to me: "What's the problem? How come he doesn't have a job?" And my husband isn't one that can talk to his parents.

Another daughter-in-law said that she talked with her mother-in-law when her husband

wasn't very happy with [their baby] when she was born. She picked up on that and I told her how I felt about it.
Was she supportive?
Yeah. She couldn't understand him.

In these examples, sympathy from the mother-in-law is not experienced as disloyalty to the husband, because the young wife can assume that she and her mother-in-law (unlike her mother) both care about her husband. Whereas daughters almost always expressed discomfort about their mothers' criticisms of their husbands, they tended to *joke* with their mothers-in-law about their husbands' faults. "My mother-in-law will kid me about living with Bob—about his not being an easy person to live with . . . Sometimes I'll even go and ask her how to get around him on something. He's very stubborn."

There is another reason why mothers-in-law and daughters-in-law talk about the son/husband. In the quote above, the daughter-in-law remarked that her "husband isn't one that can talk to his parents." This silence of sons/husbands was implied in the interviews with a number of the married daughters:

Do you talk about your relationship with your husband when you talk with your mother-in-law?

Yeah—[not] as much about our relationship as about him because he's very secretive with her. Especially since she wants to know so much so she asks me a lot of things about him. Sometimes I don't tell her but it's hard for me then—to lie or tell her half truths unless there's a real reason not to. Consequently she's been getting a pretty good picture.

How does George [husband] feel about that?

I don't think he cares—'cause he knows what's going on. I think he's glad 'cause she bothers him less. Sometimes I say, "This isn't fair. I'm taking on your parent problems." I basically like my mother-in-law and it's so infrequent I can deal with it. If we were ever to live closer it might be a problem.

After I had interviewed married daughters and their mothers, I did a follow-up study[13] (in Minneapolis) on married sons and their relatives. In that study, I also found evidence for the "silence" of married sons and the mediary role of their wives. In my sample of married men, only about one-quarter spent time alone with their mothers. Perhaps even more suggestive is that nearly three quarters of the men reported that their wives spend time alone with their (the men's) mothers! In some ways, this should not be surprising— that is, if we infer that mothers-in-law and daughters-in-law spend time alone together in gender-defined activities (such as shopping, meal preparing, and child care). But time alone provides a structure for intimacy. At the very least, it is hard to imagine developing or sustaining an intimate relationship when people almost always see each other in larger groups. The implication is that extended family structure may be more conducive to intimacy between mother-in-law and daughter-in-law than between mother and son.

I also found that when sons become fathers, they seem to have decreasing involvement with their own mothers. For example, the sons with children were *much less* likely than the childless sons to say that they talk to their mothers "most of the time" if they "have a problem." Moreover, the men with children were more than twice as likely as the childless married men to express negative feelings about their own mothers. The mother-son bond is likely to reflect the tension between mothers-in-law and daughters-in-law. Most husbands and wives indicate very similar amounts of conflict with the husbands' mothers. It is probably no coincidence that the birth of grandchildren leads to increased strain both between daughters-in-law and mothers-in-law and between married sons and their mothers.[14]

To some extent, both husbands and wives mediate between their parents and their spouses. In my research, I have come across a number of examples of wives asking husbands to intervene with their mothers-in-law, and vice-versa. But in many families, wives also serve as intermediaries between their husbands and their husbands' mothers. I have not found any examples of husbands playing a comparable mediary role between daughters and their mothers.

THE OTHER MOTHER

Daughters-in-law often couch their complaints against their mothers-in-law in comparative terms: "I have such and such a problem with my mother-in-law; she is *different* from my mother . . ." This is another form of "negative identity." The daughter is saying: I am not like—and I do not want to be like—his family. By emphasizing the negative qualities of her mother-in-law, the daughter-in-law implicitly confirms her ties to her own mother and her own family side.

Why do daughters, as young mothers, seem to welcome their own mothers' involvement in their lives while they resent and resist their mothers-in-law? There are many reasons for antagonism between in-laws. They come from different family cultures. There is a potential competition over the child/spouse. And they are, at the same time, both kin and strangers to one another. All of these underlying sources of strain potentially create problems in in-law relationships—in general. But what explains why these relationships change? When daughters become mothers there seem to be opposite kinds of changes in their relationships with their mothers and their mothers-in-law. It seems that daughters have less strain and conflict with their own mothers and more tension in their relationships with their mothers-in-law. Are these opposite reactions somehow related to each other?

In most families, by the time the daughters have children, their rebellion against their mothers—their struggle for separation and independence—seems largely over. There appears to be a new equilibrium in their relationships with their own mothers—at least temporarily. As new mothers, they relax some of the barriers that they had erected against intrusion by their mothers. They let their mothers into their lives in terms of both seeing them more often and being more willing to recognize their emotional need for their mothers. In various ways, daughters as new mothers seem to have a renewed dependence on their own mothers.

But why do some daughters seem to rebel all over again in their relationships with their mothers-in-law? Possibly, their resistance toward their mothers-in-law is a kind of counterbalance to the intrusion on their lives by their own mothers. With their mothers-in-law, the daughters-in-law confront a new kind of parent-child hierarchy. As in their adolescent relationships with their mothers, they try to be free of supervision—by avoiding advice and resenting "interference." Just as a daughter begins to acknowledge a new kind of hierarchy in her relationship with her mother—a new dependency, at least temporarily—she reasserts her independence by negating her need for her "other mother." At the same time, and perhaps more important, she reinforces her husband's independence and separation from his mother.

6

WHEN MOTHERS
BECOME FRAIL

There seem to be important changes in the mother-daughter relationship that are initiated by the daughter's maturation, marriage, and motherhood. What happens later? How does the mother's aging affect her relationship with her daughter? There may be a last stage in the mother-daughter relationship—a final transition—when a mother becomes frail and a daughter takes responsibility for her mother's care.

Many recent studies[1] have shown that daughters are particularly likely to provide long-term health care for their elderly mothers—especially if their mothers are widowed. This means that a mother's health problems can have a direct impact on her daughter and on their relationship. There is a popular imagery of "role reversal" in relationships with elderly mothers. This would suggest that there is a cycle in the mother-daughter relationship: Their relationship begins with a parent-child hierarchy, with the mother in charge of the daughter's care. They become more like peers after the daughter becomes an adult. And eventually, the daughter takes over the mother's role and their relationship comes full circle. How accurate is this cyclical model?

Aging is a slow and barely noticeable process. But frailty may come either quickly or gradually—from a sudden illness or a decline in health. Some daughters are in their sixties or even seventies when they become parent caregivers; others are young adults—in their twenties or thirties. Some are "responsible daughters" when they are teenagers, or even younger. But not all mothers become incapacitated, frail, or otherwise in need of care; and adult daughters do not necessarily become caregivers for their mothers.

In this chapter I will discuss interviews with fifteen caregivers (including two sisters) and eleven of their parents (a total of fourteen family cases). This was a study of parents who required posthospital care.[2] (A description of this research appears in Appendix A.) Most of the caregivers were daughters and most of the parents were mothers[3]—so that about half of the family cases consisted of mother-daughter relationships. In this chapter, I will compare mothers who have daughters as caregivers with other parent-caregiving relationships. To some extent, frail parents have similar needs whether they are mothers or fathers; and daughters and sons share common experiences when they become parent caregivers. Nonetheless, as I have discovered, gender is a central factor in these relationships.

BECOMING FRAIL

The parents had been hospitalized for a variety of serious health problems—fractures, strokes, cancer, heart attacks, etc. Many had had a combination of several disabilities. At the time of the interviews, about a month after hospitalization, their short-term and long-term prognoses tended to be uncertain. Some had moved to a nursing home as a result of their latest illness. For others, their long-term care needs were not yet clear.

The elderly parents found their lives transformed by their illness. Most hoped that their incapacitation would be temporary; and it appeared that most probably would recover their health to a degree. It was likely, however, that they would be left with lingering disabilities. Moreover, they would be haunted by the possibility of further health failure—whether another fall or another stroke. Some would be frail for the rest of their lives—in pain, confused, walking only with difficulty, shrinking in size because of a loss of appetite, and often suffering from a variety of other functional disabilities. For some, there was the possibility of imminent death.

A mother (age eighty-seven) described her health change as "sudden"—resulting from a fall:

I came back from the doctor. I just stood up and went down.

That must have been scary.
Oh, God, I don't want to think of it now. Of course, it could have been worse, I could have split my head open. But to think that all this happened—that I can't walk and everything on account of that.

This woman was suffering from a combination of serious health disorders—heart disease, digestive problems, and fractures; and she appeared to be very frail. After leaving the hospital, she had returned to the home of her daughter and son-in-law, where she had been living for many years. She expressed despair at being useless—no longer being able to help her daughter with household work and having nothing to do to fill her days. She was frustrated at not being able to walk: "It's really depressing. And I can't go out now with the bees, they're terrible, so that I have to stay in, which I don't like . . . I get lonely during the day . . . I'm not able to do things I feel I should . . ."

One father (age seventy-two), who had just had his fourth stroke, noted that "it was quite sudden. There really wasn't time to adapt." This man suffered from uncontrollable crying fits—probably produced by the stroke—and was both embarrassed and angry that he had lost control over his emotional and physical life. He said that the "routine of my life" had been "changed drastically." After leaving the hospital, he had been taken to a nursing home, where he complained "somebody else is structuring [my] life and they don't know how. I'm the only person who could structure my own life."

Another mother (age eighty-one) also described the sudden transformation of her life when she had cancer:

. . . you have the shock. Because I've been very active and—you know—into everything. And then all of a sudden to be in bed for month after month with two bad infections, and be isolated in a little room for months . . . and to try to keep up your disposition is difficult. But I did . . . I could move mountains and do everything—play tennis and do things that people wouldn't think of doing at my age. And then all of a sudden I became so ill. So you never know.

This woman exerted considerable energy to keep from being depressed: "I know there's nothing worse for a person who has cancer [than] to keep thinking about it, and worrying and fretting about it. It will get you down. And you just have to take each day as it comes and do the best you can and try to be as happy as you can. Don't you think?" Her way of coping—her strategy—was to deny her feelings of depression: "I saw my brother die of cancer and I saw him waste away. And that's why I don't dwell on it, because if you do you can make yourself sick . . ." She also referred to a little girl who had recently died of leukemia. ". . . all the horrible things . . . really if I dwelled on it I would have lost my mind—because, if you think, it could happen to me. And I don't want to think about it. That's why I trust in the Lord."

Almost all of the parents described their latest health crisis as "sudden," unexpected, and traumatic. Nonetheless, virtually all of the elderly parents in my study had experienced a series of health problems over the past decade or so. When I asked about how difficult or easy it was to adjust to being in the hospital, many of them indicated that they were used to being in a hospital—this was just the latest in a series of hospitalizations.

For these parents, their "life structures" had been transformed by their health crises—temporarily or permanently. In Chapter Three, I defined "life structure" as the "subjective definition of self now and into the future." A serious health problem affects the "subjective definition of self" in several ways. First, and perhaps most significant, the loss of functional health may harbinger the loss of independence and the label (by self and others) as "frail." It appears that one of the major causes leading to frailty is osteoporosis (degenerative bone disease)—particularly for elderly women. A fear of falling is a major concern for many elderly and their adult children. Over a third (five out of fourteen) of the parents had fallen when they were alone in their own homes or apartments. One mother, for example, had fallen on a Sunday morning and was unable to reach the telephone because of a broken hip. She lay on the floor for almost six hours until her neighbors noticed that she had not taken in her Sunday paper and they called her son. Not only does a bone fracture limit the ability to function independently, but the fear of such a fracture may mean that the elderly person as well as the children may choose to avoid an independent, unsupervised living environment.

A second effect of a health crisis on a person's life structure is a shrinking of the social world. Of course, being in pain, being confined to bed and/or being house-bound restricts the ability to socialize with others. But there also may be more subtle consequences of health problems. Several of the parents commented on their loss of mobility—no longer being able to drive a car or travel to visit distant friends or relatives. Now the loss of mobility meant, for example, that they would never be able to visit a distant daughter, son, or sibling. Because of their disabilities, their friends and relatives would have to come to them, which in most cases reduced their visiting time by much more than half.

Finally, their life structures had been transformed by the emotional impact of their health problems. Almost all of the parents appeared either to be depressed or to be going through some process of denial to deal with depression. Several of the mothers portrayed themselves as stoical—insisting that they just had to accept their health problems ("there was nothing I could do about it . . .") and that they did not want to burden others with their problems ("I don't discuss it much with her [daughter] or anybody. She knows that my leg bothers me a lot . . ."). Many of these parents appeared to be mourning for the life-style that they had just lost.

The mothers and fathers were about equally likely to appear depressed; but there were some striking differences by gender. The mothers tended to express their depression by withdrawal, passively disengaging from emotional commitments. Several of the mothers told their children that they were just waiting to die. One of the mothers said: "I seem to have lost interest in everything." Her daughter stated:

> She was extremely depressed—to the point when I brought her in the nurse took one look at her and said: "That is a very depressed woman—just look at the eyes, the hanging of the head . . ." I brought her into the doctor's office and all she said to the doctor was "I am so ill. What are you going to do for me? I'm dying I'm so ill." And he looked at me, not knowing what to do, 'cause her vital signs were fine. He said: "Do you think we should put her in the hospital?" So I guess I made the decision . . .

The three fathers in my family cases were as depressed as any of the mothers. But while the women tended to become passive when depressed, the men expressed anger, aggression, and paranoia. At various times, all three were angry at their doctors and/or their children. All of them were suspicious about their medical treatment. They questioned the competence of their physicians; they wondered if their nurses had mixed up their medications; and they displayed a surprising familiarity with medical terminology. If the mothers tended to portray themselves as simply recipients of medical care, the fathers presented themselves as guardians of their own health. Moreover, the men were far more likely than the women to "act out"—by refusing to cooperate and by speaking abusively to their family members or hospital staff.

For half of the mothers and fathers, their health problems had affected their mental functioning. For the most part, it was the children, and not the parents, who discussed the resulting "confusion" and changes in personality. Confused patients rarely seem to understand or acknowledge their condition. The term "confusion" refers to a variety of mental disorders, which may or may not be permanent. An extreme form of confusion is associated with Alzheimer's disease. This disorder begins insidiously—when a person may have a little difficulty remembering things and may begin to behave in strange ways. But there are many possible causes for such changes in personality and behavior. Patients with Alzheimer's disease and related disorders often are angry, and they may become abusive toward those around them. It is hard to know exactly what confused patients are feeling. Possibly their anger reveals a sense of frustration, because being confused means losing control over one's own physical and mental life. We can guess that confusion turns the taken-for-granted world upside down and in this sense may be much more traumatic than physical ailments.

REVERSING ROLES

For an elderly mother, her health crisis is experienced largely as an internal issue—as a problem that concerns her as an individual. The changes in her life structure affect her resources, her self-perception, and her emotional well-being. But while the mother has undergone an individual crisis, the transition for the daughter is relational. What has changed is the nature of interactions with the mother. For a daughter, her parent's health needs create a new role—caregiver, which often is intensive, time-consuming, and emotionally draining.

I was struck by how differently the parents and their adult children described recent events in their relationships. When asked how their relationships had changed because of the health problems, most of the children (about three-quarters) mentioned that they now had more contact and more involvement with their parents. The only exceptions—that is, daughters who did not mention increased contact—had been parent caregivers and/or had been living with their parents for a number of years before the most recent health problems. In contrast, only two of the parents noted an increase in contact as an important change in their relationships with their children. Not surprisingly, moreover, the daughters and sons were almost twice as likely as the parents to mention the "burdens" of caregiving.

For the caregiving daughters, their increased contact, involvement, and responsibilities had created major disruptions in their lives. During the peak of the crisis almost all of the daughters had seen their parents daily and had provided ongoing services. A number of the caregivers mentioned that they and/or their siblings had postponed or forgone vacations because of the parents' illness. For many, their daily responsibilities persisted long after the hospitalization.

Implicit in the notion of filial responsibility is a process of role reversal. Virtually all of the adult children portrayed themselves as being "protective" of their parents. Both daughters and sons indicated not only that they provided services but also that, in various ways, they tried to cushion their parents' experiences and to serve as a buffer between their parents and others. For instance, in the case of the father who had uncontrollable crying fits after his stroke, his daughter noted that she often had to "calm him down . . . I will not leave him in a state like that. If it takes me twenty minutes to get him calmed down, that's what it takes and that's what I do . . ." Her insistence on getting her father "calmed down" suggests that she took responsibility for his inner emotional state, to the extent that she could. Another daughter commented that she did whatever her mother wanted her to do "because I've wanted her life to be pleasant."

Some families were in the process of renegotiating their parent-child hierarchy. One son, for example, commented:

> I don't think she accepts the fact that we are grown up, we're adult, we have families, we make our own decisions now and maybe know a little bit what's better for her. My sister has gone through quite a bit of medical training. She's not a doctor by any means but yet she knows some things that are good and what's not so good for my mom. My mom does not accept the fact that, hey, we might know what might be good for her now as compared to when we were growing up. So she has trouble, I think, accepting that, and that creates conflicts because we're looking out for her better and she doesn't accept that fact.

In this case, the ambiguity of the positions of mother and children is reminiscent of the relationship between adolescent and parent. Just as a parent and adolescent child are likely to disagree about whether or not the adolescent has achieved adult status, there may be disagreement across generations about whether or not the parents should be considered "postadults."

For over half of the adult children, what they were most concerned about was their parents' depression and/or personality changes—including forgetfulness and confusion. In a number of cases, the adult children reported that their parents told them that they were just waiting to die. The daughters who mentioned such statements indicated that they responded with a sense of frustration and exasperation: They refused to allow their parents just to "give up."

For some of the caregivers, it was the personality change that created a need for a role reversal. For instance, in one family a mother's "hallucinations" undermined the mother's credibility for her son and convinced him that he had to make decisions for her. A daughter noted: "One of the things that kind of bothered me is that she doesn't want to take a newspaper anymore . . ." The transformation of the parent's personality means that the parent is lost—

as he or she once was. One of the daughters talked about how her father's "personality just switched" when he became paralyzed:

> It sounds terrible to say, I guess, but I could have better handled the fact that he was in pain, because you can control pain with medication, than I handled the fact that he wasn't himself. He wasn't the person that I remembered him being—the caring, lovable person that he was. That was harder for me to adjust to than the fact that he had cancer and was probably going to die soon . . .

Almost none of the parents themselves suggested that they were aware of a personality change (the only exception being the man who could not control his crying episodes). Thus, while both generations are undergoing a process of mourning, they actually are experiencing different kinds of losses. The parent has lost physical control over his/her life. For the children, the crisis is social and interpersonal, since their interactions with their parents are transformed.

Both confusion and depression can lead to greater emotional dependence on the daughter. For instance, one of the mothers, who was suffering from some degree of mental confusion, needed to be reminded continually of necessary dates, etc. The daughter noted:

> If there are plans that she's going someplace—there's a wedding or this or that—I tell her the date and everything. She gets very nervous that she's not going to remember it, even if I write it down. So I try not to tell her the day before, because she gets very nervous about it, although she wants to attend everything, but she doesn't want it on her mind.

This daughter is protective of her mother's anxiety about being forgetful. She did not want her mother to be interviewed for this study because she believed that her mother would feel distressed if she was not able to remember answers to simple questions.

Depression tends to entail a process of disengagement. With the health crisis, the parent may begin to withdraw emotionally from the relationship, partly in response to pain, partly from despair about the loss of functional abilities. But there is a paradox in this disengagement process: The mother's disengagement leads the daughter to become increasingly involved and active in the relationship—both instrumentally and emotionally, as the daughter becomes depended upon for services and takes on a protective role toward her mother.

In my interviews, I did not ask directly whether or not the parents and their adult children had experienced a role reversal in their relationships. It seemed to me that that would be a leading question and might evoke agitation or anger—particularly in the parents. Nonetheless, in *all* the cases the adult child either described a very protective relationship toward the parent and/or explicitly labeled this relationship a *role reversal*. All but one of the daughters declared specifically that they had experienced a role reversal:

> I think now the roles have been reversed. I think she's the child and I'm the parent . . .

> Her role changes as you grow older, and I consider her the child and me the mother now. And I don't like that, but that's the way it turns out to be . . .

> I've become her mother. It's not a mother-daughter relationship anymore, because she's so dependent on me . . .

> I have this need to be the mother . . .

It is striking that *none* of the elderly parents described this process of reversal and almost none expressed a sense of their children's protectiveness toward them. That daughters are conscious of a process of reversal may reflect social norms about aging—that is, that the aged are "postadults" and that filial responsibility is very much like parental responsibility. The fact that the elderly parents do not mention this process suggests either that they do not think they are experiencing this kind of change in their relationships with their children and/or that they feel uncomfortable with such a reversal.

If the parents do not acknowledge the change, is there really a reversal of parent-child roles? Adult children often seem to feel disappointed when their parents give up their parental roles. For example, one daughter was distressed when her father insisted that she come to the hospital at two in the morning to sit with him. She said that if he were "himself" he "wouldn't have wanted me out by myself at that hour of the night." In other words—ordinarily, her father had been protective of her; when he failed to worry about her, he was not acting appropriately as her father. For many adult children, their parents' dependency is difficult—not so much because of the work involved, but because there may be no one left with whom they can be a "child," protected and cared for. Despite the fact that all but one of the daughters said that their roles had been reversed, they also said—usually in the next breath—that they did *not like* this reversal of roles!

It is also striking that such explicit declarations of role reversal were made only by daughters about their relationships with their *mothers*. Sons portrayed themselves as having protective relationships toward their parents but they did not say that they were now in the role of father. Similarly, caregiving daughters behaved protectively toward fathers as well as mothers; but in the two father-daughter cases, neither daughter said that she saw her father as her "child."

Why should there be an explicitly depicted role reversal *only* in daughter-mother relationships? I can categorize my sample of elderly parents and their daughters and sons into two groups: daughter-mother pairs and all others. All of the "other" categories of intergenerational pairs involve males—as sons and/or fathers. A reversal of parent-child roles is considerably more difficult in relationships that involve males—because "father" has a different meaning from "mother." In both language and family structure, the position of father is more hierarchical than is the position of mother. For a son to be a father to his parents is a much more radical reversal of the parental hierarchy than for a daughter to take on a mothering (or nurturing) role. In a similar way, if a daughter were to insist that she has reversed roles with her father, she would be challenging and undermining his position in their family hierarchy.[4]

In Chapter Three, I noted that the most common type of relationship between young adult daughters and their mothers is Type IV—mutual mothering—especially for daughters who are in their mid-twenties or older. For the caregiving daughters and their elderly mothers, most of their relationships probably have evolved over the years from Type IV to Type II ("responsible daughters . . ."). For a daughter to "mother" her mother may be an extension of a mutual-mothering relationship. In that sense, the daughter's filial protective role is not so much a reversal or revolution in their relationship as an evolution or extension of an ongoing theme in the mother-daughter relationship.

DAUGHTERS IN THE MIDDLE

Caregiving is largely a woman's issue. There is, perhaps, an irony in the fact that women are both more likely than men to be care-givers—as wives, daughters, and daughters-in-law—and are less likely to be home care receivers. Most elderly men are married and receive caregiving from their spouses. Most elderly women are widowed and, if they need caregiving, they rely on their children or they go to live in a nursing home.[5]

Almost all studies of adult children as caregivers have found that daughters are more likely than sons to be parent caregivers.[6] Of course, geographical distance is a basic factor that determines which adult children are caregivers. Obviously, someone who lives far away cannot do much to help with daily routine care. But when parents have both daughters and sons who live nearby, it seems that daughters are far more likely to be their caregivers. Of the fifteen caregivers in my study (including two sisters), only four were sons. Moreover, in all of the families with caregiving sons, there was no daughter or no near daughter available; and in three of these cases it was actually the daughters-in-law who were providing most of the care.

A research project[7] done in New York City compared daughters and sons as caregivers. That study showed that sons as care-givers provide less actual hands-on care than daughters. Moreover, caregiving sons tend to rely on substantial assistance from their wives. In contrast, caregiving daughters just hope that their husbands remain "neutral." (One implication is that daughterless mothers may lack a form of "social insurance" for their old age.)

Why do daughters provide more caregiving than sons? There

is a simple explanation: because of the priority given to work in men's lives. Sons often essentially are excused from caregiving responsibilities because of the assumption that their career role takes priority. Interestingly, in several families a son was a parent's favorite child—even though it was a daughter who provided almost all of the services!

But many daughters also work at jobs and careers. Daughters who work outside the home feel torn between their job commitments and parent caregiving. One daughter, for example, talked about the difficulty in making a decision about posthospital care for her mother:

> . . . It was a miserable period. It's terrible to make decisions for somebody else who is [out of it] . . . and really not know where you're at. And there's not much you can do about it. You realize that when you look back on it. But it is a real difficult time to have to make a decision [to put her mother in a nursing home], knowing you have limited financial resources to work with. Plus the fact that you have a full-time job precludes taking care of somebody in your home. And I was warned about that—both by the social worker [in the hospital] and the social worker in our parish . . .

This daughter appeared to be troubled by the fact that she could not care for her mother in her home. She relied on advice from professionals, especially social workers, to articulate her priorities— that is, that she had *no choice* about working and that, ultimately, her role as a caregiver was discretionary.

Middle-aged daughters have been called the "women in the middle."[8] They are in between generations—with obligations to both aging parents and growing (or grown) children. Other responsibilities—toward work, spouse, or children—create constraints on the caregiver role. The "middle women" find themselves squeezed between a complex set of commitments: Their continuing ties with their mothers potentially compete for their time and energy against their other relationships—particularly with their husbands and children. How do caregiving daughters make choices and balance their competing commitments?

The pull between a husband and a mother was illustrated in a rather vivid way in the case of a fifty-one-year-old daughter whose mother and husband were in the hospital on two different floors.

Although they were in the same hospital, she could not visit both: "I felt very badly because he was in intensive care and she was in isolation with a staph infection; and the doctors told me that running back and forth between the two was not the wisest thing I could do, so I'd stand outside of her room and wait, but I would see her . . ."9

In another family, a daughter found herself having to tell her mother "no"—that her mother could not live in her (the daughter's) home. When her mother first needed care, she had lived for a while with her daughter. But there were problems. The mother had had a stroke and the daughter described conflicts that had occurred while her mother was in her home.

> . . . the one [conflict] that was really bad my kids [were involved in], and that was very difficult for them. It was the summer and all the kids were home. My boy had saved money for an aquarium, and he'd been after me and after me: "When can we go and get the fish." And I finally said: "We'll go get it." And he said: "Can David [friend] come with me?" And I said: "Yes." And Carol [daughter] wanted to come with [us]—and, of course, little Sandy [other son] would have to come with [us], because it didn't always work when they'd been home with Grandma.
>
> And I really had a carful at that point. And it was ninety-nine degrees; it was hot. And my mom said: "I want to go too." And I knew the problem involved . . . What she liked to do was get in the car and wait for us; and it was just too hot that day. It was simply too hot. And I told her that and she didn't understand it. She said: "That boy [grandson's friend] means more to you than I do. You are taking him with [you]."
>
> And I said, "No, that's not true."
>
> And she said, "You can leave your car running with the air conditioner on when you are shopping."
>
> And I thought, Oh, my husband will think that's real nifty. And I just said, "No, I just cannot do it. You will have to stay home."
>
> It was maybe a half hour–hour trip to run and get the two fish, but she couldn't deal with that; and she started to scream at me. And she hit the table, went to her room, and slammed the door . . . No one loved her and "everyone is mean to me."

This daughter's middle position is illustrated in this story in two ways. First of all, the daughter has demands placed on her by both her children and her mother. She views her son's claim for her services as legitimate—especially since she had put off running this errand for him (she says that he had been "after me and after me"). Possibly, the mother's recent stroke has induced childlike behavior—her temper tantrum. In any case, the daughter has a "maternal" orientation toward both her children and her mother. At least as she reports this incident, her tone toward her mother is rather calm, firm, and authoritative—which appears to reflect her parenting style. But she feels exasperated. This daughter is "in the middle" in a second way—when her mother's demands conflict with her husband's implicit attitudes. In this story, she alludes to this potential source of tension in her comment about leaving the air conditioner on while her mother would be waiting in the car—"Oh, my husband will think that's real nifty."

The mother was living in a nursing home at the time of her interview. She wanted to return to her daughter's home. But she said that her daughter told her that was impossible. "I tell my daughter but like she said, 'There's nothing I can do, Mother.' Well, I understand that. She's got three children and they're all in something—ball players. And he [grandson] takes drum lessons." The grandson's drum lessons may be used to legitimate keeping the mother out—by suggesting that the house would be noisy and therefore not a good place for the mother. In any case, this mother was implicitly acknowledging that parental responsibilities take priority over filial obligations.

At least for a short while, virtually all of the caregivers found themselves overwhelmed by responsibilities. One daughter said:

> Every waking hour it seems in the last six weeks or so has been concerned with hospital visits or arranging for this, or a phone call to there, or selling the trailer, cleaning up the garage . . .

Despite large numbers of hours and considerable energy expended, however, many of these caregivers insisted that they did not feel burdened.[10] For instance, one daughter described bringing food to her mother daily before her mother went to the nursing home and mentioned that she continues to attend to various of her mother's instrumental and emotional needs, although her mother's daily routine and medical care are done by health care professionals. But she insisted that it had not been a lot of work to bring meals to her mother: "I would send food over there all the time, because she really couldn't do any cooking . . . She did not want the meals-on-wheels. I felt she did need it. So I was the meals-on-wheels. I didn't mind."

A daughter in another family said that she coordinates the care among six sisters and brothers who share responsibility for visiting. They have a schedule so that the father receives a visit from at least one child daily. This daughter said that she herself visits her father about four or five times a week. The father's nursing home is at least a half-hour drive from her home and she reported spending at least an hour during each visit. This daughter has two preschool children and a full-time job and also has a serious health problem (she was about to have her second operation for cancer). But rather than seeing herself as overburdened, she asserted that the caregiving has helped to take her mind off her own health problems:

> Sometimes I think Dad's stroke at this time was a godsend for me, or maybe I would be a basket case. Because it's been a long wait between May and now, getting this second surgery scheduled . . .

The daughter who didn't "mind" bringing daily meals to her mother conveys a common attitude expressed by the daughters and sons in this sample—that their responsibilities toward their disabled parents were taken for granted among their interpersonal obligations. But many daughters report being pulled in many directions at once—by children, work demands, and the extra tasks of "running two households."[11]

The daughter who had cancer, quoted above, was one of the caregivers who had postponed her family vacation because of her father's illness. Nonetheless, she ultimately decided to take her vacation—for the sake of her *children:*

> . . . We were scheduled to leave that Friday night to go on vacation. My family—my brothers and sisters—said, "Go. You have to get out of here, Susan. You can't take any more." We waited

until Sunday afternoon before we left. We went to [northern Michigan], and I called him twice a day to make sure that everything was all right. It really wasn't a vacation vacation, because my mind and so much of me was back here. But the kids had been promised and I know with this surgery coming up that I had to live up to certain things, and this was one of them that I had to. If his condition had been critical, I wouldn't have gone.
When you say 'live up to certain things'—do you mean for yourself or for your family?
My family—because that's right. They're still number one. That was a tough decision for me to make, and my family is the one that made me—my brothers and sisters made me realize that—that your family comes first.

This daughter was bound by a complex set of commitments and loyalties—to her spouse and children, to her father, to her siblings, to her job, and also (although she tried to belittle this) to herself and her personal sense of well-being. In what seems like a stereotypical feminine way, she portrayed herself as deriving pleasure through giving to others. This led to her somewhat ironical depiction of her father's stroke as a "godsend"—which allowed her to focus on helping him rather than worrying about her own illness.

Despite this daughter's commitment to her role as parental caregiver, she clearly articulated that she had another commitment that took precedence—her children. In the several families with young children, a similar theme was stated—that responsibility to children comes first. This daughter, in fact, seemed to be ambivalent about her priorities. Her promise to her children would not come first if her father's illness had been sufficiently serious. She justified her vacation for the sake of her children—and not for herself. This woman might be expected to be selfish: She had cancer; and she knew the seriousness of her situation because her mother had died of a similar kind of cancer when the daughter was about sixteen. But she diffused her self-concern through an almost frenetic sense of responsibility to "her family"—a term she used to mean both her nuclear and her extended families.

This family was rather unusual in the involvement of such a large network of family caregivers. This daughter's overwhelming sense of responsibility toward her father was counterbalanced, at least somewhat, by the support she received from her sisters and brothers. They gave her emotional support—insisting that she has more to life than her parental caregiving commitment—and they shared the caregiving role. The fact that she shared her responsibility with her siblings limited her accountability.

But, in most of the families, the caregivers were essentially alone in their responsibility for their parents. In this sense, the caregiving role is strikingly parallel to the role of mother. In both roles, there are diffuse responsibilities concentrated in one person—usually a woman. In both roles, also, the "caring" responsibilities compete with other commitments in a woman's life.[12]

There appears to be an underlying rule of filial responsibility—that adult children have a responsibility to provide at least some caregiving to their parents. They "do not mind" helping their parents—to the extent that "helping out" is part of their relationship. Their filial responsibility emerges from their "linked lives"—their continuing attachment. This attachment tends to be strongest between daughters and mothers; and caregiving is more likely in this than in other intergenerational relationships. But filial caring is found across all of these relationships. Nonetheless, there is a corollary to the filial-caring rule—that is, that other relationships—or other commitments—come first.

WHO'S IN CHARGE?

When elderly parents become dependent on others to take care of them, this often means that others—family members, physicians, etc.—make decisions on their behalf. Major decisions, such as what medical interventions to use and where the patient will go for posthospital care, are confronted during a health crisis.[13] Some of the parents indicated that they were only vaguely aware of what happened while they were in the hospital. For example, asked about her adjustment to the hospital, one of the mothers commented: "I guess I was out of it. I didn't know much, but they were very nice there and I really haven't any complaint." When the parents were "out of it," their adult children made decisions for them.

In all but one of the families, the decision about posthospital care was made primarily by the daughter or son. It was the daughters, sons, and daughters-in-law, also, who did most of the work for making posthospital care arrangements. For most of the families, the children and not the parents conferred with the social workers. After receiving information from the hospital social workers, they almost always had to do a considerable amount of leg work on their own—such as contacting nursing homes, visiting at least two facilities, and/or considering the range of options available and their relative costs. In several families, the parent learned about the possibility of a move to a nursing home only *after* the daughter or son had gathered information and had begun to make some preliminary arrangements.

This did not mean, however, that the parents were completely acquiescent in their posthospital care decisions. In almost two-thirds of the cases, there was some controversy or conflict over posthospital care arrangements. In the majority of such cases, the adult children "won"—that is, the plans were implemented according to their own and not their parents' direct wishes. In most of the remaining cases, the plans were still under negotiation—with the parent having been placed in a care setting that the parent and/or the children believed would be temporary. In only one family was the parent the "winner"; in the story recounted below, the posthospital care plan was arranged by the mother, and the daughter was not entirely happy with the arrangement. This mother appeared to be unusual—much more independent than the other mothers and much more insistent on making decisions and plans for herself. She also appeared to be somewhat wealthier than most of the other parents.

An Independent Woman   Ethel Smythe was a rather well-to-do widow. She lived in an upper-class suburb where she owned a large, well-kept home with a swimming pool. She liked to travel and did so quite frequently before her latest illness. Her illness—cancer—had not affected her mental functioning. At age eighty-one, Mrs. Smythe did not appear to be "frail." She managed her own investments and also saw herself as in charge of her own posthospital care. She had some help from her daughter Helen, who lived in the same town, and her other daughter, Martha, who lived about a hundred miles away. But she said that she did not talk very much about her health problems with Helen "because she's a very nervous person. I'm a great one to pretty much go on my own."

When Ethel came home from the hospital, she hired a home health aide through the public health nurse at the hospital and a local home health service. Shortly afterwards, also on her own initiative, she fired the aide—an inexperienced young woman:

> . . . They sent me a terrible girl. She was young and inexperienced. She really and truly was. Well, she'd been on drugs. She'd been in a home. And maybe the poor thing was trying to do the right thing now. I hope so. But she couldn't cook. And here I was—so helpless . . . I kept her two days and finally the third day I told her that I thought she had better go home and that my sister would come 'cause she just couldn't . . . the poor thing couldn't cook. She couldn't boil water.

Her daughter Helen described her mother as "very particular. And she questions everybody . . . Well, I mean the whole thing was bizarre. And the more that my mother found out, the more she disliked the girl." Ethel put together a patchwork-style care plan for herself. Her sister (whom Ethel previously had cared for when her sister was ill) came for a while. Then her distant daughter, Martha, stayed with her for two days. Finally, Mrs. Smythe managed to find two nuns who came and provided home care. (Her daughter commented: "There was really nothing she could question about the nuns.")

What is striking about this parent, and substantially different from the other elderly parents, was Ethel Smythe's independence— her insistence on taking charge of her own health care arrangements. This daughter had little input on her mother's arrangements. She was the only "caregiver" who could give almost no details about how the posthospital care plan was made. She said that she gave some information (to the doctor and social worker) about what she saw as her mother's needs—but she was not really involved in making the plans. However, Helen was worried about her mother's living arrangement. She thought it was too difficult for her mother to care for her own large house: "I'm sure she's trying to do too

much"—like "trying to clean leaves out of the swimming pool."
Although she and her sister, husband, and children had suggested
other living arrangements, her mother remained where she
wanted—because "she wants her own home."

Despite this mother's independence, however, her daughter
described a role reversal in her relationship with her mother—"it's
almost like she's the daughter and I'm the mother"; and she made
a number of statements that indicated she was supervising her
mother's behavior. For example, she said that since her mother's
latest illness "I don't let her drive anymore." Also, her mother had
a skin infection which the daughter thought was related to her
scratching herself—so "everytime I catch her scratching, I take
her hand away." Helen calls her mother every day to make sure
she takes her medication. But she does not drive over to her mother's home daily, because, she says, her mother "never expected
that."

In this relationship, we find an interweaving of dependence
and independence. Not only does Ethel want to manage her own
life, but her daughter is equally insistent on placing boundaries
around her filial role:

> She has a great tendency to want others to do these things for
> her . . . But you see I don't think that's right . . . I mean if they're
> capable of doing these things—like picking up the phone and
> calling the doctor. I feel silly calling the doctor and saying "My
> mother doesn't feel well" when he knows she can pick up the
> phone herself and say it.

We might argue that the issues of control and independence were
being negotiated in this family and were subject to change. Clearly,
Ethel Smythe does not view herself as a "postadult"—that is, as a
person who has surrendered her status as an independent adult.
For the mother, her children constitute just one among several
resources on which she can rely. For the daughter, her mother's
status is less clear. On the one hand, she fosters her mother's independence and therefore supports her mother's ability to control
decisions over her own life. On the other hand, she is frustrated by
her inability to protect her mother. As in other cases in this study,

in the "role reversal" analogy the mother's role is much more comparable to an adolescent status rather than a reversion to early childhood. And, as in families with adolescents, the issues of power and independence are sources of negotiation and conflict.

Power and Reciprocity A parent's position of dependence implies a lack of reciprocity. It is this asymmetry that underlies the sense of powerlessness. According to "power/dependency" theory,[14] in any relationship the person who has more of a need for the other has less power. This theory is used, for example, to explain why wives who are non–wage-earners have less power in their marriages than their husbands—and also less power than employed wives. Similarly, children depend on their parents for economic (and other) support and therefore tend to be less powerful than their parents when there are disagreements. In a comparable way, we might assume that frail parents need their children more than the other way around—and therefore that parents are more likely than their children to "give in" when there is a disagreement.

I have pointed to Mrs. Smythe as atypical—possibly as the "exception that proves the rule." This mother has an exceptional number of resources with which to confront her health problems—her money, her intelligence and mental awareness, her social contacts (she knows physicians personally as peers), and her family. She is rather unusual in her ability to manage her own caregiving needs. But her daughter views even this very independent mother as increasingly dependent and thinks that there is a reversing of the parent-child hierarchy.

In a similar way, although the other parents have had decisions made for them, it is an exaggeration to assert that they simply have surrendered decision-making control to their children. In most of the families—in various ways—there is evidence for a continued assertion of parental independence and power.

There are several types of evidence to suggest that the power hierarchy between adult children and their frail parents is not simply reversed—at least not entirely. One piece of evidence is inferential. If the parent's powerlessness is based on a lack of reciprocity, then perceived reciprocity might provide a subjective base of power. In over a third of the families, the parents and/or the adult children attempted to depict the relationship in an exchange framework. In other words, they explained the current asymmetry against a background of exchanges in the past. One daughter commented: ". . . she knows there are things she can no longer do and that she has to rely on us and she doesn't like it much. [She] talks about being a nuisance. [But] I think that somewhere in there she has a feeling that we pretty much stick together and take care of each other and that she's done a lot of the taking care of." Another caregiving daughter insisted that "I think Mother has always given *more* help. I think that's something you realize when you become a parent . . . if you total up over the years . . . what a mother [gives]. You never stop giving . . ."

Perhaps even more striking is the fact that two of the daughters-in-law explicitly commented on the lack of reciprocity in the history of their in-law relationships. One of these daughters-in-law said about her father-in-law: ". . . it's always been us doing it for him—cooking him meals, baking him stuff, sending him home care packages, doing his laundry . . ." In contrast, she viewed her own mother as having a more legitimate right to expect caregiving: ". . . like with my mother—she ended up going into a nursing home, but at a much younger age. And for the last—probably a year— we gave a lot for her. But before that she gave an awful lot to us— by staying with us when we had our children. And she lived with us for a while and took care of our kids . . ." Similarly, another daughter-in-law, when asked about help from her mother-in-law (for whom she was now serving as a caregiver) and other family members, complained:

> I think it's always been—not always but a great deal of it—has had to come from us. George's family is not a close family. His family . . . were never that supportive of us . . . You heard what I've been doing this summer. I would never have gotten that from their family. John, our oldest son, has polio. [He has been] ill for four years. [There has been] very little support—no particular offers of child care. . . . It's always been whatever we have done was pretty much what we have done . . .

If the father-in-law and mother-in-law, alluded to above, do not "deserve" (or have not "paid" in advance for) the care that they are receiving, their position as care recipients is less legitimate—and therefore more powerless—than is the position of other parents. The issue of power becomes clearer when we consider the range of people who can provide health services. A husband can demand services from a wife—or (perhaps only slightly less so) a wife from a husband. Conversely, an aunt may be less able to ask for caregiving from a nephew or niece. By implication, a husband has more "power" over a wife than an aunt has over a niece. The relationship between elderly parents and their adult children lies between these extremes. The rights of parents vary across cultures and ethnic groups; and this variability affects the amount of involvement. But, despite ethnic differences, the underlying rationale for filial responsibility is that there is a life cycle of reciprocity. Elderly parents are viewed, not simply as being needy, but as having a legitimate right to command services.

There is also another type of evidence by implication for a continuity of parental power: In many families arrangements for a parent's long-term care require a long process of negotiation—possibly over many months or even years! Although the choosing of a nursing home may appear to be a sudden decision—which may be made quickly before the patient is discharged from the hospital—often this possibility has been considered and rejected and considered again. In part, the nursing home decision may be postponed because family caregivers are reluctant to send their parents (or other relatives) to an institution. In many cases, however, the length of this process is implicit evidence of parental control in care planning.

One daughter, whose mother has severe back pains and has limited mobility, remarked:

> We've talked a long time about retirement homes or apartment houses with elevators in them, or something to alleviate this problem of her walking without help; and she would deny that she wanted to go anywhere. [She insisted] that she wanted to stay there. Finally, I think it got to her that she had to do something, but by this time it was too late to go to a private apartment, even if it had an elevator . . .

This daughter used a hospital admission as part of her strategy for placing her mother in a nursing home. The stay in a hospital both facilitated finding a good nursing home and helped her mother accept the necessity of this change.

> ... I had not had any success finding a nursing home for her previous to this hospital visit so I, in frustration, called the doctor and said I can't stand this any longer. We've got to do something. So he said we would put her in and see if he could check on her back pain again, and see if there was more damage or whatever. And then we would have the social service department at the hospital work on a nursing home for me . . .
>
> [It was easier to get a good nursing home] from in the hospital than trying to do it from home . . . There were long waiting lists. I was given times of from one month to two years to get in any nursing home—the ones I visited, I shouldn't say any . . . When you finally get to this decision that this is what you are going to have to do, then you want it to happen right away. A month away is a long time for my mother, who needed some care, I felt. But apparently once you are in a hospital they have a priority list . . .
>
> [When she was in the hospital] my mother knew that she was going to a nursing home from there, wasn't very happy about it, but accepted it . . .
>
> I think I have a fairly good relationship with my mother. She may be a little unhappy with me for getting this nursing home situation evolved. However, I think she also realizes that she really can't take care of herself as well as she would like to. So I think she's becoming more adjusted to it. It's only been a few weeks . . .

As part of my research on posthospital care, I interviewed three hospital social workers who, together, described their one-month case loads of seventy elderly patients. In over half of the social workers' cases, a nursing home was considered by the family as a possible destination for posthospital care. However, I found that in about half of those situations the patient had actively resisted going to a nursing home. And, in fact, patients who resisted were much less likely to go to nursing homes than patients who did not resist. Moreover, gender seemed to be a crucial factor in both the likelihood and the success of patient resistance. In the social work cases, over two-thirds of the men compared to only about two-fifths of the women resisted transfer to nursing homes. Among those who resisted, men were much more likely to be "successful": 89% of the men compared to 50% of the women managed to delay nursing home placement. These findings suggest that fathers are more likely than mothers to exert control over their health care arrangements.

In my interviews with elderly parents and their caregiving children, I found explicit as well as implicit evidence of parental power. One way that parents overtly exert control is through negative—or angry—behavior. All three fathers were angry at some point. For two of the fathers, their anger was directed at medical staff but not at their children. Nonetheless, their anger—or the anticipation of anger—placed constraints around their children's ability to manage their health care. In one of these families, for example, a daughter interceded when a certain physician was called in to treat her father:

> I found out that they had called this Dr. Summer, who does not get along with my dad. She's a female doctor and she's the one that put Dad in the hospital in December. And if Dad's life depended on it, he would not see that doctor. Well, I intercepted that immediately. I said if [Dr.] Summer comes over here, somehow he is going to get up out of here and he is going to leave. And that's not going to benefit anybody. So then they called another doctor . . .

One of the fathers directed his anger at everyone—including the medical staff and his children. This father was circumspect during his interview and appeared to be suspicious of the research project—even though he had agreed to participate. When asked if he would like to change his relationship with his children, he answered tersely: "Yes. They take over my finances too much." In this family the daughter-in-law was the main caregiver. When asked about the impact of her father-in-law's illness on family relationships, she referred to his anger and paranoia:

> I don't think it's changed our feelings toward [him], but it seems to be changing his feelings toward us tremendously, which is, I suppose, a natural thing—because he's striking back at the people

that's closest to him, or the people that are trying to help him the most . . . I guess it's a natural thing to happen, but there's not much you can do about it. I think for me—I'm probably into the point of frustration, because I was the one that's always done things for him. And it was probably—what, two weeks ago, three weeks ago—where he told me I was taking over too much, and I was being too pushy about things. And I tried to explain to him that I was only trying to do what he couldn't do, and to pick up his loose ends. And he still said that he was eighty-eight years old and he could take care of his own business and that I shouldn't be so pushy. Which angered me—because I thought I was trying to help and instead I'm coming out as the pushy broad type of thing . . .

There are two factors that affect the power dynamics in this family. First of all, it is particularly difficult for an in-law to impose decisions. One of the other daughters-in-law alluded to an almost identical difficulty with her mother-in-law. When her mother-in-law needed surgery, the daughter-in-law insisted that "I will not be a part of that decision, because I don't want to hear [for] the rest of my life that it was my decision . . ." Second, fathers appear to be more likely than mothers to resist the loss of control over their lives. Although the three fathers in my cases were dependent on their children and their children had made decisions for them about their health care, these fathers attempted to reverse their dependency. All of these fathers viewed their current health care situations as temporary or transitional. In contrast, only a fifth of the mothers saw themselves as being in "transitional" caregiving settings.

The expression of anger and resistant behavior are forms of coercive power, which entails the use of "punishment" or other negative sanctions. Fathers seem to be more likely than mothers to use coercive power. This might lead us to conclude that fathers are more powerful—and therefore more able than mothers to demand compliance from their children. An alternative interpretation, however, is that coercive power tends to be an ineffective power base (which is found in "dysfunctional" families)[15] and the fact that mothers are less likely to behave unpleasantly may be evidence for their greater attachment to their children.

In any case, some mothers also exert coercive power. In my

family cases, two of the mothers were described by their daughters as "very demanding." One daughter (quoted earlier in this chapter discussing her mother's temper tantrums) said that her mother's health problems "had a great change on our relationship—because it made her insecure and therefore it made her not meaning to be demanding but very demanding, because there's no one else to turn to for her." Another daughter suggested that her mother has always been demanding—particularly in her relationship with her daughter:

> I don't think I'm good for my mother to be around a lot, because I think then she'll always complain. When I'm not there, she's just wonderful. The people at [the nursing home] just love her, because she's a . . . giver, not a taker. But with me it's a different story. With me, something's always wrong. She'll just fall apart at the seams . . .
> *Can you give me an example?*
> If her food isn't there on time—she's very excitable. It passes. Thursday there was a barbecue there, so my youngest daughter and my husband and I went. We went to see my mother-in-law first [in the same nursing home], who can't go out to the barbecue. By the time we got back my youngest daughter went to tell my mother I was in line. Well, she was having a fit, because some people had been served and where was I? By the time I came with her food, she didn't say anything to me—but that's her. She's very excitable and she'll let her steam off at me.
> *Has she changed—or has she always been that way?*
> No, it's always been—so it has nothing to do with her illness. She lets off steam and she can say all kinds of things and it comes from her mouth, not her heart.
> *You don't feel hurt?*
> No, I know . . . really . . . Inside it probably still eats me up, but I know that this is her.
> *Is she critical of you in particular?*
> No, I don't think that. I just think—she just knows that who else is she going to yell at like that? No one else is going to take it. I'm the scapegoat.

Another daughter gave a similar portrayal of her mother, who had died of cancer two years earlier. She currently was caring for her father, who also had cancer. This daughter described her mother as the "dominant" one in the family. (Even so, her father, like the other fathers in the study, was not an easy or compliant patient.) She said that the nurses and social workers at the hospice where her mother had last lived had described her mother as "such a lovable and caring person." But that was not how she knew her mother. She said about her mother: "I felt like I was never forgiven for anything" and "No matter what I did I was always wrong." She related an incident that had occurred while her mother was dying:

> . . . My cousin brought up a whole bunch of strawberries. They had been out picking strawberries and my mother loves strawberries, so Ellen said: "Well, I'll bring some up—we'll come visit for the day and we'll bring some up."
>
> I wasn't going to make strawberry jam when we were leaving that same afternoon. So I was going to freeze some—leave some whole and fresh and freeze some. I don't know why I remember this; I suppose because it hurt so much when she said it.
>
> I was in the kitchen doing this. They brought more strawberries than they ever should have—just big ice-cream buckets full. And I was cleaning the strawberries and slicing them . . . And I went into the living room to ask Mom if she wanted me to freeze them with sugar or without sugar.
>
> [She said] "Well, don't freeze them; they're no good if they're frozen." And they were already washed and you have to freeze them once you wash them. I said, "Well, I'm leaving quite a few." And she said: "I don't care." I went back into the kitchen to finish, thinking: What am I doing anyway? Why did I even start?
>
> And she said to Dad: "Well, she just wants them in the freezer so that after I'm dead, she can eat them when she comes up here to visit you."
>
> So I just left them. They just sat and rotted in the sink . . .

What is particularly striking about these three families is that the daughters became outlets or targets for their mothers' anger, depression, and anxiety. Whereas these mothers presented themselves as compliant toward others, they were almost abusive—in an emotional sense—toward their daughters. The daughters with angry/demanding mothers are atypical; they are like the small proportion of daughters (discussed in Chapter Two) who have had negative or problematic relationships with their mothers. Nonetheless, it is important to realize that *some mothers—even if they are old, frail, and mentally impaired—are overtly powerful figures in their families—particularly in their relationships with their daughters.*

FAMILIES AND HOSPITALS

How does the mother-daughter relationship change when an aging mother is hospitalized? Once their mothers have been admitted to a hospital, the daughters' caregiving role is redefined within the context of the health care system. One way that hospitalization transforms family relationships is that "private" interactions now take place in a "public" setting. Hospital doors tend to be kept at least partially open, so that patients can be monitored. This means that visitors also are in public view and that nurses and other health care staff witness family behaviors that might otherwise occur inside households and behind closed doors. To some extent health care professionals are reluctant witnesses who endeavor not to intrude on families. One nurse commented: "It's an invasion of privacy if I overheard [some kind of misinformation], so I wouldn't just go in there and say, 'Hey I heard what you said and you're all wrong.'" But hospital staff—particularly those involved in discharge planning—often need to assess the capability of a patient's home health care providers. In order to do this, they observe family behavior and evaluate relationships. Thus, families lose privacy not just in spatial terms but also in the sense that outsiders (that is, professionals) become involved with their family system.

A daughter's responsibilities may increase or decrease after a mother is hospitalized. Social workers, physicians, nurses, etc. sometimes facilitate greater caregiver involvement; at other times they counsel against the continuation of a caregiver role. In any case, hospital staff often are implicated in planning the future of the mother-daughter relationship.

Hospital staff emphasize the importance of family involvement. The head nurse of the neurology ward, for example, insisted that it is her "personal philosophy" to "involve the families and really keep the families informed as to what's going on with the patient.

And I think that's what I have related to my staff so I think my staff become very involved with families." Clearly this nurse was concerned with more than next-of-kin notification (in case of death). But why should hospital staff be interested in family involvement?

The sociologist Eugene Litwak[16] has argued that there is a partnership between "formal" health care providers (such as hospitals and nursing homes) and "informal" caregivers (such as family, neighbors, and friends). According to Litwak, the functions served by family members cannot be replaced by institutions. In my research on family caregivers there was much evidence to support his assertion.

A major role for adult children is to serve as a linkage between the patient and the health care system. Daughters serve as advocates for their mothers in the hospital. In this role, they speak on their parents' behalf. Earlier, I alluded to the fact that adult children often make decisions for their parents when their parents are physically and/or mentally "out of it." This is only one part of their linkage or advocacy role.

Probably the most obvious component of this linkage role— and the reason why health care staff say that they value family involvement—is for family members to provide supportive care. For example, daughters often help with the admission process: They give information about their mothers' medical and personal needs; they help to orient their mothers in their hospital rooms; they bring in familiar objects from home (slippers, etc.); they encourage parents-as-patients to follow prescriptions from physicians and nurses; and they reassure their mothers that they are not surrounded by "strangers." Daughters vary in how much supportive care they provide during the hospital stay. One nurse told of a case where the patient "needed to be encouraged to eat . . . So the daughter was there when the dietitian filled out the diet with the patient and she was there at mealtime and helped us a lot. Because we could come in, but what's a stranger trying to help you to eat. It's better if it's a family member." In other cases, however, family members "leave at mealtime . . . they use that [bringing in the tray] as an excuse to leave."

When daughters serve as advocates for their parents, one

result is that they preserve their parents' "personhood." Implicitly, all of the adult children, by virtue of their presence—their daily visits—helped to define their parents as persons, with connections and lives beyond the hospital walls. One daughter was bothered by the fact that the health care staff were receiving a negative image of her father. She and her siblings tried to revise this image:

> When he was really having the depression and [having] a hard time sleeping . . . and he was very demanding, we tried to make them aware of the fact that normally he's a very easygoing, kind, gentle person that, rather than bother somebody, even if he needed help . . . he would do without. If it meant putting somebody on the spot or if it meant you going out of your way to help him, he'd rather you didn't . . .
> *His behavior was demanding when he was in the hospital?*
> He was incredible. He was a totally different person. We wanted them to know that he wasn't just being an old grump. This wasn't him. . . . That was our big concern—that the nurses not treat him like he had always been a crazy old grouch, that they had to understand, for his sake, and I guess for ours too, to know that he was the most easygoing person . . .

Possibly this daughter worried that her father's care might suffer if the hospital staff did not like him. But she was concerned not just with the kind of care he received but with the kind of person he was and is. Whereas the nurses saw him as a patient (an obstreperous one, who made it difficult for them to do their job), she continued to see him as her father. By drawing on her relationship with him, she created a past and future for him that transcended his definition as a patient with a specific illness.

The advocacy role also may mean that daughters supervise the hospital care. One daughter noted that her mother's "chart said soft foods and once she got steak and once ribs. I said I didn't think that qualified." Another daughter investigated when she found out her mother was taking a pill that she did not know about:

> . . . toward the end of her [stay in the] hospital, the nurse came in and gave her a pill, and I said, "I didn't think she was on any medications."
> And she said, "Well, we started this three days ago."

> And I said, "What's it for?" And she said, "Her blood pressure."
>
> And I said, "I don't understand that. Her blood pressure was so low they were having trouble reading it."
>
> And so she went out. I saw her going through some manuals. She came back in, and she said, "I checked up on the medication for your mother, and it's either for blood pressure or confusion." So apparently they were giving it to her because of her confusion . . .

These daughters were mediating between their mothers and a large bureaucracy—the hospital. Despite the ostensible efficiency of a hospital organization, with its reliance on professional expertise, occasional errors are likely to occur. The caregiving daughters were in a position to minimize the effects of such errors by paying particularly close attention to the patients whom they care most about.

A major function of the advocacy role of adult children or other family members is to make their particular relatives visible to hospital staff. In the following example, a daughter and her family found themselves in adversary positions with hospital staff when they were monitoring the hospital care.

An Angry Family   Mrs. Johnston had lived with her daughter, son-in-law, and grandchildren for over twenty years—ever since she had been widowed. At age eighty-seven, she had multiple health problems—including osteoporosis, congestive heart failure, and digestive disorders. Mrs. Johnston said that she remembered little of what happened while she was in the hospital. She thought that almost everybody was "very kind"—although she remembered one "mean" nurse who flopped her down on her bed uncomfortably.

However, her daughter, Barbara Hogan, was very angry about the hospital experience. According to Barbara, she and her children (two grown sons and a daughter) constantly battled with the staff on her mother's behalf. (Mrs. Johnston never mentioned such fights.) For example, Barbara said that her mother had been left on a bedpan for long periods of time—with the staff seemingly forgetting that it had been placed there. She also complained that they ignored her mother's serious back problems:

When she had gone in there . . . I said that I thought she had injured her back. She had osteoporosis—which is softening of the bone. And I said to one of the nurses, when you lift her out of bed, I think she's injured her back. But they didn't look at that at this point, because they were so concerned about the pneumonia. So this one nurse said to me: "We all have back problems." She was like a yo-yo—in and out of bed . . .

Bert [grandson] noticed, when they said they would like to take her out of bed, like a half an hour before eating . . . the screaming, with the back, you could hear her all over the floor. And no one took any notice of it. So he spoke to the nurse in charge there and said could something be done. So they agreed, yes, they would give her a pain pill half an hour before getting her out of bed, because they really felt she should sit in a chair. So that was a big advantage . . .

[However, the next morning the grandson asked:] "Is it marked in the record that she should be given a pain pill before being out of the bed?" That was not indicated at all in the records and chart, which it should have been . . .

Mrs. Hogan and her children had a conference with her mother's physician, who commented, "I can see that you are a very angry family." In large part, their anger emerged from their strong attachment to the mother/grandmother. Mrs. Hogan (Barbara) explained their frustration with the hospital care by noting that they were "really upset, because she means a lot to us . . ." But their anger also was a functional part of their role as patient advocates. From their perspective, their mother/grandmother's acquiescent behavior made her vulnerable to neglect. Their anger may have been a somewhat extreme manifestation of patient advocacy—but it had a purpose. By pressing their claims and insisting that nurses and physicians attend to their mother/grandmother, they saw themselves as protecting her well-being.

There are, however, several important constrictions around the patient advocacy role of adult children. First of all, daughters and sons, to varying degrees, are emotionally involved parties and therefore are not entirely objective in their advocacy role. It is perhaps not coincidental that the angriest family—Barbara Hogan and her children—had lived for many years in the same household with Barbara's aging mother. In a sense, the physician dismissed their concerns about hospital services by labeling Barbara and the grandchildren as an "angry family"—and thereby suggesting that their evaluation was more emotional than real.

A second major difficulty that the adult children face is their lack of expertise in both health care and governmental policies. The daughters, quoted above, who expressed doubt or frustration about their mothers' care also admitted that they *did not know* what specifically ought to be done. With perhaps two exceptions (daughters who had some medical training), almost all of the adult children had very limited understanding of their parents' medical condition. Moreover, many of them expressed bewilderment about Medicare and other insurance benefits—which often seemed capricious in what was and what was not covered.

Finally, their advocacy role was limited by their need to establish working relations with the hospital staff. There is a delicate dividing line between "concern" and "overconcern" on the part of adult children. Several hospital staff members attributed overconcern to adult children who really had not been involved with their parents before and felt guilty when their parents were sick:

> A lot of times you can take that [their guilt] by their being critical of everything you do for the person—not always, but if they're questioning everything . . . they're just doing that to us in order to counteract their own feelings.

From the perspective of the hospital staff, obstreperous family members are not much easier to deal with than difficult patients; these families also interfere with the staff's ability to fulfill their responsibilities. The parents—as patients—may be limited in their ability to represent their own interests while they are sick in the hospital. If they are compliant, they may be relatively ignored, given the many demands that are placed on nursing staff. If they are demanding, they risk arousing anger in those on whom they are dependent for their care. Their adult children are less vulnerable personally and therefore may have somewhat more freedom to serve as advocates. Nonetheless, as allies of their parents, adult children confront similar risks.

The Caregiving Alliance In the hospital "system," there is a triangle made up of patients, their families, and hospital staff. There are potential alliances along all sides of this triangle. When adult children serve as advocates for their parents as patients, they essentially are cementing a patient-family alliance. Occasionally, there is a temporary alliance between patients and hospital staff. For example, one nurse said that she helped to prevent a patient from returning home to the care of her husband, who was alcoholic and abusive. However, my interviews with patients, family caregivers, and hospital staff indicated that a "caregiving alliance"— between family caregivers and the hospital staff—was the most visible and the most influential partnership within this health care setting.

To call these family-staff alliances "conspiracies" would be an exaggeration. For the most part, families and the physicians, nurses, and social workers with whom they consulted shared a benign concern for the parent-patient. Nonetheless, these tended to be "controlling" alliances, which occasionally entailed keeping secrets, at least temporarily, and sometimes led to decisions that the parents opposed. There appeared to be two issues around which family caregivers and staff became allies: information management and arrangements for posthospital care. The hospital staff whom I interviewed insisted that they were "open" with both patients and family members about managing information. They said that they did not conceal information—including a prognosis of imminent death. However, when asked to describe specific cases, various staff mentioned circumstances when they occasionally deceived patients—at least partially or temporarily—in order to reduce anxiety. But they could not think of any instance when they kept back information from family members.

In my interviews with adult children and their parents, I did not come across any cases where medical information about their condition actually had been concealed from the parents. There were several illustrations, however, of information being delayed, so that doctors and family members decided together how to talk to the patient/parent. Notice, in the following quote, for example, how the daughter sets the stage to inform her father about his cancer:

> The doctor had called me because he wanted to make sure that he [father] got all of the information clear, so he called me with the results, and I would transfer the information to Dad and my brother and sister-in-law . . . I was hoping that we could get everybody together and then have Dad come and we would talk about it together. But Dad was here when I got home and I had to get everybody together under the pretext that we were just going to . . . to have a nice little afternoon together. And then . . . when I told him the doctor had called and that they had found several spots on his bones that were probably cancer, he was shocked at first . . .

As I have noted above, almost all of the daughters and sons made decisions about posthospital care plans for their parents. Also, when there is some dissension about posthospital care, the plans proposed by the adult children tend to prevail over the expressed wishes of the parents. These findings suggest that when elderly parents become patients in a hospital, they lose some decision-making control over their own lives.

The issue of decision-making control can be explained, in large part, by the context of care planning. A major factor is that decisions about posthospital care usually have to be made quickly. Elderly patients and their families often think that Medicare will supplement the hospital stay until an adequate posthospital care plan has been arranged. This is not so. Patients are allotted a limited number of days (and these limitations have become much more severe with recent changes in Medicare reimbursement policies). Because patients tend to leave the hospital when they are still at least somewhat incapacitated, others—such as physicians or family members—may have to make decisions for them.

In my interviews with the hospital social workers, I asked them to discuss their specific case loads over a period of one month. In a number of these cases, the social workers described themselves as mediators between the patient and the family caregiver. Those situations tended to have some conflict between the elderly patient and the caregiver—usually a daughter or son—about where the patient would go after leaving the hospital. When I compared the cases in which the social workers mediated with those where there was also some dissension but the social workers did not mediate, I found that social worker mediation greatly increased the chance that the outcome would be institutionalization.

Social workers tend to give both implicit and explicit support to the family caregivers, particularly daughters and sons. Implicit support meant viewing the situation from the caregiver's rather than the patient's point of view. For example, a social worker described one father as "very unappreciative" of his son's "opening his home to him just as long as it would be a feasible situation." Explicit support meant trying to persuade the patient to acquiesce to their children's wishes or plans—". . . it took a lot of steady [convincing] from the doctor and me and the family."

There are several reasons why social workers may tend to help the adult children to gain further decision-making control. First of all, there may be age biases. The social workers were younger than most of the daughters and sons—but still closer in age to them than to the elderly parents. There was, however, little direct evidence of ageism. Second, more important, they work more with the families than the patients and therefore are likely to have a better understanding of the family caregiver's perspective. Third— because they work with the family members—they are aware of the family caregiver's stake in the arrangements. Thus, for example, in most cases where a nursing home is arranged for, a central concern is convenience for the daughter, who will be visiting and possibly providing some supplemental care. Finally, daughters and sons often are easier to work with than their parents as patients. The social workers tended to assess their cases in terms of how "realistic" or "unrealistic" they found the patients and/or family members. Being "realistic" meant defining caregiving needs in medical or functional terms rather than in terms of emotional needs. The social workers were much more likely to view the daughters and sons than the elderly patients as realistic.

Are the social workers—and other health care professionals who become involved in family caregiving decisions—"objective" mediators? In some ways they are. Whereas the mothers as patients and their daughters as caregivers tend to be immersed in their emotional commitments to one another, "outsiders" (such as social workers) define the situation in terms of functional or medical needs. The professional staff lack the emotional entanglements that skew family perspectives. But they also bring their own perspectives— personal and professional. The social workers stated quite clearly that they are not supposed to make decisions for families. Nonetheless, sometimes unintentionally, they are in a position to influence decisions. For many families, a major problem is the uncertainty about how daughters can balance their care for their mothers with their other commitments. Under these circumstances, the social work staff, and sometimes physicians, may help families to define the boundaries around their responsibilities.

THE FINAL STAGE

Do daughters "mother" their mothers in this final stage of the mother-daughter relationship? According to the daughters, they do. But in most families the process of change seems to come slowly, imperceptibly shifting family interactions. Although daughters say that their roles have been reversed, they do not necessarily view this as a sudden transformation. This is something that mothers and daughters do not seem to talk about. A daughter may find herself with an overwhelming responsibility for her mother, in terms of both caring for daily needs and protecting her mother emotionally. But the reversal of roles may never be openly acknowledged.

I was struck by how immersed these daughters were in their caring role. The rhythm of their lives, at least for a while, had been turned upside down by their tasks and by the emotional responsibility of being caregivers. So it is not surprising that they referred to themselves as "mothers" to their mothers. Through that analogy, they described their sense of entering another all-consuming role— a role in which they had taken total responsibility for the well-being of another person. In this way, parent caregiving is a quintessential woman's role—very much like motherhood.

But there are inherent contradictions in this later-life relationship between elderly mothers and their grown daughters. Some basic assumptions about family relationships are turned around—

such as, who is supposed to be the "parent" and the necessity of adult daughters having "their own lives." Daughters are faced with uncomfortable choices: Where does their loyalty lie? How can they juggle their various commitments? How much care can they give to their mothers? And their mothers, also, confront a moral dilemma: If they face a future of increasing dependency, how much can they ask their children to care?

7

MOTHERS AND DAUGHTERS AS WOMEN

Mother-daughter relationships vary in many ways. Even within the same family, a mother may have different kinds of relationships with each of several daughters. If there is so much variability within the same family, we can assume that there is even more diversity in expectations for mothers and daughters across cultures, societies, and historical periods. Having come to the end of this book, what, then, can we conclude about mother-daughter relationships in general?

A central question that I have addressed in this book is: How do mother-daughter relationships change as daughters mature and mothers age? Psychological studies of adult development[1] have emphasized that there is much stability in personality over time, so we might anticipate that mothers and daughters would stay the same over the years. However, throughout this book, I have shown how mother-daughter relationships are shaped by their "social environment." The social environment includes the particular set of other relationships that surround each mother and daughter. In various ways, there are "structural" changes in their family relationships. When a daughter marries, the presence of the daughter's husband places constraints around mother-daughter interactions. For example, mothers need to be careful about intruding on their daughters' marital relationships, in terms of both what they do and what they say. Similarly, when daughters have children and when mothers become frail, there are changes in their life structures as individuals, and these changes create new conditions for their relationships with one another. One conclusion from my research is that mother-daughter relationships do change—because of these transformations in family structure and despite the fact that as they grow older their personalities may remain much the same.

But change in mother-daughter relationships is not a simple process of development in one direction. Rather, mothers and daughters have complex relationships. There are opposing demands that are placed on both daughters and mothers through their other family roles; they are pulled together and pushed apart. They are in some ways like peers and, at the same time, they retain a parent-child orientation toward one another. The complexity of the mother-daughter bond reflects inherent contradictions in the structure of their family relationships.

There is also a broader meaning to the term "social environment"—that is, not just the particular family setting, but the norms and roles that come from the wider society. On a societal level, gender is *the* critical factor in defining the structure of mother-daughter relationships. The bond between an adult daughter and her mother is a woman-to-woman relationship. In past research, when anthropologists, psychologists, and sociologists have talked about mothers and daughters, they often have taken this obvious fact for granted. Why else are mothers and daughters usually closer than fathers and daughters, mothers and sons, or fathers and sons? When I began my own research on mothers and daughters, about ten years ago, I also saw gender as a background factor, which explains why mothers and daughters have "linked lives." Over the years, as I have worked on the research for this book, I have been further convinced that gender is a central factor in family relationships and in social relationships in general. But I have begun to question why this should be so. Of course, I am not alone in asking such questions. Social scientists, popular writers, politicians, and many others seem to be raising questions about the rigidity or flexibility of gender roles in our society. Some of the most important sociological issues of our day concern the fluidity of gender roles—with questions such as: To what extent are social positions, such as positions in work, family, and community, defined by gender? How much change has there been in personal relationships between men and women? How much flexibility in gender roles is possible in the future?

Gender has a number of meanings. On the most obvious level,

it is a form of self-identifier. Mothers, daughters, and all girls/women can say about themselves: "I am a female." Gender is also associated with social roles—particularly family roles. In English, and perhaps all languages, there are separate terms for most family relationships by gender—mother and father, sister and brother, etc. I do not believe that gender is the only factor that determines family roles, but it is a crucial one. A daughter's identification with her mother's role as a mother transcends their generic identity as females. Gender also is associated with status—to the extent that men and women in our society are seen as both different and unequal. The status of women in our society is bound up with their roles as mothers.

If we were to imagine the mother-daughter relationship without motherhood as a factor, what would their relationship be like? First of all, if a daughter's mother did not "mother" her—that is, serve as her primary parent—the mother and daughter might lack the initial foundation of their attachment. In recent years a number of social scientists and other concerned citizens have raised questions about "who will care for the children?"—if mothers fail to take seriously their children's need for a primary attachment. There is some debate about whether or not children need one mother figure and about the capability of fathers to "mother" their infants and small children. When we ask, If a daughter were not "mothered" (adequately) by her mother, would she still have a special attachment to her mother? the answer is complicated by the generalized expectations of motherhood. As I have shown, some mothers are more nurturant than others and mother-daughter relationships vary. In the very beginning of Chapter One, I described a woman who talked about her mother as "cold" and not very nurturant. She said that as she was growing up she knew that she was missing something and when she became a mother herself she realized what was wrong with her own mother. This daughter clearly had a general image about what mothers were supposed to be like. Despite variability in the way mothers actually interact with their daughters (and sons), there are expectations imposed on *all* mothers.

What happens to this relationship if the daughter does not replicate her mother's role—that is, if the daughter never becomes a mother herself? Given the design of my research, I do not have findings to address this question, since almost all of the daughters that I interviewed either were or anticipated becoming mothers at some time in their lives. This question may be important for future research, however, especially if more and more women remain childless. Since daughters seem to become closer to their mothers when they become mothers themselves, we might suppose that daughters who reject motherhood may not develop adult-adult intimate attachments with their mothers. This prediction, however, might not be accurate for two rather opposite reasons. First of all, it is unlikely that the daughter's motherhood is a necessary condition for mother-daughter attachment. There is evidence in my interviews, as well as in other studies,[2] that mothers take pride and vicarious pleasure in the various achievements of their daughters. Given the restrictions that older generations of mothers have experienced in their own career lives, possibly some mothers may prefer that their daughters *not* follow them in motherhood.

Second, daughters who do not become mothers nonetheless may be affected by motherhood. Motherhood is only one type of caring relationship. There is some evidence that caring—for children, for parents, and for others—is central in the lives of most women. Bernice Neugarten,[3] who has written extensively on human development and aging, interviewed middle-aged men and women. She reported that men tend to gauge the length of their lives on a work "clock" whereas women are more attuned to the timing of family events—*even women who never had children!* Furthermore, other studies have shown that single daughters are particularly likely to serve as caregivers to their mothers. This caring orientation brings together mothers and daughters in multiple ways—through nurturing their children/grandchildren, caring for each other, and being available to care for others.

Even so, it seems that for each generation daughters have lives that are very different from their mothers' lives. The mothers and daughters that I interviewed often emphasized these differences. Occasionally, they talked about new problems that exist today—like the availability of drugs and the new sexual morals. More often, however, both daughters and mothers recognized that there are more opportunities for women now. I was surprised, frankly, that the mothers were not more bitter about this. Possibly their feelings reflected their socialization—not simply in the sense that they had learned specific female roles, but that they had learned to accept the constrictions on their lives as women. Perhaps some of their daughters are less fully socialized in this acceptance and may be more disappointed if their achievements do not far surpass their mothers'.

How different are daughters' lives from their mothers' lives? In some ways, there seems to be no similarity at all. Daughters today often shun "traditional" patterns. A large proportion of them cohabit before they marry and they marry at later ages than generations before them. They not only anticipate working after they marry but their wage-earner role has become increasingly essential to maintaining their standard of living. They are having fewer children. And they are divorcing in record numbers. With all these social trends, what do mothers and daughters have in common?

Given the magnitude of these trends, the research in family sociology from the 1950s and 1960s—which shows continuity in the lives of mothers and daughters—may seem irrelevant today. And yet, many of my own research findings have been similar to results from those earlier studies. Perhaps the enormity of social change has been exaggerated. One factor to keep in mind is that the trends that we are witnessing in the late seventies and the eighties really began much earlier—so that the generation of their mothers also took part in those trends.[4] More important, perhaps, is the fact that there is much continuity in the social arrangements of mothering. Daughters may be wage earners and they may have fewer children; nonetheless, they almost always are the primary caregivers for their children.

Many working mothers find themselves in a bind. They may need to work to help support their families and they also may want to work, for their own satisfaction. But they are likely to spend a large proportion of their paychecks for baby-sitters and, even then, they often have doubts about the quality of care. Daughters and wives with a parent or husband who needs care face a similar dilemma. There are some striking similarities between the mothering role and the parent-caregiving role. Both of these roles tend to be done by women; the responsibilities generally are concentrated on one person; and these roles require diffuse and unbounded time commitments. The nature of the responsibilities—taking care of a dependent child or a dependent adult—means that someone has to be available, on call, all the time. Formal caregivers—professionals—can be hired to care for children or adults. But there are problems. Continuous care is expensive and the quality of care may not be as good if it is not based on personal commitment and attachment.[5]

Why do women seem to specialize in caring work? There is an economic explanation that is circular: Despite the rising trend of women working in the paid labor force, the ratio of men's to women's salaries has remained about the same: Women earn about 60¢ for every dollar that men earn. One reason for the salary differential is that women tend to lack consistent work histories— that is, they take out time for raising children. Women's lower earning power then reflects back on decisions about family caregiving. From the perspective of individual families, women's labor is cheaper and therefore more expendable on time-consuming care.

But the economic argument, which emphasizes mothering as a kind of forced labor, is incomplete because it misses an essential point about women's lives and about their relationships as mothers and daughters: Caring comes from intimacy and from the linking of their lives. The actual labor of mothering lasts for only a small proportion of their years, especially in families with few children. But their commitment to and involvement with their children stretches over the length of their lives. The birth of grandchildren, at least in some measure, revives their mothering responsibilities. They also may provide "mothering" care to their own mothers and, in their turn, when they are very old, they may find themselves "mothered" by their daughters. The family roles of women provide a meeting ground for the interweaving of generations. The caring orientation of adult daughters and their mothers—the centrality of mothering in both of their lives—means that their lives are linked from generation to generation.

APPENDIX A

Research on Mothers
and Daughters

I have studied two sources of change in the mother-daughter relationship: the maturation of daughters (when daughters enter adult family roles) and the aging of mothers (when mothers become frail and daughters become their caregivers). In order to study these relationships at two times of change, I have done two separate research projects—one on daughters' transitions to marriage and motherhood and another on the health crises of elderly parents. The following descriptions provide an overview of these projects:

A STUDY OF YOUNG ADULT DAUGHTERS
AND THEIR MOTHERS

The purpose of this research was to determine how mother-daughter relationships change when daughters marry and have children of their own. For this project, I did in-depth interviews with forty-three daughters and thirty-nine of their mothers. In half of my mother-daughter pairs, the daughter was married with a two-year-old child. The other half of the daughters were divided between childless married daughters and single daughters. A central feature of this project is a cross-sectional comparison of mother-daughter relationships by the daughters' marital/parental status. The sample was further split in about half between mothers and daughters who lived near each other (within twenty miles) and those who lived at a distance (fifty miles away or farther). I used geographical distance as part of my sample design so that I could examine the effects of physical proximity. All of the near mothers and daughters lived in the same or a nearby town; if they wanted to, they could see each other daily. All of the far mothers and daughters could not possibly have such frequent access to one another. Unfortunately, I found that geographical distance is correlated with education and other indicators of social class. Daughters who live at a distance tend to have more education and come from more educated families than daughters who remain in the same town after they are grown. The confounding of these variables, especially in a small sample, means that it is not always possible to distinguish between the effects of social class and the separate impact of geographical distance.

The daughters ranged in age between twenty-one and thirty-one. The mean age for the daughters was twenty-six and two-thirds of the daughters were twenty-three to twenty-eight. The daughters with children were older than the married childless daughters, who were a little older than the single daughters. If we think of the cross-sectional design as mimicking a developmental profile, we would expect to have daughters be somewhat older at "later" developmental stages. There is more variability in the ages of the mothers, who range in age between forty-three and sixty-four. The mean age for the mothers was fifty-four and two-thirds of the mothers were forty-eight to sixty-one.

I did the interviews for this research in 1978, while I was at the University of Massachusetts. I obtained the names of almost all the daughters from past birth and wedding announcements in the archives of a local newspaper and from town street lists. All of the daughters lived in small towns in western Massachusetts. Their mothers lived in Massachusetts and in many different states throughout the United States. I interviewed all of the near mothers and daughters in person, almost always in their own homes; and I tape-recorded and transcribed these interviews verbatim. I did the interviews with the distant mothers over the telephone; I took copious notes while we were talking; and immediately after the interview was finished, I typed up both what was directly in my notes and what I had "recorded" in my short-term memory.

The interviews consisted largely of life-history data. The daughters and mothers were interviewed separately and each was asked a structured set of questions about the history of their relationship. They were asked both general questions about their feelings and perceptions and also about their specific experiences together.

In addition to the interviews, I gave self-administered questionnaires to the daughters and their mothers, mothers-in-law, and husbands. By gathering data from mothers, daughters, and other family members, I was able to compare and contrast their perspectives on their relationships. As part of my study, I compared the mother-daughter bond to the daughters' relationships with fathers and mothers-in-law. I also analyzed how relationships with other family members—such as husbands and fathers—affect the mother-daughter relationship.

The findings discussed in Chapters Two through Five come from this research project, unless otherwise indicated. Where I discuss findings from other studies that I have done or from other researchers, I note the appropriate sources.

A STUDY OF PARENT CAREGIVING AND POSTHOSPITAL CARE

I collected the data for this study in 1982, as a kind of follow-up to my research on young adult daughters and their mothers. I wanted to study a later-life transition in the mother-daughter relationship—when mothers become frail. By the time I began my research on parent caregivers, I had come to the University of Minnesota. The research began as a case study of one hospital, which is located in a well-to-do suburb of Minneapolis.

This project entailed in-depth interviews with elderly parents who had recently been hospitalized and their adult children who were designated as "caregivers." The family cases in this study comprise a specialized sample, selected according to the following criteria: The patient was over sixty-five, widowed, recently discharged from the hospital, required some kind of posthospital care, had a local son or daughter, and was able to give "informed consent." The subjects were obtained from the case loads of the three hospital social workers (who made the initial contact and obtained permission to release names and addresses to the researchers). The adult children in the sample were those who maintained contact with the social workers.

There were fourteen family cases—based on interviews with eleven daughters (including two sisters), two sons, and two daughters-in-law (all of whom were the prime caregivers). The sample of parents was comprised of nine mothers and two fathers (three parents were not interviewed). The mean age of the parents was eighty; for the daughters and sons it was forty-five. It turned out that the adult children were overwhelmingly both daughters and youngest children, with the exceptions being cases where there was no daughter and/or no youngest child residing locally.

The study also included interviews of hospital staff and two surveys of patients. I did in-depth interviews with nurses, physicians, social workers, occupational therapists, etc. The two patient surveys consisted of (1) a one-month census of elderly patients in the neurology ward (fifty cases) and (2) a one-month census of the case loads from the three hospital social workers (seventy cases).

APPENDIX B

A Note About
Qualitative Research and
Life-History Data

My interviews consist of "life histories" of mother-daughter relationships. The raw data are comprised of over one thousand pages (single spaced) of interview transcripts, along with questionnaires. Each case has been analyzed and interpreted in terms of the structural features of their family relationships. An underlying assumption of my research is that the idiosyncratic experiences of mothers and daughters emerge from and reflect the structure of their family roles. "Stories" about events in the lives of mothers and daughters have been used both to provide illustrations of mother-daughter interactions and to generate hypotheses. Variables were coded from the interview data in order to test these hypotheses by examining major differences between variables. In addition, precoded data from questionnaires have been used to compare mother-daughter perspectives and to cross-check findings from the interviews. Thus, this research integrates "qualitative" life-history data with a "quantitative" analysis of the case material.

In analyzing my life-history interviews, I have been influenced by the methodology that William Foote Whyte described in the Appendix to his book *Street Corner Society.* That research was a participant observation study of an urban community. My study is about the life history of relationships, and I have used in-depth interviews rather than observations. What I have drawn from Whyte's methodology is his systematic approach to qualitative data. Like Whyte, I have asked a constant stream of questions from my data; I have developed mini-theories out of my impressions; and I have tested hypotheses both qualitatively, through an analysis of the content of the interviews, and quantitatively, through coding, counting, and cross-tabulating my data.

An important part of analyzing case studies is to ask, How is this case different from others, and why? Throughout much of this book I have discussed relationships that I have portrayed as "atypical." To some extent, of course, all people and all relationships are different from all others; no one is "typical." Nonetheless, there is a range of variability for any particular dimension of a relationship. For each dimension, a comparison of outlying cases with modal patterns helps to illuminate the structural features of these relationships.

Life-history data have a number of advantages over survey data. First of all, the data are "concrete"—that is, the information is closer to actual experiences than are the precoded summary items on surveys. For example, in a survey, I might ask mothers and daughters to indicate if they argued "frequently," "sometimes," or "almost never." By providing these precoded answers I am asking my respondents to summarize their experiences and give me their best estimate of the frequencies of their arguing. In an open-ended interview, I would ask respondents to describe in detail specific arguments that they have had. Having open-ended responses means that I, as the researcher, can make my own interpretations and analyses of these experiences, rather than relying on the respondent to summarize life events. In my research, I also have used some summary questions; and, for much of my analysis, I have cross-checked my interpretations of open-ended data with the precoded responses.

A second advantage of using life-history data is that the narratives trace connections between events in their lives. Thus, life-history material is useful for understanding the development of individuals or relationships over time. There are problems, of course, with relying on memory. But surveys also often rely on recall—at least implicitly. When doing a life-history interview, the researcher can ask probing questions to check for accuracy and to help the respondent remember events.

Finally, an important benefit of qualitative data is that the understandings and interpretations of the actors can be included as part of the analysis. The meanings that people give to their experiences shape the way they interact with one another and guide their expectations for the future. The mothers and daughters who have participated in my studies have been both respondents and coresearchers. My understandings of their relationships were stimulated by their insights. This did not mean that I simply accepted their interpretations as representing "reality." Sometimes mothers and daughters have divergent interpretations of their relationships; there may be multiple versions of reality. The fact that mothers and daughters (or mothers-in-law and daughters-in-law) sometimes have divergent perceptions reveals potential sources of strain in their relationships. Precisely where these inconsistencies occur is an important part of the data.

But there are problems with life-history data, as well as with other forms of qualitative research (such as participant observation). The major criticism of qualitative research methods is that there are too few cases and too much data. The fact that the sample may be both small and non-random makes it difficult to draw generalizable conclusions from this type of research. With a small sample, only large differences between categories are meaningful—especially since, with non-random samples, it is inappropriate to use tests of statistical significance. But the subtlety of this research comes, not from statistical differences, but from a careful analysis of the wealth of material.

The large amount of data means that the analysis of qualitative data tends to be cumbersome and inefficient. Moreover, the qualitative researcher is faced with another problem which the survey researcher tends to ignore: The case material emphasizes the idiosyncrasies of individual lives. The researcher seems to be faced with a choice—either to take into account individual idiosyncrasies or to code the material and then to analyze the data statistically. Either of these options, alone, is problematic.

When cases are treated descriptively, as interesting stories, the researcher and reader never know to what extent any individual case is representative of or similar to others in the sample. Some respondents tell more interesting stories than others. This means that "noisy" respondents will be overrepresented in the analysis—leading to possible biases in interpretation. Moreover, if cases are treated individually, as interesting stories, it seems wasteful to interview a whole sample. If most of the cases essentially are ignored, the study might just as well be focused on one or two individuals, with a thorough analysis of these cases. There is an opposite problem when the qualitative data are coded and the idiosyncratic nature of the data is ignored. This approach is wasteful in a different way. If all of the data are coded and analyzed numerically, it is not clear why these data were collected as open-ended responses. The end product is equivalent to survey research—gathered very inefficiently. The challenge of doing qualitative research is to do *both*—to incorporate the idiosyncrasies of the case material with a systematic analysis of the range of cases in the total sample.

Notes

The quotation on the dedication page comes from *Belle of Amherst: A Play Based on the Life of Emily Dickinson,* by William Luce, Boston: Houghton Mifflin, 1976, p. 69.

1. MOTHERS' LIVES/DAUGHTERS' LIVES

1. Cf. Raymond Firth et al., *Families and Their Relatives,* 1970; Peter Townsend, *The Family Life of Old People,* 1957; Peter Willmott and Michael Young, *Family and Class in a London Society,* 1960.

2. Sigmund Freud, *New Introductory Lectures,* 1933, p. 133; *see also* Therese Benedek, "Parenthood as a Developmental Phase," *Journal of the American Psychoanalytic Association,* vol. 7, 1959, pp. 389–417; Grete Bibring et al., "Considerations of the Psychological Processes in Pregnancy," *The Psychoanalytic Study of the Child,* vol. 15, 1959, pp. 113–21; Helene Deutsch, *The Psychology of Women,* 1944.

3. Elizabeth Bott, *Family and Social Network,* 1957.

4. M. G. Boulton, *On Being a Mother,* 1983, p. 207.

5. Diane Ehrensaft, "When Women and Men Mother," in J. Trebilcot, ed., *Mothering,* 1984; Alice Rossi, "Gender and Parenthood," *American Sociological Review,* vol. 49, 1984, pp. 1–18.

6. Nancy Chodorow, *The Reproduction of Mothering,* 1978, p. 39; *see also* Alice Rossi, "A Biosocial Perspective on Parenting," *Daedalus,* 1977; Lionel Tiger and Joseph Shepher, *Women in the Kibbutz,* 1975; Simone de Beauvoir, *The Second Sex,* 1949.

7. Myra Leifer, *Psychological Effects of Motherhood: A Study of First Pregnancy,* 1980, p. 89.

8. Cf. Nancy Chodorow, "Family Structure and Feminine Personality," in M. Z. Rosaldo and L. Lamphere, *Women, Culture and Society,* 1974, pp. 43–66; Dorothy Dinnerstein, *The Mermaid and the Minotaur,* 1976; *see also* Deutsch, op. cit.; Freud, op. cit.

9. Willmott and Young, op. cit.

10. Townsend, op. cit., p. 53.

11. Bert Adams, *Kinship in an Urban Setting,* 1968; Lucy Rose Fischer, "Married Men and Their Mothers," *Journal of Comparative Family Studies,* vol. 14, 1983, pp. 393–402.

12. Elaine Brody, "Women in the Middle and Family Help to Older People," *The Gerontologist,* vol. 21, 1981, pp. 471–80; Amy Horowitz,

"Sons and Daughters as Caregivers to Older Parents," paper presented at the annual meetings of the Gerontological Society, 1981; Helen Mederer, "The Transition to a Parent Caring Role by Adult Children: A Model of Ease of Role Transition and Difficulty of Role Performance," unpublished doctoral dissertation, University of Minnesota, 1982.

13. George S. Rosenberg and Donald F. Anspach, *Working Class Kinship*, 1973.

14. Adams, op. cit.

15. Firth et al., op. cit., pp. 404–5.

16. Gordon Streib, "Intergenerational Relations: Perspectives of the Two Generations on the Older Parent," *Journal of Marriage and the Family*, vol. 27, 1965, pp. 469–76.

17. Leifer, op. cit.; Ann Oakley, *Subject Women*, 1981.

18. Marvin Sussman and Lee Burchinal, "Kin Family Network: Unheralded Structure in Current Conceptualizations of Family Functioning," *Marriage and Family Living*, vol. 24, 1962, pp. 231–40.

19. Mederer, op. cit.; Betsy Robinson and Majda Thurnher, "Taking Care of Aged Parents," *The Gerontologist*, vol. 19, 1979, pp. 586–93.

20. Cf. Sylvia Weishaus, "Aging Is a Family Affair," in P. Ragan, *Aging Parents*, 1979.

21. Joan Aldous, *Family Careers*, 1978; Nancy Friday, *My Mother, Myself*, 1977.

22. Alice Balint, "Love for the Mother and Mother-Love," in M. Balint, ed., *Primary Love and Psychoanalytic Technique*, 1965; *see also* Chodorow, 1978, op. cit.

23. Dinnerstein, op. cit., pp. 111–12.

24. There is also a third possible model of change in the mother-daughter hierarchy—a cyclical model—that mothers and daughters become like peers when daughters become adults, and then the hierarchy is reversed in the mother's old age and the daughter "mothers" her mother. I have discussed the dynamics of role reversal in Chapter Six, "When Mothers Become Frail."

25. Cf. Ralph Turner, *Family Interaction*, 1970.

2. THE ADOLESCENT YEARS

1. Alice Rossi, "Aging and Parenthood in the Middle Years," in P. Baltes and O. Brim, eds., *Life Span Development and Behavior*, vol. 3, 1980.

2. Ralph Turner, *Family Interaction*, 1970, p. 400.

3. Nancy Chodorow, *The Reproduction of Mothering*, 1978, p. 135.

4. Marjorie Lowenthal et al., *Four Stages of Life,* 1975.

5. John Scanzoni, *Sexual Bargaining: Power Politics in the American Marriage,* 1973.

6. Nancy Friday, *My Mother, Myself,* 1977, p. 238.

7. Cf. Vern L. Bengtson and Joseph A. Kuypers, "Generational Difference and the Developmental Stake," *Aging and Human Development,* vol. 2, 1971, pp. 249–60; Turner, op. cit.

8. P. Berger and H. Kellner, "Marriage and the Construction of Reality," *Diogenes,* vol. 46, 1964, pp. 1–25; Turner, op. cit.

9. James Alexander, "Supportive and Defensive Communication in Family Systems," *Journal of Marriage and the Family,* vol. 35, 1973, pp. 613–17.

10. See the discussion of Buber's I-Thou dialogue, in Ivan Boszormenyi-Nagy and Geraldine Spark, *Invisible Loyalties,* 1973, p. 7. For both mother and daughter, their intimacy can serve as a "mutually confirming dialogue."

11. Evelyn Duvall, *Family Development,* 1977.

12. In all the cases with inconsistencies in perspectives—that is, the daughter depicting the relationship as distant, and the mother describing a close relationship—the mothers and daughters currently live at a distance from one another. Possibly, daughters who feel distant from their mothers may choose to live far from them. More important, geographical distance allows these mothers and daughters to sustain their differing perspectives. The far mother who has little contact with her daughter can assume that without the physical separation they could see each other very frequently. Conversely, a near mother and daughter would have much more difficulty in maintaining a "fiction" of closeness; lack of contact would be much more likely to be interpreted as lack of interest. For the daughters, geographical distance may mean that they retain their adolescent images of their mother. Thus, their physical separation may interfere with the development of adult-adult relationships between mothers and daughters.

13. Lowenthal et al., op. cit.

14. Mirra Komarovsky, *Blue Collar Marriage,* 1967; Peter Willmott and Michael Young, *Family and Class in a London Society,* 1960.

15. Education is one indicator of social class status. In addition, presumably education improves people's vocabulary, their knowledge, and their ability to communicate.

16. On a 1 to 7 scale, with 1 high and 7 low, these daughters gave their mothers a mean rating of 5 = "below average," compared to the overall sample mean of 3 = "above average." Whereas most daughters in the sample rated their mothers as better than or equal to themselves in mothering ability, all but one of these daughters rated their mothers as *worse* than themselves in mothering ability.

17. This helplessness may explain the silence and lack of intervention by many mothers when fathers physically or sexually abuse their children.

18. Frieda Fromm-Reichmann, *Psychoanalysis and Psychotherapy*, 1959.

19. Greer Litton Fox, "The Mother–Adolescent Daughter Relationship as a Sexual Socialization Structure," *Family Relations*, vol. 29, 1980, pp. 21–28.

20. Chodorow, op. cit.

21. Female silence about sexuality tends to be characteristic of our culture. Compared with males, few women talk about, inspect, or touch each other's bodies (cf. The Boston Women's Health Book Collective, *The New Our Bodies, Ourselves*, 1984). By far the most prevalent attitude of the daughters in my sample toward their mothers' sexuality was *not to know* anything about it. One implication of mother-daughter silence about sexuality is that daughters lack female sexual role models. Silence among females means that most daughters learn about sexuality when they become sexually active. Thus, female sexuality becomes a *male creation*—viewed from a male perspective and defined in terms of the needs of the male partner.

3. MATURATION, MARRIAGE, AND MOTHERHOOD

1. Gunhilde Hagestad and R. Snow, "Young Adult Offspring as Interpersonal Resources in Middle Age," paper presented at the annual meeting of the Gerontological Society, 1977.

2. Irving Rosow, *Social Integration of the Aged*, 1967.

3. Raymond Firth et al., *Families and Their Relatives*, 1970; Carol Stack, *All Our Kin*, 1974.

4. In this case, the mother, after spending her child-rearing years at home, returned to finish her undergraduate degree at the same time that her daughter was in college. The daughter describes her resentment at her mother taking on a peerlike role:

> I was just thinking—the question about the worst time with my mother. It was when she was in school, when she was going to college and I was going too. I kind of resented that—I don't know why . . . she'd always be talking about her classes and she really learned things from going to school. I didn't feel as though I was. She was really absorbing it and was always talking about it—what marks she got. Oh that really bugged me . . . she used to say how the kids in her class would confide in her, talk to her about things. I never wanted to listen to it . . . Now that I think about it I really acted pretty badly . . . Friends of mine would say, I met your

> mother—that's so great that she's going to school. To me I didn't think it was that great. She wasn't there. I didn't think she was doing what she should be doing . . .

This daughter found herself in an uncomfortable but muted rivalry with her mother; she did not want to hear about her mother's academic or social achievements. She also expresses a sense of abandonment—her mother "wasn't there . . . doing what she should." It was apparently of little comfort to the daughter that other students would "confide" in her mother. Her refusal to type her mother's papers symbolized, to her, a rejection of her mother—retaliated abandonment. She notes that she cheerfully agreed to type her father's papers when he was taking classes around the same time! Thus, she now feels guilty because—out of competitiveness and jealousy—she purposely neglected her mother.

5. Reuben Hill et al., *Family Development in Three Generations*, 1970; Mederer, op. cit.

6. Sandra L. Titus et al., "Family Conflict over Inheritance of Property," *Family Coordinator*, vol. 28, 1979, pp. 337–46.

7. Irwin Deutscher, "The Quality of Post-parental Life," *Journal of Marriage and the Family*, 26, 1964, pp. 52–59; Marjorie Lowenthal et al., *Four Stages of Life*, 1975.

8. Michael Young and Peter Willmott, *The Symmetrical Family*, 1973.

9. Type II—responsible daughters/dependent mothers—does not appear to be related to the daughters' marital status in any systematic way. The mother's (as well as the daughter's) personality is probably the most important factor in shaping these relationships.

10. Cf. Evelyn Duvall, *Family Development*, 1977; Rhona Rapoport, "Transition from Engagement to Marriage," *Acta Sociologica*, vol. 8, 1964, pp. 36–55.

11. Lucy Rose Fischer, "Married Men and Their Mothers," *Journal of Comparative Family Studies*, 14, 1983, pp. 393–402.

12. In the case (just quoted) of the married childless daughter who describes her life as "unsettled," the mother is the one (referred to earlier) who states: "I try not to tell her what to do."

13. Alice Rossi, "Transition to Parenthood," *Journal of Marriage and the Family*, vol. 30, 1968, pp. 26–39.

14. Lucy Rose Fischer, "Metamorphosis in the Mother-Daughter Bond," unpublished paper; *see also* Lucy Rose Fischer, "Transitions in the Mother-Daughter Relationship," *Journal of Marriage and the Family*, 1981, pp. 613–22.

15. Rossi, op. cit.

16. Sheila Klatsky, *Patterns of Contact with Relatives*, 1968.

17. Cf. Grete Bibring et al., "Considerations of the Psychological

Processes in Pregnancy," *The Psychoanalytic Study of the Child,* 15, 1959, pp. 113–21; Helene Deutsch, *The Psychology of Women,* 1944; Myra Leifer, *Psychological Effects of First Motherhood: A Study of First Pregnancy,* 1980.

4. GENDER AND GENERATION

1. Chodorow, *The Reproduction of Mothering,* 1978.
2. Oakley, *Subject Women,* 1981, p. 272; *see also* Helena Lopata, *Occupation Housewife,* 1971.
3. Cf. Marcia Guttentag and Paul Secord, *Too Many Women?* 1983; Alice Rossi, *The Feminist Papers,* 1973.
4. Mirra Komarovsky, *Blue Collar Marriage,* 1967; Peter Willmott and Michael Young, *Family and Class in a London Society,* 1960.
5. A 10% difference in a small sample is not really meaningful.
6. Cf. Lillian Breslow Rubin, *Worlds of Pain: Life in Working Class Families,* 1976.
7. Almost all of the daughters (with just two exceptions) rated themselves as either very similar to or very different from their mothers in terms of cleaning. In contrast, a quarter of the daughters with children did not check either column about child care—thus giving neutral responses. There is, of course, an obvious explanation: It is relatively easy to assess and compare cleaning styles. Moreover, the issue of cleaning is likely to have been a source of discussion or argument during the daughter's adolescence, if not subsequently.
8. The first two items, child discipline and housecleaning, seem to relate to "instrumental" components of roles; whereas the last item refers to an "expressive" dimension. One conclusion, then, might be that there is more intergenerational transmission of instrumental than expressive components of roles. But these items all have multiple referrents, which makes interpretation difficult. For example, how a person cleans a house relates to a combination of specific skills, personality, time (or opportunity), norms, environment, and developmental factors. Moreover, disciplining children might be viewed as both instrumental and expressive.
9. Dorothy Dinnerstein, *The Mermaid and the Minotaur,* 1976.
10. Neal E. Miller and John Dollard, *Social Learning and Imitation,* 1941.
11. Vern L. Bengtson and Joseph A. Kuypers, "Generational Difference and the Developmental Stake," *Aging and Human Development,* 2, 1971, pp. 249–60.
12. Bert Adams, "Isolation, Function and Beyond: American Kinship in the 1960s," *Journal of Marriage and the Family,* vol. 32, 1970, pp. 575–97.

13.   Anne Seiden and Pauline Bart, "Woman to Woman: Can Sisterhood Be Powerful?" in N. Glazer-Malbin, ed., *Old Family/New Family*, 1975.

14.   It is not easy to assess the meaning of these responses. Even when husbands *say* that they "share equally" in certain tasks, it is not clear that they actually *do* half the work or take half the responsibility. Anecdotal evidence from these interviews and numerous other studies indicate that "equal parenting" is very rare. But these responses can be interpreted in a relative sense—that is, compared to participation in other chores done around the home, husbands' participation in child care may be more nearly equal. *See also* Rossi, "Gender and Parenthood," *American Sociological Review*, 49, 1984, pp. 1–18.

15.   *See* Myra Leifer, *Psychological Effects of Motherhood: A Study of First Pregnancy*, 1980.

16.   *See* Robert Blood, Jr., and Donald Wolfe, *Husbands and Wives*, 1960.

17.   *See* Anne Seiden and Pauline Bart, op. cit.; Jessie Bernard, *The Future of Marriage*, 1973.

18.   Table 12 suggests that there are some differences between daughters with and without children in terms of their use of confidants. The daughters with children in this sample were more likely to say they confide in their husbands than the daughters without children. When we add the first two categories (confiding in husbands—with and without qualifiers), we see that the daughters with children are almost twice as likely as the daughters without children to mention confiding in their husbands. Conversely, daughters without children say they confide in friends more than the daughters with children. Possibly, because the daughters with children have been married somewhat longer, their "friendships" with their husbands may be more developed. However, the husbands with and without children are virtually the same in their use of confidants (see Table 11). Potentially, the lack of other supports for the daughters with children reflects a process of isolation for mothers with small children. The young mothers are the most likely women in the sample to mention their husbands as confidants. Nonetheless, only about half of these women indicate relying freely (that is, without qualifiers) on their husbands for emotional support.

19.   Peter Pineo, "Disenchantment in the Later Years of Marriage," *Marriage and Family Living*, vol. 23, 1961, pp. 3–11; Joan Cuber and Peggy Harroff, *Sex and the Significant Americans*, 1966.

20.   Michael Young and Peter Willmott, *The Symmetrical Family*, 1973; John Scanzoni, *Sexual Bargaining: Power Politics in the American Marriage*, 1973.

21.   These negative reactions to daughters' husbands were *in ad-*

dition to the reluctance of some mothers to see their daughters married "too young."

22. Gunhilde Hagestad, "Problems and Promises in the Social Psychology of Intergenerational Relations," in R. Fogel et al., eds., *Aging: Stability and Change in the Family,* 1981, p. 29.

23. Betty Friedan, *The Feminine Mystique,* 1963; Alice Rossi, "Equality between the Sexes: An Immodest Proposal," *Daedalus,* vol. 93, 1964, pp. 651–52.

24. Reuben Hill et al., *Family Development in Three Generations,* 1970.

25. Whether or not technological changes necessarily improve the quality of life is open to debate. Some social historians and feminists have argued that the improvements in cleaning technology just lead to higher standards—with the result that women in different generations have spent similar portions of their time cleaning. *See* Ruth Schwartz Cowan, *More Work for Mother: The Ironies of Household Technology from the Open Hearth to the Microwave,* 1983.

26. Leon Festinger, *A Theory of Cognitive Dissonance,* 1957.

27. It is possible, of course, that the daughters may enter "male" professions later. However, most professional careers require a number of years both for training and for climbing career "ladders." People who embark on such careers relatively late are handicapped in several ways: (1) They will need to invest in educational training at a time when they will have responsibilities for earning an income. (2) Late beginners will always be behind their age peers on their professional career ladders. (3) The later they begin their training, the fewer the years of payoff. (4) There are age biases in hiring and promotions. In short, it is unlikely that large numbers of these daughters will radically reorient their career lives.

28. Bengtson and Kuypers, op. cit.; Erik Erikson, *Childhood and Society,* 1963.

29. This phrase was initially penned by Alphonse Karr in a pamphlet entitled *Les Guêpes,* 1849. The comment is in reference to the political revolutions of 1848.

30. Diane Ehrensaft, "When Women and Men Mother," in J. Trebilcot, ed., *Mothering,* 1984.

5. HER MOTHER VERSUS HIS

1. Evelyn Duvall, *In-laws: Pro and Con,* 1954.

2. Anthropological research on kinship has indicated that in-law relationships in many cultures are problematic and sometimes are surrounded by rules of "avoidance." In some societies, in-laws—particularly a son-in-law and mother-in-law—need to be very careful to avoid meeting

each other, even if this means going far out of their way so that their paths do not cross. Culturally prescribed avoidance and joking are both ways of coping with a difficult relationship in which there is likely to be tension. Cf. Duvall, *In-laws: Pro and Con,* 1954; A. R. Radcliffe-Browne and Darylle Forde, eds., *African Systems of Kinship and Marriage,* 1950; John Schlien, "Structure-function, Kinship Terminology, and the Mother-in-law," paper presented to the Annual Symposium of the Committee on Human Development, 1965.

3.   Duvall, op. cit., p. 12.

4.   In middle-class American society, children traditionally have been cared for exclusively by their mothers—with little help from either fathers or female relatives. We can contrast this social pattern with the child-rearing customs in other cultures—such as an American black ghetto or a peasant community in Thailand. In the black ghetto and Thai communities, children not only have multiple female kin who help to rear them but also they are sometimes "borrowed out"—adopted, permanently or temporarily, by other kin. Thus, more people than the biological mother may be viewed as having "maternal" rights in the child. In middle-class American society, on the other hand, the isolation of mothers with their children may foster a highly exclusive child-mother bond. The mother, of course, may have intimate bonds with multiple children. But from the child's perspective, there is only one mother and a fierce loyalty is owed this person. Thus, a married daughter who has had a fairly remote relationship with her father and has no aunts or grandmothers that have helped to rear her confronts a tie with her mother-in-law as a new kind of relationship. She has had no experience in dealing with "another mother." Because her bond with her mother has been and is supposed to be exclusive, she may interpret attachment to another mother as disloyalty to her own mother. Cf. Carol Stack, *All Our Kin,* 1974; Herbert Phillips, *Thai Peasant Personality,* 1966.

5.   Cf. Bertram Raven, Richard Centers, and Aroldo Rodriguez, "The Bases of Conjugal Power," in R. Cromwell and D. Olson, eds., *Power in Families,* 1975, pp. 217-32.

6.   Actually, most of the daughters in my sample have barely discussed the topic of sexuality with their mothers—such discussions having ended with instructions about menstrual pads and tampons.

7.   It is possible that the increase in conflict indicated by responses from mothers-in-law is a conservative estimate. The non-response rate from mothers-in-law is especially high in cases where the daughter-in-law has children (six non-responding mothers-in-law, compared with only one non-response from these mothers). The mean conflict rating from daughters-in-law in cases with non-responding mothers-in-law is 5.2, whereas in cases with responding mothers-in-law the comparable daughter-in-law

rating is 4.3 (where a higher number means more conflict). It seems, then, that some of the mothers-in-law with the most conflictful relationships with their daughters-in-law may be among the non-respondents. Findings from paired perspectives of daughters-in-law and (responding) mothers-in-law should underestimate the amount of conflict in in-law relationships after the daughter-in-law's first maternity. Moreover, these findings may also minimize the divergence of their perspectives.

8. Erving Goffman, *The Presentation of Self in Everyday Life,* 1959.

9. These quotes come from a study I did in Minneapolis on grandmothers and young mothers; *see* Lucy Rose Fischer and Jane Silverman, "Grandmothering as a 'Tenuous' Role Relationship," paper presented at the Annual Meetings of the National Council on Family Relations, 1982.

10. *See* Lucy Rose Fischer, "Transition to Grandmotherhood," *International Journal of Aging and Human Development,* vol. 16, 1983, pp. 67–78; Eva Kahana and Boaz Kahana, "Theoretical and Research Perspectives on Grandparenthood," *Aging and Human Development,* vol. 2, 1971, pp. 261–68.

11. Fischer and Silverman, op. cit.

12. Cf. Bert Adams, *Kinship in an Urban Setting,* 1968; George S. Rosenberg and Donald F. Anspach, *Working Class Kinship,* 1973.

13. Cf. Lucy Rose Fischer, "Married Men and Their Mothers," *Journal of Comparative Family Studies,* 14, 1983, pp. 393–402.

14. In another paper (Fischer, op. cit.), I have suggested that men's relationships with their mothers resemble in-law bonds. An in-law relationship is a kinship link *through a spouse.* Anthropological and sociological studies have characterized in-law relationships as (a) mediated, (b) emotionally distant, and (c) problematic. My own research and other studies suggest that these characteristics also apply to the relationships between married men and their mothers.

The differences in the mediating role of spouses is illustrated by Horowitz's description of the parent-caring role of sons versus daughters. Horowitz notes that when married sons provide care to their aged parents they tend to rely on a considerable amount of instrumental assistance from their wives. In contrast, married daughters, as parent carers, tend to expect, at best, neutrality from their husbands. (Amy Horowitz, "Sons and Daughters as Caregivers to Older Parents: Differences in Role Performance and Consequences," paper presented at the Thirty-Fourth Annual Meeting of the Gerontological Society, November 1981.)

The emotional distance between married sons and their mothers is described by Farrell and Rosenberg (*Men at Midlife,* 1981, p. 179), who view distancing from parents as a developmental issue for adult males: "The effort to find autonomy apparently required them to find alternative sources of support and strength: wives, in-laws, professional identifications, and so on."

In-law relationships tend to be problematic because in-laws are simultaneously kin and "strangers." Relationships between married sons and their mothers may be problematic for a similar reason—that is, being at the same time close and distant. Farrell and Rosenberg (p. 181) describe the men in their sample as remaining attached to their parents while needing to "keep them away."

6. WHEN MOTHERS BECOME FRAIL

1. Cf. Elaine Brody, "Women in the Middle and Family Help to Older People," *The Gerontologist*, 21, 1981, pp. 471–80; Amy Horowitz, "Sons and Daughters as Caregivers to Older Parents: Differences in Role Performance and Consequences," paper presented at the Thirty-Fourth Annual Meeting of the Gerontological Society, November 1981; Helen Mederer, "The Transition to a Parent Caring Role by Adult Children: A Model of Ease of Role Transition and Difficulty of Role Performance," unpublished doctoral dissertation, University of Minnesota, 1982.

2. The fact that my interviews were with adult children who were already caregivers has been a limitation of my study—in that I did *not* talk to non-caregiving children. Unfortunately, I have not found any research that shows why some children serve as caregivers while others do not. I can make one inference, however—that daughters are more likely to be caregivers than sons. Almost all studies of parent caregiving, including my own, have shown that caregivers are disproportionately daughters.

3. In my Minneapolis study of posthospital care there were only three fathers. This was because I selected only families where the parent was widowed. When I conducted a survey of elderly patients in a ward of the same hospital, I found a much more nearly equal distribution of elderly men and women. In fact, in the hospital ward there were more married men than married women.

4. Possibly both daughters and wives nurture their disabled fathers and husbands while maintaining these men in an ostensibly dominant position.

5. This is mostly because women live longer than men and also because men marry women who are younger than themselves. But being cared for by an adult child is not the same as being taken care of by a spouse, because spouses are more "reliable" as caregivers than children. Elderly women, since they lack spouses, are much more likely than men to live in nursing homes. For spouses, not only is there more of a moral obligation to provide care, but also their financial statuses are tied together. The eligibility requirements for Medicaid and other governmental programs

often give spouses no choice but to provide care at home—for "free." *See* Lucy Rose Fischer, with Carol Hoffman, "Who Cares for the Elderly: The Dilemma of Family Support," in M. Lewis and J. Miller, *Research in Social Problems and Public Policy*, vol. 3, 1984.

6. Brody, op. cit.

7. Horowitz, op. cit.

8. Brody, op. cit.

9. Given the mortality differential between men and women, it may be somewhat common for caregiving daughters to provide health care services at the same time to their mothers and their husbands.

10. If we want to understand to what extent the adult children are "burdened" by their caregiving role, we need to ask, Compared to what? For instance, worry might also be a burden—so that a daughter or son who is not providing needed care might be subjectively more stressed than the one who is assured that appropriate care is provided by his/her own hands-on assistance.

11. Most adult children have parents who live in separate households. Thus, parent caregiving requires managing two households—their own and their parents'. Multigenerational residences are rare in American society today—less than 8% of households. But the statistics may be somewhat misleading. While only a small proportion of elderly live with their children at any one time, a considerably larger percentage—possibly over a third—may reside with their children at *some* time in their lives—when they are in need of care; cf. Betsy Robinson and Majda Thurnher, "Taking Care of Aged Parents," *The Gerontologist,* 19, 1979, pp. 586–93.

12. Brody, op. cit.

13. Fischer with Hoffman, op. cit.

14. *See* J. W. Thibaut and H. H. Kelley, *The Social Psychology of Groups,* 1959; Robert Blood, Jr., and Donald Wolfe, *Husbands and Wives,* 1960.

15. *See* Bertram Raven et al., "The Bases of Conjugal Power," in R. Cromwell and D. Olson, eds., *Power in Families,* 1975, pp. 217–32.

16. Eugene Litwak, *Helping Networks of Older People: From Health to Institutionalization,* 1985.

7. MOTHERS AND DAUGHTERS AS WOMEN

1. *See* Howard Moss and Elizabeth Susman, "Longitudinal Study of Personality," in Orville Brim and Jerome Kagan, eds., *Constancy and Change in Human Development,* 1980, pp. 530–95.

2. *See* Arlie Hochschild, *The Unexpected Community,* 1973.

3. Bernice Neugarten, "The Awareness of Middle Age," in B.

Neugarten, ed., *Middle Age and Aging,* 1968, pp. 93–98.

4.   Andrew Cherlin, *Marriage, Divorce and Remarriage,* 1981.

5.   Eugene Litwak, *Helping Networks of Older People: From Health to Institutionalization,* 1985.

References

Adams, Bert, "Isolation, Function and Beyond: American Kinship in the 1960s," *Journal of Marriage and the Family,* 32, 1970: 575–97.
———, *Kinship in an Urban Setting,* Chicago: Markham Publishing Co., 1968.
Aldous, Joan, *Family Careers,* New York: John Wiley and Sons, 1978.
Alexander, James, "Supportive and Defensive Communication in Family Systems," *Journal of Marriage and the Family,* 35, 1973: 613–17.
Balint, Alice, "Love for the Mother and Mother-Love," in M. Balint, ed., *Primary Love and Psychoanalytic Technique,* New York: Liveright Publishing, 1965.
Benedek, Therese, "Parenthood as a Developmental Phase," *Journal of the American Psychoanalytic Association,* 7, 1959: 389–417.
Bengtson, Vern L., and Joseph A. Kuypers, "Generational Difference and the Developmental Stake," *Aging and Human Development,* 2, 1971: 249–60.
Berger, Peter, and H. Kellner, "Marriage and the Construction o Reality," *Diogenes,* 46, 1964: 1–25.
Bernard, Jessie, *The Future of Marriage,* New York: Souvenir Press, 1973.
Bibring, Grete, Thomas Dwyer, Dorothy Huntington, and Arthur Valenstein, "Considerations of the Psychological Processes in Pregnancy," *The Psychoanalytic Study of the Child,* 15, 1959: 113–21.
Blood, Robert, Jr., and Donald Wolfe, *Husbands and Wives,* New York: Free Press of Glencoe, 1960.
Boston Women's Health Book Collective, *The New Our Bodies, Ourselves,* New York: Simon and Schuster, 1984.
Boszormenyi-Nagy, Ivan, and Geraldine Spark, *Invisible Loyalties,* New York: Harper & Row, 1973.
Bott, Elizabeth, *Family and Social Network,* London: Tavistock Publications, 1957.
Boulton, M. G., *On Being a Mother: A Study of Women with Pre-school Children,* London: Tavistock Publications, 1983.
Brody, Elaine, "Women in the Middle and Family Help to Older People," *The Gerontologist,* vol. 21, no. 5, 1981: 471–80.
Buber, Martin, *Between Man and Man,* London: Routledge & Kegan Paul, 1947.

Cherlin, Andrew, *Marriage, Divorce and Remarriage,* Cambridge, Mass.: Harvard University Press, 1981.

Chodorow, Nancy, "Family Structure and Feminine Personality," in M. Z. Rosaldo and L. Lamphere, *Women, Culture and Society,* Stanford, Calif.: Stanford University Press, 1974, pp. 43–66.

————, *The Reproduction of Mothering,* Berkeley: University of California Press, 1978.

Cowan, Ruth Schwartz, *More Work for Mother: The Ironies of Household Technology from the Open Hearth to the Microwave,* New York: Basic Books, 1983.

de Beauvoir, Simone, *The Second Sex,* New York: Alfred A. Knopf, 1953.

Deutsch, Helene, *The Psychology of Women,* New York: Grune and Stratton, 1944.

Deutscher, Irwin, "The Quality of Post-parental Life," *Journal of Marriage and the Family,* 26, 1964: 52–59.

Dinnerstein, Dorothy, *The Mermaid and the Minotaur,* New York: Harper & Row, 1976.

Duvall, Evelyn, *Family Development,* Philadelphia: J. B. Lippincott Co., 1957.

————, *In-laws: Pro and Con,* New York: Association Press, 1954.

Ehrensaft, Diane, "When Women and Men Mother," in J. Trebilcot, ed., *Mothering,* Totowa, N.J.: Rowman and Allanheld, 1984.

Erikson, Erik, *Childhood and Society,* New York: W. W. Norton, 1963.

Farrell, Michael, and Stanley Rosenberg, *Men at Midlife,* Boston: Auburn House, 1981.

Festinger, Leon, *A Theory of Cognitive Dissonance,* Stanford, Calif.: Stanford University Press, 1957.

Firth, Raymond, Jane Hubert, and Anthony Forge, *Families and Their Relatives,* London: Routledge & Kegan Paul, 1970.

Fischer, Lucy Rose, "Married Men and Their Mothers," *Journal of Comparative Family Studies,* 14, 1983: 393–402.

————, "Metamorphosis in the Mother-Daughter Bond," unpublished paper.

————, "Transition to Grandmotherhood," *International Journal of Aging and Human Development,* 16, 1983: 67–78.

————, "Transitions in the Mother-Daughter Relationship," *Journal of Marriage and the Family,* August 1981: 613–22.

————, with Carol Hoffman, "Who Cares for the Elderly: The Dilemma of Family Support," in M. Lewis and J. Miller, *Research in Social Problems and Public Policies,* vol. 3, JAI Press, 1984.

————, and Jane Silverman, "Grandmothering as a 'Tenuous' Role Relationship," paper presented at the Annual Meetings of the National Council on Family Relations, October 1982.

Fox, Greer Litton, "The Mother-Adolescent Daughter Relationship as a Sexual Socialization Structure," *Family Relations,* 29, 1980: 21–28.

Freud, Sigmund, *New Introductory Lectures,* New York: W. W. Norton, 1933.

Friday, Nancy, *My Mother, Myself,* New York: Delacorte Press, 1977.

Friedan, Betty, *The Feminine Mystique,* New York: W. W. Norton, 1963.

Fromm-Reichmann, Frieda, *Psychoanalysis and Psychotherapy,* Chicago: University of Chicago Press, 1959.

Goffman, Erving, *The Presentation of Self in Everyday Life,* New York: Doubleday, 1959.

Guttentag, Marcia, and Paul Secord, *Too Many Women?* Beverly Hills, Calif.: Sage, 1983.

Hagestad, Gunhilde, "Problems and Promises in the Social Psychology of Intergenerational Relations," in R. Fogel, E. Hatfield, S. Kiesler, and E. Shanas, eds., *Aging: Stability and Change in the Family,* New York: Academic Press, 1981.

————, and R. Snow, "Young Adult Offspring as Interpersonal Resources in Middle Age," paper presented at the Annual Meeting of the Gerontological Society, 1977.

Hill, Reuben, Nelson Foote, Joan Aldous, Robert Carlson, and Robert MacDonald, *Family Development in Three Generations,* Cambridge, Mass.: Schenkman Publishing Company, 1970.

Hochschild, Arlie, *The Unexpected Community,* Berkeley: University of California Press, 1973.

Horowitz, Amy, "Sons and Daughters as Caregivers to Older Parents: Differences in Role Performance and Consequences," paper presented at the 34th Annual Meeting of the Gerontological Society, November 1981.

Kahana, Eva, and Boaz Kahana, "Theoretical and Research Perspectives on Grandparenthood," *Aging and Human Development,* 2, 1971: 261–68.

Klatsky, Sheila, *Patterns of Contact with Relatives,* Washington, D.C.: American Sociological Association, 1968.

Komarovsky, Mirra, *Blue Collar Marriage,* New York: Vintage Press, 1967.

Leifer, Myra, *Psychological Effects of Motherhood: A Study of First Pregnancy,* New York: Praeger, 1980.

Litwak, Eugene, *Helping Networks of Older People: From Health to Institutionalization,* New York: Guilford Press, 1985.

Lopata, Helena, *Occupation Housewife,* New York: Oxford University Press, 1971.

Lowenthal, Marjorie, Majda Thurnher, and David Chiraboga, *Four Stages of Life,* San Francisco: Jossey-Bass Publishers, 1975.

Mederer, Helen, "The Transition to a Parent Caring Role by Adult Children: A Model of Ease of Role Transition and Difficulty of Role Performance," unpublished doctoral dissertation, University of Minnesota, 1982.

Miller, Neal E., and John Dollard, *Social Learning and Imitation,* New Haven, Conn.: Yale University Press, 1941.

Moss, Howard, and Elizabeth Susman, "Longitudinal Study of Personality," in Orville Brim and Jerome Kagan, eds., *Constancy and Change in Human Development,* Cambridge, Mass.: Harvard University Press, 1980, pp. 530–95.

Neugarten, Bernice, "The Awareness of Middle Age," in B. Neugarten, ed., *Middle Age and Aging,* Chicago: University of Chicago Press, 1972, pp. 93–98.

Oakley, Ann, *Subject Women,* New York: Pantheon Books, 1981.

Phillips, Herbert, *Thai Peasant Personality,* Berkeley: University of California Press, 1966.

Pineo, Peter, "Disenchantment in the Later Years of Marriage," *Marriage and Family Living,* 23, 1961: 3–11.

Radcliffe-Browne, A. R., and Daryll Forde, eds., *African Systems of Kinship and Marriage,* London: Oxford University Press, 1950.

Rapoport, Rhona, "Transition from Engagement to Marriage," *Acta Sociologica,* 8, 1964: 36–55.

Raven, Bertram, Richard Centers, and Aroldo Rodriguez, "The Bases of Conjugal Power," in R. Cromwell and D. Olson, eds., *Power in Families,* New York: Halstead Press, 1975, pp. 217–32.

Robinson, Betsy, and Majda Thurnher, "Taking Care of Aged Parents," *The Gerontologist,* 19, 1979: 586–93.

Rosenberg, George S., and Donald F. Anspach, *Working Class Kinship,* Lexington, Mass.: Heath and Co., 1973.

Rosow, Irving, *Social Integration of the Aged,* New York: Free Press, 1967.

Rossi, Alice, "Aging and Parenthood in the Middle Years," in P. Baltes and O. Brim, eds., *Life Span Development and Behavior,* vol. 3, New York: Academic Press, 1980.

———, "A Biosocial Perspective on Parenting," *Daedalus,* 106, #2, 1977, pp. 1–31.

———, "Equality between the Sexes: An Immodest Proposal," *Daedalus,* 93, 1964: 651–52.

———, *The Feminist Papers: From Adams to de Beauvoir,* New York: Columbia University Press, 1973.

———, "Gender and Parenthood," *American Sociological Review,* 49, 1984: 1–18.

————, "Transition to Parenthood," *Journal of Marriage and the Family,* 30, 1968: 26–39.

Rubin, Lillian Breslow, *Intimate Strangers,* New York: Harper & Row, 1983.

————, *Worlds of Pain: Life in Working Class Families,* New York: Basic Books, 1976.

Scanzoni, John, *Sexual Bargaining: Power Politics in the American Marriage,* Chicago: University of Chicago Press, 1973.

Schlien, John, "Structure-function, Kinship Terminology, and the Mother-in-law," paper presented to the Annual Symposium of the Committee on Human Development, 1965.

Seiden, Anne M., and Pauline Bart, "Woman to Woman: Can Sisterhood Be Powerful?" in N. Glazer-Malbin, ed., *Old Family/New Family,* New York: Van Nostrand, 1975, pp. 189–228.

Stack, Carol, *All Our Kin,* New York: Harper & Row, 1974.

Streib, Gordon, "Intergenerational Relations: Perspectives of the Two Generations on the Older Parent," *Journal of Marriage and the Family,* 27, 1965: 469–76.

Sussman, Marvin, and Lee Burchinal, "Kin Family Network: Unheralded Structure in Current Conceptualizations of Family Functioning," *Marriage and Family Living,* 24, 1962: 231–40.

Thibaut, J. W., and H. H. Kelley, *The Social Psychology of Groups,* New York: John Wiley and Sons, 1959.

Tiger, Lionel and Joseph Shepher, *Women in the Kibbutz,* New York: Harcourt Brace Jovanovich, 1975.

Titus, Sandra L., Paul C. Rosenblatt, and Roxanne M. Anderson, "Family Conflict over Inheritance of Property," *Family Coordinator,* 28, 1979: 337–46.

Townsend, Peter, *The Family Life of Old People,* London: Routledge & Kegan Paul, 1957.

Turner, Ralph H., *Family Interaction,* New York: John Wiley and Sons, 1970.

Weishaus, Sylvia, "Aging Is a Family Affair," in P. Ragan, ed., *Aging Parents,* Los Angeles, Calif.: University of Southern California Press, 1979.

Whyte, William Foote, *Street Corner Society,* Chicago: University of Chicago Press, 1943.

Willmott, Peter, and Michael Young, *Family and Class in a London Society,* London: Routledge & Kegan Paul, 1960.

Young, Michael, and Peter Willmott, *The Symmetrical Family,* New York: Pantheon Books, 1973.

Index

Adams, Bert, 6
adolescence, 14–45
  arguments in, 19, 22, 24, 45
  child vs. adult status in, 15
  confidences vs. censorship in, 22,
    24, 29, 41
  daughters vs. sons in, 15–16
  detachment patterns in, 22–24
  emotional withdrawal in, 23, 24
  holding on vs. letting go in, 16,
    25–26, 45
  mothers's criticism in, 19
  mother's praise in, 20, 27–28
  physiological changes in, 14, 39–
    41
  rebellion in, 23, 45
  sexuality as issue in, 39–44
  social changes in, 15, 39
advice:
  on child care, 95–96, 101, 127,
    148
  from daughter, 54
  daughter-in-law's acceptance of,
    146, 148
  daughter's acceptance of, 51, 59,
    147, 148
  on daughter's marriage, 101
  on domestic tasks, 95, 148–149
  from mother, 51, 59, 95–96, 147,
    149, 150
  mother-daughter bond and, 150
  from mother-in-law, 127, 146,
    150

advice: *(cont.)*
  mother's rejection of, 54
  sought by daughter, 51, 95, 101,
    146, 148–149, 151
  sought by daughter-in-law, 146,
    148–149, 151
Alzheimer's disease, 161
Anspach, Donald F., 7

"backstage" behavior, 139
Balint, Alice, 10
Bengston, Vern L., 90

careers:
  daughter's, 108–110
  "female" vs. "male," 109
  generational continuity provided
    by, 110
  motherhood vs., 111–114, 200
  mother's, 107, 112
caregivers, caregiving, 156, 173
  conflicting obligations of, 168–
    170, 171–172, 173, 200–201
  geographical distance and, 167
  hospital social worker's support
    of, 193
  hospital staff's alliance with, 186,
    191–194
  hospital staff's evaluation of, 185
  life disruptions experienced by,
    162
  mothering role assumed by, 173,
    200–201

caregivers, caregiving *(cont.)*
  overwhelming responsibilities of, 170–171, 194
  primary concerns of, 163
  protective role assumed by, 162–166
  as quintessential woman's role, 194, 201
  sons as, 167
  see also parent-caregiver relationships
child care:
  husband's participation in, 94–95, 105, 114
  mother-in-law's advice on, 127, 148–149
  mother's advice on, 95, 148–149
  primary responsibility for, 3–4, 17, 114, 200
children:
  adult status for, 11
  emotional support provided by, 46
  as focus of concern, 75, 78–79
  health care decisions made by, 173–174, 186, 192
  mother-in-law/daughter-in-law relationship affected by, 126–130, 141–150
  parental approval sought by, 9
  parents judged by, 9
  as source of confusion, 71–72
  see also caregivers, caregiving
Chodorow, Nancy, 3–4, 15–16
cognitive dissonance, 107
cohorts, 104–105
confidants:
  daughters as, 25, 29, 30–31, 32–33, 34, 37–38
  husbands as, 97, 98
  limitations of husbands as, 99, 100–101
  mothers as, 16, 22, 29, 34, 40–41, 101, 136

confidants: *(cont.)*
  mothers-in-law as, 126–128, 136
  wives as, 97, 98
continuity:
  career advancement and, 110
  generational, need for, 110
  in mother-daughter relationships, 16, 19, 44, 117, 173, 200, 201
  motherhood issue and, 110–111, 115–116
control:
  daughter-dominated, 54
  over decision-making, 192, 193
  definition of, 48
  frail parent's loss of, 182, 192, 193
  mother-dominated, 51–52
  mutual avoidance of, 56
  mutual exercise of, 58, 59–60
  over single daughter, 67, 68

daughters:
  adult status established by, 49, 70, 78
  advice accepted by, 51, 59, 147, 148
  advice given by, 54
  advice sought by, 146, 148–149
  birth order of, 34–35
  career aspirations of, 109
  career vs. caregiving responsibilities of, 168, 200
  childcare as priority of, 168, 170, 171–172
  with children, 73–79
  educational advantages of, 105–108, 110
  emotional withdrawal in, 23, 28
  femininity encouraged in, 20
  financial advantages of, 105
  as focus of concern, 52, 53, 68
  future as viewed by, 66–67, 70–72, 90, 112

daughters: *(cont.)*
 "homesickness" of, 61–62, 63
 hospital care supervised by, 187–188
 as hospitalized parent's advocates, 186–190
 hospital staff's cooperation with, 190
 life structures of, 66–79
 marital advantages of, 105
 marital/parental status of, 64–80
 maturity of, 68, 146
 medical expertise lacked by, 190
 middle position of, 167–173
 mother evaluated by, 73–74, 75
 mothering sought by, 59, 63, 79
 mother's advice sought by, 51, 95, 101, 151
 mother's approval sought by, 61
 as mother's colleagues, 5, 46, 73
 mother's criticism of, 19, 20, 137
 mother's life envisioned by, 67
 mother's praise of, 20, 27–28
 negative feelings of, toward mother, 35–36
 as parent caregivers, 6, 9, 156–195, 162–173, 174–177, 194, 199, 201
 peer attachment in, 24
 pretransitional, 70–71
 protective role assumed by, 36, 37–38, 53, 162–163, 164–166, 194
 responsible, 53–55
 role reversals understood by, 165–166
 sense of individuality in, 88, 90
 separation struggles experienced by, 16, 19, 22–24
 as service providers to mother, 76, 96, 145–146
 as silent about sexuality, 43–44
 as similar to mother, 83, 87–88

daughters: *(cont.)*
 single, 64–65, 66–69, 87, 199
 as "substitute sons," 35
 as targets for mother's negative behavior, 184–185
 unfulfilled aspirations of, 109
 uninvolved, 63
 as unobjective in advocacy role, 189–190
 viewed as needing care, 50
daughters-in-law:
 advice accepted by, 146, 148
 advice sought by, 146, 148–149, 151
 baby-sitting as viewed by, 142–143
 described by mother-in-law, 119, 131–132
 distrust of, 143, 146
 gifts as viewed by, 141–142
 help given by, 145
 as mediators, 150–154
 mother-in-law not known by, 120
 mother-in-law rejected by, 123–124
 mother-in-law's advice accepted by, 146, 148
 mother-in-law's criticism of, 137
 as obligated to mother-in-law, 124, 143
 as outsiders, 131
 priorities for, 133
 self-sacrifice in, 134, 135
 treated as daughters, 123–124, 146, 150
depression, 159–161
 anger caused by, 161
 denial of, 159
 emotional disengagement caused by, 164–165
 in mothers vs. fathers, 160–161
 paranoia caused by, 161
 withdrawal caused by, 160

Dinnerstein, Dorothy, 10
domestic tasks:
   adult status demonstrated by, 70
   husband's participation in, 93–94
   mother-daughter relationships
      and, 95–96, 148–149
   mother-daughter sharing of, 92
   mother-in-law/daughter-in-law
      relationships and, 138, 148–
      149
   mother's evaluation of, 70
   see also child care
Duvall, Evelyn, 118, 119, 123

educational attainment:
   changing priority of, 106
   of daughter vs. mother, 105–108,
      110
   mother-daughter identification
      and, 83, 90
   role models and, 84
"Equality between the Sexes: An
      Immodest Proposal" (Rossi),
      105

Family and Class in a London
      Society (Willmott and Young),
      2, 6
Family Interaction (Turner), 15
family structure, 12–13
family systems:
   British vs. American, 3
   dominated by women, 6
   marital disruption in, 28–29, 31–
      32
   size of, 28
   social class and, 3
father-child relationships, power in,
   10, 43
father-daughter relationships:
   as alliance against mother, 36–37
   confidences exchanged in, 16, 33–
      34

father-daughter relationships: (cont.)
   daughter's sexual maturation and,
      41–43
   mother-daughter relationships vs.,
      16–19, 20, 30–32
   role reversals and, 166
fathers:
   as allies against mothers, 36–37
   autocratic, 54
   daughters as protective of, 165
   daughters' negative feelings
      toward, 35–36
   depression in, 161
   hierarchical position of, 38–39,
      166
   loss of control resisted by, 182
   mother-daughter alliances against,
      30, 34
   mothering capabilities of, 198
   mothers' relationships to, 32
   as outsiders, 18, 39
   power exerted by, 182
   problem, 30–31, 34, 36, 37, 53
   as role models, 84
   as "sexual guardians," 41–43
fathers-in-law:
   care recipient status of, 178–179
   husbands discussed with, 151
   negative feelings toward, 119
Feminine Mystique, The (Friedan),
      105
femininity:
   encouragement of, in daughters,
      20
   self-sacrifice stereotype in, 134,
      172
feminism:
   domestic roles and, 92–93
   mother-daughter identity and,
      82–83
   mothering roles and, 105
filial responsibilities:
   boundaries imposed on, 176, 194

filial responsibilities: *(cont.)*
  as engendered by parent-child
    attachments, 173
  life cycle of reciprocity and, 179
  parental responsibilities vs., 165,
    170, 173
  role reversals in, 162
Firth, Raymond, 7
focus of concern:
  on children, 75, 78–79
  on daughters, 52, 53, 68
  definition of, 48–49
  effect of marriage on, 69
  on mothers, 55
  of mothers vs. mothers-in-law,
    138
  reciprocity and, 57
frail parent-child relationships:
  asymmetry in, 177, 178
  power hierarchy in, 177
  reciprocity in, 177–178
  see also parent-caregiver
    relationships
Friday, Nancy, 18
Friedan, Betty, 105
Fromm-Reichmann, Frieda, 38
"front stage" behavior, 139

gender:
  and allocation of domestic tasks,
    92–95
  family roles determined by, 198
  and health care decisions, 180–
    181
  as important in family
    relationships, 197
  in mother-daughter identification,
    82–83, 91
  as self-identifier, 197–198
  social changes and, 82–83
  status associated with, 198
  structure of mother-daughter
    relationships and, 197

generational continuity:
  career advancement and, 110
  educational attainment and, 105–
    108, 110
  motherhood as priority in, 110,
    115–116
Goffman, Erving, 139
grandmothers:
  advice given by, 146–150
  as baby-sitters, 77–78, 96, 141
  emotional attachment of, 141
  geographical distance of, 140, 141
  grandchildren's contact with, 140
  help given by, 141–146
  "parenting" rights of, 150

Hagestad, Gunhilde, 46, 104
health care decisions:
  dependence vs. independence in,
    176
  hospital social worker and, 191,
    192–196
  made by children, 173–174, 186,
    192
  negotiations leading to, 179
  parent's gender and, 180–181
  parent's input and, 174–181,
    192–193
  parent's resistance to, 180
  urgency factor in, 192
health problems:
  decision-making and, 173–176
  depression caused by, 158–159,
    160–161
  fears caused by, 159
  frustration caused by, 158, 161
  life structures affected by, 159–
    162
  mental functions affected by, 161
  mother-daughter relationships
    affected by, 156–157, 162
  parent's view of, 159
  social world restricted by, 160

hospitalization:
  daughter's responsibilities
    changed by, 185
  decision-making control lost
    during, 192
  family involvement as important
    during, 185–189
  mother-daughter relationships
    and, 185–195
  privacy as issue in, 185
hospital social workers:
  caregiver supported by, 193
  health care decisions aided by,
    191, 192–196
  objectivity of, 193–194
  as parent-caregiver mediators,
    192–193
hospital staff:
  caregiver evaluated by, 185
  caregiver's alliance with, 186,
    191–194
  daughter's cooperation with, 190
  mother-daughter relationship
    affected by, 185
  patient's alliance with, 191
housekeeping, *see* domestic tasks
husbands:
  competition for, between wife and
    mother, 151
  domestic tasks performed by, 93–
    94
  as excluded from motherhood
    experience, 89
  as financial decision-makers, 96–
    97
  as lifelong friends, 91
  mother-daughter access affected
    by, 96–97
  as wives' confidants, 97, 98, 99,
    100–101
husband-wife relationships:
  confidentiality of, 101, 102
  mother-daughter bond as
    competitive with, 8, 88–89, 92

husband-wife relationships: *(cont.)*
  mother-daughter bond
    strengthened by, 92
  mother-daughter relationship
    limited by, 8, 101–104, 196
  power/dependency theory and,
    177
  as strengthened by motherhood, 8

Intimate Strangers (Rubin), 100

Kinship in an Urban Setting
    (Adams), 6
Kuypers, Joseph A., 90

Leifer, Myra, 5, 95
life structures:
  definition of, 66, 159
  loss of independence and, 159
  loss of mobility and, 160
  mental functions and, 161
  motherhood and, 75
  "newly settled," 66, 69
  "settled in," 66, 73
  "unsettled," 66–69
Litwak, Eugene, 186

marriage:
  adult status demonstrated by, 70
  advice about, 101
  barriers created by, 70, 72, 196
  disenchantment with, 100
  focus of concern affected by, 69
  life transformed by, 92
  mother-daughter relationship
    changed by, 64, 69–73, 80,
    101–104, 196
  mother's disapproval of, 101–102
  reasons for, 91–92
  sources of emotional support in,
    97
  wife's protectiveness toward, 103
Medicare, 190, 192

men:
  identity established in, 4
  priority given to, 82
  work as priority of, 168
menstruation, daughter educated
    about, 39–41, 43
Mermaid and the Minotaur, The
    (Dinnerstein), 10
mother-daughter bond:
  advice giving and, 150
  as basis for self-esteem, 82
  as competitive with husband-wife
    ties, 88–89, 92
  complexity of, 197
  daughter's acknowledgement of,
    81–82
  as strengthened by husband-wife
    ties, 92
mother-daughter identification, 4
  children and, 83
  daughter's awareness of, 87
  daughter's rejection of, 81–82,
    83, 89
  dualistic nature of, 5
  educational attainment and, 83,
    90
  gender roles and, 82–83, 91
  geographical distance and, 90
  housewife role in, 85, 86
  mother role in, 85–86, 116
  mother's lifestyle and, 90, 91
  mother's negative status and, 82,
    89, 90–91
  multiple meanings of, 83
  social changes and, 82–83
  social class and, 83, 90
  spousal role in, 85, 86
mother-daughter relationships:
  as alliance against father, 30–31,
    34
  attachment in, 20–21, 24
  caution in, 147, 148
  censorship in, 22, 24, 29, 41
  changing nature of, 196–197

mother-daughter relationships:
    (cont.)
  closeness vs. distance in, 11–12
  as closest in family, 5–6
  confidence exchanged in, 16, 22,
    29, 30–31, 32–33, 34, 37–38,
    40–41, 101, 136
  continuity of, 16, 19, 44, 173,
    200, 201
  daughter's age and, 65
  daughter's marital/parental status
    and, 64–80
  daughter's sexual maturation and,
    39–41
  dependent daughter in, 49–53,
    65, 79, 80
  dependent mother in, 53–55, 58–
    60, 164
  detachment patterns in, 22–24
  detachment vs. attachment in, 23,
    24, 31
  domestic tasks and, 95–96, 148–
    149
  effect of marriage on, 64, 69–73,
    80, 101–104, 196
  ethnic background and, 11
  father-daughter relationships vs.,
    16–19, 20, 30–32
  father's absence and, 29, 31
  as friendship, 46, 47, 55–58
  geographical distance and, 47, 53,
    59, 62, 75–78
  highly involved, 27–28, 29
  holding vs. letting go in, 16, 25–
    26
  hospital staff and, 185
  husband-wife relationship and, 8,
    101–104, 196
  interdependence in, 6, 29, 58
  "intimacy at a distance" in, 7, 8,
    13
  limitations to, 7–8
  loosening of ties in, 5

mother-daughter relationships: *(cont.)*
  motherhood and, 2–5, 8, 46, 73–80, 146, 198–199
  mother-in-law/daughter-in-law relationships vs., 117–118, 121, 126–130, 135–139
  mother's health problems and, 156–157, 162
  mother's hospitalization and, 185–195
  mutual mothering in, 58–60, 64, 166–167
  parent-caregiver relationship as similar to, 200–201
  parenting vs. peership in, 11–12, 79–80
  peerlike, 10, 32, 34, 38, 55–58, 64, 78, 80, 121, 156
  phone calls vs. visits in, 76
  pretransitional, 49
  reciprocity in, 49–51
  remote, 27, 28–29, 31, 48, 63–64
  responsible daughter in, 53–55
  responsible mother in, 49–53, 65
  role reversal in, 156, 161–167, 176–177, 194
  as shaped by social environment, 196–197
  social class and, 3, 6, 11, 28, 47
  superficial harmony in, 7
  systematic misreadings in, 60
  as viewed by caregiving daughter, 162
  as viewed by elderly mother, 162
  as woman-to-woman relationships, 197
  see also parent-caregiver relationships; parent-child relationships
motherhood:
  adult status established by, 78
  as all-consuming role, 112, 114–115, 116, 194

motherhood: *(cont.)*
  asymmetry in, 10, 78
  careers vs., 111–114, 200
  daughter's dependence renewed by, 79, 80, 155
  daughter's hindsight affected by, 75
  dualistic nature of, 5
  educational opportunities limited by, 108
  financial burdens of, 79
  as forced labor, 201
  generational continuity provided by, 110–111, 115–116
  as highest priority, 108–115, 116
  husband-wife bond strengthened by, 8
  life structures affected by, 75
  mother-daughter relationships and, 2–5, 8, 46, 73–80, 146, 198–199
  parent-child hierarchies changed by, 73, 78
  preparation for, 4, 5
  psychological basis for, 4, 5
  as source of identification, 2
  "traditional" ideology about, 110–111
mother-in-law/daughter-in-law relationships:
  adolescent rebellion repeated in, 118, 155
  barriers in, 124
  caution in, 131–132, 134–135, 146, 147–148, 150
  censorship in, 130, 131, 132, 136
  children and, 126–130, 138, 141–150
  confidences exchanged in, 126–128, 136
  continuity in, 117
  distorted perceptions in, 132
  domestic tasks and, 138, 148–149

mother-in-law/daughter-in-law
relationships: *(cont.)*
educational attainment and, 136
family ties sustained by, 130, 131,
136
friendship pattern of, 120–122
"front stage" vs. "back stage"
behaviors in, 139
geographical distance and, 122
interdependence in, 146
intimacy lacked in, 121
minimally involved pattern of,
122–123
mother-daughter relationships vs.,
117–118, 121, 126–130, 135–
139
mythical negativity of, 118
nonvoluntary nature of, 120
as quasi-mother-daughter
relationships, 123–124, 143,
150
son/husband linkage and, 151
tension as likely in, 119
as viewed by daughters-in-law,
129–130
mothers:
adolescent daughters as viewed
by, 16, 25–26
advice given by, 51, 59, 96, 147,
149, 150
advice rejected by, 54
advice sought from, 51, 95, 146,
149, 150, 151
as allies against fathers, 30, 34
as approachable for arguments,
20
as baby-sitters, 143
after children's departure, 63
cognitive dissonance in, 107
daughters as dependent on, 49–
53, 58–60, 65, 79, 80
daughters as protective of, 36,
37–38, 53, 162–163, 164–165,
194

mothers: *(cont.)*
daughters as similar to, 83, 87–
88
daughters criticized by, 19, 137
daughters' evaluation of, 73–74,
75
daughters' future as viewed by,
66–68
daughters' mothering abilities
assessed by, 67–68
daughters' negative feelings
toward, 35–36
daughters praised by, 20, 27–28
demanding, 183–184
as dependent on daughters, 53–
55, 58–60
depression in, 161
in family planning decisions, 72–
73
father-daughter alliances against,
36–37
fathers' relationships to, 32
financial aid given by, 96, 144
as focus of concern, 55
holding on vs. letting go by, 25–
26
inexpressive, 27, 28, 198
limitations of confiding in, 101–
104
loss of control resisted by, 182
mothers-in-law as substitutes for,
123–124
as necessary vs. intrusive, 10, 19
negative family status of, 82, 89,
90–91
negative feelings for mothers-in-
law vs., 119
permissive, 54
power exerted by, 182–185
problem, 36–37, 53, 121
protectiveness felt by, 33
regret lacked by, 107–108
rejection felt by, 25–26
responsible, 49–53, 65
as role models, *see* role models

mothers: *(cont.)*
  as sources of sexual
    information, 39–41, 43
  stereotypical loneliness of, 63
  unfulfilled aspirations of, 106
mothers-in-law:
  advice given by, 127, 146, 150
  advice sought from, 146, 148–
    149, 151
  as baby-sitters, 133–134, 141,
    142
  care recipient status of, 178–179
  child care advice from, 127
  competition with, 151
  as confidants, 126–128, 136
  daughters-in-law criticized by,
    137
  daughters-in-law described by,
    119, 131–132
  financial aid given by, 141, 143–
    144
  gifts given by, 141, 143–144
  as intrusive, 149
  negative feelings for mothers vs.,
    119
  not known by daughters-in-law,
    120
  obligations created by, 124, 143
  rejection of, 123–124
  as substitute mothers, 123–124
  as underinvolved, 136, 137–138
  visits to, 122–123
  women's vs. men's attachment to,
    118
My Mother, Myself (Friday), 18

Neugarten, Bernice, 199

Oakley, Ann, 82
osteoporosis, 159

parent-caregiver relationships:
  age and, 156–157
  hospitalization and, 185–195

parent-caregiver relationships:
    (cont.)
  mediated by hospital social
    workers, 192–193
  mother-daughter relationships as
    similar to, 200–201
  parent-adolescent relationship as
    similar to, 163, 177
  parenting obligations vs., 168,
    170, 171–172
  role reversals in, 161–166
  see also frail parent-child
    relationships
parent-child hierarchy, 8–9
  continuation of, 52–53, 61
  cyclical model of, 156
  daughter's sexuality and, 44
  father-daughter role reversals
    and, 166
  maternal dominance in, 50–51
  motherhood and, 73–78
  mother-in-law/daughter-in-law
    relationship as, 155
  negated by adult children, 9
  renegotiation of, 163
parent-child relationships:
  adolescence and, 15
  affection vs. power in, 10
  asymmetry in, 9–10
  gender as important to, 15
  peerlike, 9–10
  power/dependency theory and,
    177
  see also frail parent-child
    relationships; parent-caregiver
    relationships
parents, frail:
  confusion in, 161, 164
  control exerted by, 181–183
  daughters as advocates for, 186–
    190
  daughters as caregivers to, 6, 9,
    156–157, 162–173, 174–177,
    194, 199, 201

parents, frail: *(cont.)*
 decision-making control lost by,
  192
 dependent position of, 177
 depression in, 159–161, 164–165
 effects of health problems on,
  157–161
 fear of falling in, 159
 health care decisions and, 174–
  181, 192–193
 hospital staff's alliance with, 191
 independence lost by, 159
 mobility lost by, 160
 negative behavior of, 181–185
 as oblivious to role reversals, 165
 parental roles forsaken by, 165–
  166
 personality changes in, 163
 as "postadults," 163, 176
 power of, 177–179
 sense of powerlessness in, 177
 sons as protective of, 166
 see also frail parent-child
  relationships
"postadults," 163, 176
post-parents, 8–9
power:
 of children, 179
 coercive, 182
 continuity of, 179
 as defined by need, 177
 exerted by fathers vs. mothers,
  182
 exerted by mothers, 182–185
 in father-child relationships, 10,
  43
 of frail parents, 177–179, 182–
  185
 in in-law relationships, 178–179,
  182
 methods of exerting, 181–183
 of wives, 179
power/dependency theory, 177

*Psychological Effects of Motherhood,
 The* (Leifer), 5

Reproduction of Mothering, The
 (Chodorow), 3–4, 15–16
reproductive bond, 43
 as competitive with husband-wife
  bond, 8
 daughter's sexual maturation and,
  39–41
responsibility:
 daughter-dominated, 54
 hierarchy of, 47–48
 mother-dominated, 51
 mutuality of, 58, 60–61
role models:
 educational attainment and, 84
 fathers as, 84
 mothers as, 74, 82, 84–91
 mothers rejected as, 82, 91
 nurturant qualities in, 84
 personality characteristics in, 84,
  89
 social class and, 84–85
role reversals:
 caused by personality changes,
  163–164
 daughter's awareness of, 165
 daughter's dislike of, 166
 evolution of, 167, 194
 in father-daughter relationships,
  166
 in mother-daughter relationships,
  156, 161–167, 176–177, 194
 in parent-caregiver relationships,
  161–166
Rosenberg, George S., 7
Rossi, Alice, 105
Rubin, Lillian, 100, 150–151

self-esteem:
 children's departure and, 63
 mother-daughter bond as basis
  for, 82

self-sacrifice:
    in caregiving daughters, 172
    in daughters-in-law, 134, 135
    in stereotype of femininity, 134,
        172
sexuality:
    ambivalence about discussing, 41
    father-daughter relationships and,
        41–43
    mother-daughter relationships
        and, 39–41
    parent-child hierarchy and, 44
    silence about, 43
sibling rivalries, 61–62
social environment, 196–197
    mother-daughter relationships
        shaped by, 196–197
    society in general as, 197
    surrounding relationships as, 196
sons:
    as caregivers, 167
    as protective of frail parents, 166

sons-in-law, 125
    criticisms of, 103
    dissatisfaction with, 92, 102

Townsend, Peter, 6
Turner, Ralph, 15

Willmott, Peter, 2, 6
wives:
    as confidantes, 97, 98
    husbands as confidants of, 97, 98,
        99, 100–101
women:
    caring orientation of, 199, 201
    earning power of, 201
    identity established in, 4
Working Class Kinship (Rosenberg
    and Anspach), 7
*Worlds of Pain: Life in Working
    Class Families* (Rubin), 150–
    151

Young, Michael, 2, 6